Post-Conviction Relief: Winning Claims

Kelly Patrick Riggs

FREEBIRD
PUBLISHERS

Freebird Publishers
www.FreebirdPublishers.com

Freebird Publishers

221 Pearl St., Ste. 541, North Dighton, MA 02764
Info@FreebirdPublishers.com
www.FreebirdPublishers.com

Copyright © 2018 Updated 2019
Post-Conviction Relief: Winning Claims
By Kelly Patrick Riggs

All Freebird Publishers titles, imprints, and distributed lines are available at special quantity discounts for bulk purchases for sales promotions, premiums, fundraising educational or institutional use.

ISBN-13: 978-0-9996602-6-3
ISBN-10: 0-9996602-6-8

Printed in the United States of America

SCOPE AND PURPOSE

This book is written from the same perspective as my first three. Its purpose is to give you sound ideas with which you can identify winning claims for *habeas corpus* relief. When studying your own criminal case or that of another, the task becomes much easier when you can compare the facts of your case to cases that have prevailed in the past.

It's my desire that you develop a vocabulary you can use to express yourself intelligently in a court of law. Learning the information contained herein will provide you with that. These pages focus on winning cases that you can refine into your very own winning claims.

TABLE OF CONTENTS

INTRODUCTION

This book was intended to be the one and only all-encompassing guidebook to lead the nonprofessional through to *habeas corpus*. I initially presented "A David and Goliath Story" to Freebird Publishers in an unreadable format. It was during this time, through attempts to correct our technical difficulties, that I discovered that a 700-page book was doomed to fail in reaching my goal. My intent was to reach the needs of the layman and the underprivileged who had been deprived of justice. What I had done, however, was what every other lawyer who writes a book has done: I wrote right over the head of anyone who has not been to law school.

After realizing my error, I broke my book down into seven different installments called the "Post-Conviction Relief" series. In the first three installments, I have taught you what *habeas corpus* is and how to file petitions, the entire appeal process with step-by-step instructions, and how to learn and think in the legal arena. Here, now, I present to you the principles of the *habeas corpus* practice, along with ideas for relief you can base your claims on.

Make no mistake – this is not a cite book that provides random decisions from random courts. These cases are doctrine cases that all *habeas* courts follow, and the winning *habeas corpus* cases that followed them. This book is not written for the sole purpose of selling copies. It is the heart of the over 2,000 winning cases I have, in one way or another, been involved in. Once published, it will be the guidebook for everyone in my non-profit organization, "Release of Innocent Prisoners Effort, Inc."

I now introduce you to the winners and the doctrines they followed: Welcome to "Post-Conviction Relief: Winning Claims."

SECTION ONE
CHAPTER ONE

THE STANDARD OF A CLAIM

This is a good time for me to regurgitate years of education and once again drive you back to the dictionary – just like most other legal books, to baffle you with bull. The bottom line is that if you have followed sound reasoning and the advice I have provided thus far, you deserve more. So here it is: *habeas corpus* claims are governed by simple standards; it is unfortunate that lawyers twist and pervert these standards to take advantage of the less fortunate. The basis of the standard is whether your sentence, conviction, and/or detention are in violation of the Constitution or statutes.

The decisions and/or waivers that are evident in your particular case narrow this standard, however. After a criminal conviction, you have a right to appeal – and other additional remedies for State prisoners. Those decisions by the Court of Appeals – or the waiver thereof – affect the scope of claims you can raise in a petition or motion for a writ of *habeas corpus*. Remember also that the right to appeal a criminal conviction directly is not a Constitutional one, but rather a creature of statute. See *United States v. Harrison*, 777 F.3d 227 (5th Cir. 2015). I hope you can see the resemblance to 28 U.S.C. §2255 and §2254. All of which are designed to redirect you from your Constitutional right to seek *habeas* relief from illegal detention.

The purpose of the redirection is a simple one: it is time. The original writ – which is supplanted by direct appeal and the various statutory remedies – has very strict time limits. If the court and lawyers can avoid those time limits, they can avoid that dirty little word, "Justice," by confusing you and causing years of delay. Their goal is to delay your case until relief would be pointless.

What is important is to wrap your brain around the claims that remain viable under the standard. The post-conviction standard has never been better defined than the Supreme Courts explanation in *Strickland v. Washington*, 466 U.S. 668 (1984). I know you have read it at length before, so here I am going to get to the nitty gritty without wasting any words.

The claims that remain after your opportunity to seek direct appeal are limited to claims that you could not reasonably raise in direct appeal, which, prior to 2003, there were none. Of course, in 1984, the Strickland court made clear that a true showing of ineffective assistance of counsel was grounds upon which *habeas corpus* relief could be based. But that brings me to the "cause and prejudice" standard. The *Strickland* decision is clear in its holding that:

"A convicted defendant's claim that counsel's assistance was so defective as to require reversal of a conviction or death sentence has two components. First, the defendant must show that counsel's performance was deficient. This requires showing that the counsel made errors so serious that counsel was not functioning as the 'counsel' guaranteed the defendant by the Sixth Amendment. Second, the defendant must show that the deficient performance prejudiced the defense. This requires showing that the counsel's errors were so serious as to deprive the defendant of a fair trial, a trial whose result is reliable. Unless a defendant makes both showings, it cannot be said that the conviction or death sentence resulted from a breakdown in the adversary process that renders the result unreliable" (*Strickland*, 466 U.S. 687).

I know, quite a mindful. I know also that this standard seems to serve as a gatekeeper to the *habeas* review. Well, it is. You must show cause, meaning you must show why you did not raise your claim in your direct appeal. The answer is an easy one: "It was the lawyer's fault," right? Well, most likely.

Once upon a time, in federal cases – and still today in almost all state cases – a prisoner was required to show why he did not raise an ineffective assistance of counsel claim in direct appeal.

That all changed in 2003 when the Supreme Court of the United States decided *Massaro v. United States*, 538 U.S. 500. In *Massaro*, the Supreme Court held that a federal prisoner's failure to raise an ineffective assistance of counsel claim on direct appeal cannot bar review under 28 U.S.C. §2255. The Court determined that the prisoner's failure can never serve as a procedural default that precludes an I.A.C. claim in a subsequent §2255 motion. However, the high court made clear that this was a supervisory decision with no underlying Constitutional basis. As a result, however, the *Massaro* decision has no application in §2254 proceedings. Therefore, State prisoners are still required to raise ineffective assistance claims during the appeal process when State law requires.

Now, let us look at "cause and prejudice." This standard allows a *habeas* petitioner to relitigate nearly every element of his criminal proceedings if he can show that his lawyer either failed to raise the issue or was ineffective in his attempt to do so. Counsel's ineffectiveness will almost always be your "cause" to overcome procedural defaults of your valid claim. This is why I have repeatedly said two to five claims. That is because there will always be at least two in any *habeas* motion or petition; you must first show your counsel's errors are the reason that your trial process was unreliable. Here, in Section One, I am giving you hundreds of winning *habeas* cases that were based on claims of ineffective assistance of counsel.

CHAPTER TWO

OUTRIGHT DENIAL OF COUNSEL OR COUNSEL OF YOUR CHOICE

In the ordinary post-conviction case, the backbone to the claim rests squarely on defense counsel. Because of this, the Supreme Court defined the limitations in *Strickland*, which we discussed earlier. These limits were largely defined by the "cause and prejudice" standard. But this standard, just as every other standard of law, is subject to some exceptions. One of those exceptions to the "cause and prejudice" standard, is the exception set out by the Supreme Court in *United States v. Cronic*, 466 U.S. 648. The *Cronic* exception, which provides that prejudice is to be presumed, applies when a criminal defendant has been completely denied the right to counsel for a critical stage of the trial, which is an error that contaminates the entire proceeding. See also *Bell v. Cone*, 535 U.S. 685 (2002) (noting that *Cronic* "identified three situations implicating the right to counsel" in which prejudice to the defense could be presumed). The *Cronic* decision limited the presumption of prejudice to cases where defense counsel "entirely fails to subject the prosecution's case to meaningful adversarial testing" in the trial or where there is "the complete denial of counsel" at a "critical stage of the trial." *Cronic*, 466 U.S. at 659. This part of *Cronic* is very telling in what the word "counsel" means: advice or assistance. This is the first definition found in *Black's Law Dictionary*. This means that a lawyer can be by your side, and you can still be denied counsel. This condition is referred to as a "constructive denial of counsel."

It is important to note that only once, in the 33 years since the *Cronic* decision was issued, has the Supreme Court applied *Cronic* to presume prejudice. See *Penson v. Ohio*, 488 U.S. 75. Because of this, I use these cases as proof of cause alone and go on to prove prejudice in every case. My stance: no prejudice, no case.

Here are some examples of denial of counsel:

- *Gideon v. Wainwright,* 372 U.S. 335 (1963) (petitioner forced to trial without lawyer because he was indigent).

- *Koenig v. North Dakota,* 755 F.3d 636 (8th Cir. 2014) (state court unconstitutionally denied appellate counsel in misdemeanor appeal based on accused's waiver of appointed counsel at trial court level that "was limited to the issue of the right to trial counsel only").

- *Smith v. Grams,* 565 F.3d 1037 (7th Cir. 2009) (trial court improperly treated accused's "election to proceed to trial" without counsel, when confronted with "Hobson's choice" of doing so or "adjourning the proceedings and waiving his right to a speedy trial," as "knowing and voluntary waiver" of right to counsel).

- *Carlson v. Jess,* 526 F.3d 1018 (7th Cir. 2008) ("trial court's denial of [petitioner's] motion for substitution [of new retained counsel for previous counsel] and a continuance [to afford new counsel time to prepare for trial] was arbitrary and in violation of the Sixth and Fourteenth Amendments").

- *Bradley v. Henry,* 510 F.3d 1093 (9th Cir. 2007) (en banc) (trial court deprived petitioner of right to counsel of choice by refusing to substitute retained counsel for court-appointed counsel because of concerns about possible financial problems or delay without conducting adequate inquiry about these concerns or considering alternatives).

- *Cottenham v. Jamron,* 248 Fed. Appx. 625, 2007 U.S. App. LEXIS 20421 (6th Cir. Aug, 21, 2007) (per curiam) (petitioner was denied right to counsel of choice on direct appeal because appellate court initially refused petitioner's requests to discharge counsel retained by petitioner's parents. When appellate court eventually granted request, court denied replacement counsel sufficient time to prepare brief and court scheduled oral argument on date when replacement counsel was unavailable).

- *James v. Brigano*, 470 F.3d 636 (6th Cir. 2006) (trial court permitted petitioner to represent himself at trial without ensuring that waiver of counsel was knowing and intelligent).

- *Daniels v. Woodford*, 428 F.3d 1181 (9th Cir. 2005'), cert, denied, 550 U.S. 968 (2007) ("Daniels was constructively denied his right to counsel in violation of the Sixth Amendment" due to "complete breakdown in the communication between Daniels and his trial counsel." This stemmed from trial judge's refusal to acknowledge the public defender's conflict until close to the trial," the judge's refusal to appoint private attorney requested by petitioner, the appointment instead of "inexperienced former prosecutor as lead counsel," and the newly appointed counsel's failure to "conduct reasonable preparation").

- *Pazden v. Maurer*, 424 F.3d 303 (3d Cir. 2005) ("Pazden's waiver of counsel was not voluntary in the constitutional sense": "Pazden was not exercising his free will but was instead compelled to proceed *pro se* only because his attorney had not been given enough time to familiarize herself with the relevant background of the case").

- *Robinson v. Ignacio*, 360 F.3d 1044 (9th Cir. 2004) ("Sixth Amendment right to counsel was violated when the trial court denied [petitioner's] timely request for representation at sentencing based on the notion that once waived [prior to guilt-innocence trial], the right to counsel cannot be re-asserted").

- *Mitchell v. Mason*, 325 F.3d 732 (6th Cir. 2003) ("[W]e are convinced that the undisputed amount of time that [trial counsel] spent with Mitchell prior to jury selection and the start of trial-approximately six minutes spanning three separate meetings in the bullpen. When viewed in light of [counsel's] month-long suspension from practice immediately prior to trial [it] constituted a complete denial of counsel at a critical stage of the proceedings").

- *Norde v. Keana*, 294 F.3d 401 (2d Cir. 2002) (trial court violated right to counsel by denying adjournment to permit defense counsel to consult with accused who had been removed from courtroom for disruptive behavior during *voir dire*, and by communication with accused through court officer rather than counsel about accused's return to courtroom).

- *Moore v. Purkett*, 275 F.3d 685 (8th Cir. 2001) (trial court "actually or constructively denied the assistance of counsel altogether during trial court proceedings" by prohibiting counsel to speak with accused during trial despite accused's reading and writing problems, which prevented court's proposed alternative of writing notes).

- *Hunt v. Mitchell*, 261 F.3d 575 (6th Cir. 2001) ("[w]hen [petitioner] refused to waive his right to a speedy trial, the trial court effectively forced him to go to trial with an unprepared attorney" by appointing counsel and forcing counsel to start trial immediately without opportunity to confer with client).

- *Burdine v. Johnson*, 262 F.3d 336 (5th Cir. 2001) (en banc), cert, denied, 535 U.S. 1120 (2002) (petitioner was "denied counsel at a critical stage of his trial" and prejudice must presume because "defense counsel repeatedly slept as evidence was being introduced").

- *Fowler v. Collins*, 253 F.3d 244 (6th Cir. 2001) (trial court permitted petitioner to waive counsel and plead guilty without satisfying court's "duty to make [accused] aware of the dangers and disadvantages of self-representation").

- *Appel v. Horn*, 250 F.3d 203 (3d Cir. 2001) (lawyers, who were appointed by the court as "standby" counsel for a 10-day period leading up to hearing on competency to waive counsel and appear *pro se*, deprived client of counsel by failing to conduct investigation into competency. "Courts have found constructive denial of the right to counsel ... where counsel offered no assistance to defendant at plea proceedings ...; acted as a mere spectator at defendant's sentencing – ; failed to object to a directed verdict against the defendant ; and deliberately stressed the brutality of his client's crime ..." (citing cases)).

- *Barnett v. Hargett*, 174 F.3d 1128 (10th Cir. 1999) (during proceedings on remand from state appellate court to trial court, petitioner was unrepresented because of resignation of appellate defender who had handled appeal).

- *Henderson v. Frank*, 155 F.3d 159 (3d Cir. 1998) (judge's failure to ensure that accused's waiver of counsel and assertion of right to proceed *pro se* were voluntary, knowing and intelligent resulted in unconstitutional denial of right to counsel at suppression hearing, necessitating new suppression hearing and retrial).

- *Crandell v. Bunnell*, 144 F.3d 1213 (9th Cir. 1998), partially overruled on other grounds, *Schell v. Witek*, 218 F.3d 1017 (9th Cir. 2000) (en banc) (trial judge functionally denied counsel by forcing petitioner to choose between appearing *pro se* or continuing to be represented by lawyer who met with petitioner only 1-3 times over period of months, had no other communications with him, relied on state's "open file" discovery without seeking formal discovery or conducting other investigation, and pressed petitioner to accept plea without having previously developed working relationship with client).

- *Blankenship v. Johnson*, 118 F.3d 312 (5th Cir. 1997) (petitioner was constructively denied counsel when his attorney, who was elected county attorney after representing petitioner in appeal to intermediate appellate court, failed to represent petitioner at, and did nothing to secure substitute counsel during, state-requested discretionary review by state's criminal court of last resort).

- *Snook v. Wood*, 89 F.3d 605 (9th Cir. 1996) (state appellate court's failure to advise *pro se* appellant of "dangers and disadvantages" of waiving appellate counsel violated right to counsel on appeal).

- *Robinson v. Norris*, 60 F.3d 457 (8th Cir. 1995), cert, denied, 517 U.S. 1115 (1996) (petitioner was functionally deprived of counsel when judge refused to replace trial counsel with new attorney to file post-trial motion for new trial on grounds of ineffective assistance of counsel)

- *Bland v. California Dep't of Corrections,* 20 F.3d 1469 (9th Cir.), cert, denied, 513 U.S. 947 (1994) (trial court violated 6th Amendment by summarily rejecting petitioner's request for discharge of appointed counsel and substitution of different attorney without inquiring into basis of petitioner's request).

- *Bowen v. Maynard*, 799 F.2d 593 (10th Cir.), cert, denied, 479 U.S. 962 (1986) (petitioner forced to trial without retained attorney, who was injured the day before trial).

CHAPTER THREE

CONFLICT OF INTEREST

A conflict of interest can be simply defined as a condition where someone, entrusted to protect the interests of another, has opposing interests of their own. This happens in most cases where lawyers are involved. In many criminal cases, inexperienced and/or lazy lawyers take appointments where they are paid a token wage to herd criminal defendants through the system, on to conviction.

As we are taught in our childhood, the Sixth Amendment of the United States Constitution secures our right to the assistance of counsel in all felony criminal proceedings. We often overlook the fact that Congress clarified and codified this right in 18 U.S.C. §3006A. Now, we live in a time where the court is tasked with providing counsel for anyone who cannot afford counsel (*Gideon v. Wainright*, 372 U.S. 335).

What is unknown to us now is that a conflict occurred in the 1980s and then compounded in the 1990s. It was during this period that Ronald Reagan declared the drug trade a national emergency. Shortly after, George Bush Sr. declared a war on drugs. Another misnomer is that former President Bush declared war on American drug users. In actuality, he tasked the D.E.A. with the regulation of drugs, not abolishment. Thus, the "war on drugs" is, in actuality, a "war on drug addiction."

The war on addiction created a crisis concerning bed space in prisons across America. Congress responded by throwing money at the problem, hence the boom to build and supply prisons. The return of the pendulum now causes problems of its own, where many prison beds are available, along with an 800-billion-dollar budget (both federal and state). So now the beds must remain full to maintain the status quo.

All across the nation, you discover that crime, conviction, probation, and prison are a profitable business. Nearly all stock in prison-related corporations is owned exclusively by politicians, judges, and lawyers. Although this creates a simple yet serious conflict of interest, it is also one of the best-kept secrets of our modern time. What most do not see is that the same people who conduct the trials that convict the poor and underprivileged are the ones who profit from their incarceration.

It is time to realize that the modern American courtroom is a battlefield of class warfare. On one side are the citizens who believe in justice as we are taught by the government-run schools. On the other side are the lawyers, who harvest the unwitting people and profit from their pain.

> *Author's Note: As you can see, the modem day "prison-for-profit scheme" is as egregious a tyranny as the Trans-Atlantic Slave Trade propagated by Christopher Columbus. Is it not ironic that millions of minorities are taught to celebrate Christopher Columbus Day, the birth of American Slavery?*

Your court-appointed lawyer (and any paid lawyer) is a member of the bar, just like the prosecutor and the judge. They are paid by the same system as the court and prosecutor who want to convict you. They know that if they want to continue to be paid, they must play along. The court is a theater where this secret is concealed from the people. This is a conflict of interest. So, be alert to any moment that your lawyer makes the conflict known. These are some examples:

- *Salts v. Epps*, 676 F.3d 468 (5th Cir. 2012) (trial court violated *Holloway v. Arkansas*, 435 U.S. 475 (1978) by failing to inquire into potential conflict of interest caused by lawyer's joint representation of married couple charged with embezzling funds in business they operated together).

- *Boykin v. Webb*, 541 F.3d 638 (6th Cir. 2008) ("Where, as here, the facts at trial show that a defendant's best defense is to point the finger at his co-defendant, it almost goes without saying that the two co-defendants cannot be represented by the same trial counsel. Permitting an attorney to labor under such a conflict of interest would inexorably have an adverse effect on the defense of at least one of the defendants, if not both." Petitioner also was denied effective assistance of direct appeal because "the same attorney who labored under a conflict of interest at his trial controlled his subsequent appeal [and this] *Boykin* was unable to raise on direct appeal the obvious conflict of interest at trial").

- *McElrath v. Simpson*, 595 F.3d 624 (6th Cir. 2010) ("counsel's joint or dual representation of petitioner and [co-defendant] ... resulted in an actual conflict that affected petitioner's representation," in that "joint representation caused counsel to elect to pursue a joint or mutual defense [that both clients were innocent]. That was contradicted by the evidence, rather than pursuing the obviously stronger defense of pointing the finger at [co-defendant] ... and arguing that there was reasonable doubt concerning McElrath's intent to aid the commission of the offenses").

- *Lewis v. Mayle*, 391 F.3d 989 (9th Cir. 2004) (counsel previously represented "primary witness for the prosecution," who was other possible suspect in charged murder, which "only one of two people could have committed").

- *McFarland v. Yukins*, 356 F.3d 688 (6th Cir. 2004) (trial counsel's representation of petitioner and codefendant violated: (1) rule of *Holloway v. Arkansas*, 435 U.S. 475 (1978). Both petitioner and codefendant "indicated that they would defend themselves on the theory that 'someone else' owned the drugs and that they did not want to be represented by the same lawyer at trial." The trial court consequently was on "clear notice ... of a concrete conflict of interest"; and (2) rule of *Cuyler v. Sullivan*, 446 U.S. 335 (1980), because "case ... presents an actual choice by [petitioner's] counsel to forego an obvious and strong defense to avoid inculpating another client").

- *Harris v. Carter*, 337 F.3d 758 (6th Cir. 2003) (trial court failed to conduct adequate inquiry into potential conflict of interest when petitioner's counsel, who also represented another prosecution witness, reported possible conflict and requested appointment of different attorney for witness).

- *Lockhart v. Terhune*, 250 F.3d 1223 (9th Cir. 2001) (counsel simultaneously represented petitioner and other individual who was implicated in uncharged murder that state attributed to petitioner and about which state presented evidence at petitioner's trial).

- *Perillo v. Johnson*, 205 F.3d 775 (5th Cir. 2000) (counsel, who had previously represented key prosecution witness and had ongoing friendship with her, provided witness with preview of his cross-examination of her and refrained from cross-examining her about prior statements and other matters that would cast doubt on her credibility).

- *Atley v. Ault*, 191 F.3d 865 (8th Cir. 1999) (trial court failed to conduct adequate inquiry when notified that defense counsel had potential conflict of interest in that he had accepted offer to begin working at County Attorney's Office after trial ended).

- *United States v. Moore*, 159 F.3d 312 (9th Cir. 1998) (counsel's irreconcilable conflict with section 2255 movant resulted in denial of counsel).

- *Blakenship v. Johnson*, 118 F.3d 312 (5th Cir. 1997) (attorney, who represented petitioner in appeal to intermediate appellate court, had irremediable conflict of interest at time of subsequent state-request discretionary review by state's criminal court of last resort because, in interim, attorney had been elected county attorney).

- *Edens v. Hannigan*, 87 F.3d 1109 (10th Cir. 1996) (counsel, who represented petitioner and codefendant at joint trial, presented less aggressive defense for petitioner to avoid prejudicing codefendant and failed to pursue plea offer with condition of testimony against codefendant).

- *Griffen v. McVicar*, 84 F.3d 880 (7th Cir. 1996), cert, denied, 520 U.S. 1139 (1997) (counsel, who represented petitioner and codefendant at joint trial, rejected defense that was clearly favorable to petitioner but detrimental to codefendant in favor of untenable joint defense).

- *Selsor v. Kaiser*, 81 F.3d 1492 (10th Cir. 1996) (trial judge failed to inquire adequately into need for separate counsel for petitioner and codefendant, both of whom were represented by same public defender's office).

- *Ciak v. United States*, 59 F.3d 296 (2d Cir. 1995) (despite awareness that defense counsel had recently represented government witness and may have had conflicting interests, trial judge failed to conduct inquiry into need for withdrawal).

- *Lopez v. Scully*, 58 F.3d (2d Cir. 1995) (counsel had "actual conflict of interest" at time of sentencing because client had moved to vacate guilty plea on ground that counsel induced plea by threats and misinformation).

- *United States v. Cook*, 45 F.3d 388 (10th Cir. 1995) (although trial counsel's initial conflict of interest in representing section 2255 movant and codefendant was resolved by withdrawal from codefendant's case, counsel developed new conflict of interest when he complied with "district court's mid-trial instruction to advise codefendant of consequences of failure to comply with testimony agreement that counsel negotiated on her behalf").

- *Dawan v. Lockhart*, 31 F.3d 718 (8th Cir. 1994) (counsel, who previously represented defense witness when he was charged as codefendant, did not rehabilitate witness's in-court testimony by aggressively attacking his out-of-court inconsistent statements as perjurious).

- *Burden v. Zant*, 24 F.3d 1298 (11th Cir. 1994) remand from *Burden v. Zant*, 510 U.S. 132 (1994) (*per curiam*), court of appeals concludes that writ should be granted because attorney who represented petitioner prior to trial also represented another suspect and negotiated agreement for latter individual to testify against petitioner in exchange for transactional immunity).

- *Sanders v. Ratelle*, 21 F.3d 1446 (9th Cir. 1994) (counsel's previous representation of petitioner's brother, who admitted to counsel in course of representation that he committed murder with which petitioner was charged, created conflict of interest precluding effective representation of petitioner).

- *United States v. Fulton*, 5 F.3d 605 (2d Cir. 1993) (section 2255 motion granted on grounds of ineffectiveness of counsel because prosecution witness's allegation of criminal activity by counsel created per se prejudicial conflict of interest).

- *Fitzpatrick v. McCormick*, 869 F.2d 1247 (9th Cir.), cert, denied, 493 U.S. 872 (1989) (counsel represented petitioner at retrial after serving as counsel for co-defendant at petitioner's first trial).

CHAPTER FOUR

PLEA AGREEMENTS

In today's courts, a defendant faces two uniquely opposing standards concerning an ineffective assistance of counsel claim after a guilty plea.

In the first, the Supreme Court has held that under certain circumstances involving a 28 U.S.C. §2255 motion concerning a guilty plea (that the defendant failed to raise in direct appeal) prisoner would be entitled to a hearing – possible *habeas* relief – on the merits of the claim, only if the petitioner made the necessary showing of actual innocence to relieve his procedural default in failing to contest the guilty plea on appeal (see *Bousley v. United States*, 523 U.S. 614 (1998)).

In the second, however, the standard is presented as this general rule: that claims not raised by convicted federal defendants on direct appeal may not properly be raised on collateral review under 28 U.S.C. §2255, unless defendant shows cause and prejudice. This procedural-default rule is neither statutory nor a federal Constitutional requirement. Instead, this general rule is doctrine adhered to by courts (1) to conserve judicial resources and (2) to respect the law's important interest in finality of judgments. Moreover, with respect to claims of ineffective assistance of counsel, convicted defendants may properly first bring such ineffective assistance claims in collateral proceedings under §2255, regardless of whether the defendant could have raised the claim on direct appeal. While this ineffective assistance holding doesn't mean that such claims must be reserved for collateral review, this holding does mean that the defendant's failure to raise an ineffective assistance claim on direct appeal does not bar the claim from being brought in a later appropriate proceeding under §2255, for, among other factors, requiring defendant to bring ineffective assistance of counsel claims first on direct appeal would not promote the rule's objectives (see *Massaro v. United States*, 538 U.S. 500 (2003)).

The combination of these two standards are straight forward and easily understood. But, the courts – both district and appellate – have taken the latter standard a bit further. In doing so, they are able to reap the financial benefits of inordinate delay. In the recent Eleventh Circuit case, *United States v. Hanlon*, U.S. App. LEXIS 14137, Case No: 16-17457 (Aug. 2/2017), the Eleventh Circuit dismissed the appeal because they "will not generally consider claims of ineffective assistance of counsel raised on direct appeal where the district court did not entertain the claim nor develop a factual record" *United States v. Bender*, 290 F.3d 1279, 1284 (11th Cir. 2002). The preferred method of raising claims of ineffective assistance of counsel is in a motion pursuant to 28 U.S.C. §2255 (see *Massaro v. United States*, 538 U.S. 500, 500-06, 123 S. Ct. 1690, 155 L. Ed, 2d 714 (2003)). The record is not sufficiently developed for us to address in this direct appeal Hanlon's claims that his counsel was ineffective at the plea negotiation, *Bender*, 290 F.3d at 1284. For this reason, those claims are dismissed without prejudice to his raising them in a §2255 motion to adjudicate them, *Massaro*, 538 U.S. at 505-06."

In analyzing this Eleventh Circuit appeal, I want you to remember the lessons of citation signals in "Post-Conviction Relief: Advancing Your Claim." Take note that when the panel referred to the court's own precedent in *Bender*, the panel used quotes and no signal words, indicating that that is exactly what the opinion said. But, the panel' in referring to *Massaro*, used the signal word "See," which means that *Massaro's* holding follows this principle, but it is not a quote. In short, the panel's words here are not found in *Massaro*. In fact, these statements are cherry picked to deny *Hanlon's* meritorious appeal, which should have been reviewed for the plea error, under a plain error standard of review.

I hope you can see that the plea agreement stage of a criminal trial proceeding has become a defense lawyer's playground. They know that, regardless of their errors, you cannot file a direct appeal against them, where adequate counsel is a Constitutional guarantee. But, instead, your claim will be reserved for collateral proceedings under §2255, where a poor criminal defendant has no counsel to assist in formulating a claim. Moreover, the United States Attorney's Office now becomes the defense counsel for your attorney in the §2255 collateral proceeding.

The combination of these opinions, coupled with some creative thinking, allows all defense lawyers to follow the predetermined path of least resistance to maximize their own personal income. Once paid, defense lawyers seek to minimize their labor expense, thus maximizing their profit margins. This is most achievable by coercing plea agreements of even the innocent, which is now facilitated by the courts, by removing any meaningful recourse for counsel ineffectiveness. Here are some fine examples:

- *Lafler v. Cooper*, 132 S. Ct. 1376 (2012) (petitioner was denied effective assistance of counsel in plea bargaining by attorney's misadvising petitioner to reject plea offer based on view of law by counsel that state conceded was deficient, which resulted in petitioner's rejecting plea, "being convicted at trial, [and] receiving] a minimum sentence 3 1/2 times greater than he would have received under the plea").

- *United States v. Rodriquez-Vega*, 797 F.3d 781 (9th Cir. 2015) (counsel was ineffective in stating to client that a guilty plea created "'potential' of removal," rather than advising client "that her conviction rendered her removal virtually certain, or words to that effect." Although defendant "received notice that she might be removed from a provision in the plea agreement, and the court's plea colloquy under Federal Rule of Criminal Procedure lit,] … [t]he government's performance in including provisions in the plea agreement, and the court's performance at plea colloquy, are simply irrelevant to the question whether counsel's performance fell below an objective standard of reasonableness").

- *Pidgeon v. Smith*, 785 F.3d 1165 (7th Cir. 2015) (prisoner plead guilty to sexual assault based on counsel's advice "that he would [otherwise] face a mandatory sentence of life imprisonment without the possibility of parole" due to prior "serious felony" conviction, but actually prior conviction "did not qualify as a serious felony offense, meaning that Pidgeon did not face the possibility of life imprisonment," and "Pidgeon alleges that he would not have accepted the plea agreement had he received correct legal advice").

- *United States v. Bui*, 769 F.3d 831 (3d Cir. 2014) ("Bui's counsel was ineffective with respect to his advice regarding the availability of [sentence reduction under 18 U.S.C.] §3553(f)" if client accepted plea offer, and "there is a reasonable probability that, but for counsel's errors, Bui would not have pled guilty" because "Bui "gained no benefit from his plea agreement" other than potential sentence reduction).

- *Heard v. Addison*, 728 F.3d 1170 (10th Cir. 2013) (counsel "provided ineffective assistance in failing to advise [Heard] of viable defenses to the charges against him, and … but for counsel's deficient performance. Heard would not have pled guilty to these offenses").

- *Johnson v. Uribe*, 700 F.3d 413 (9th Cir. 2012) cert, denied, 134 S. Ct. 617 (2013) (counsel failed to advise client that sentence stipulated in guilty plea, to which client was ultimately sentenced, exceeded what was authorized by California law for charged crimes and enhancements and thus was unlawful).

- *United States v. Akinsade*, 686 F.3d 248 (4th Cir. 2012) (granting *coram nobis* relief to lawful permanent resident who pled guilty to crime that could result deportation after being misadvised by counsel that deportation could occur only after conviction of two felonies).

- *United States v. Juarez*, 672 F.3d 381 (5th Cir. 2012) (section 2255 movant, who pled guilty to lying about United States citizenship and illegal re-entry after deportation following conviction of aggravated felony, was misadvised by counsel who "failed to independently research and investigate the derivative citizenship defense," which "is a defense to the alienage element of both crimes to which Juarez pled guilty").

- *Tovar Mendoza v. Hatch*, 620 F.3d 1261 (10th Cir 2010) (petitioner's "no contest" plea was product of counsel's "blatant and significant misrepresentations about the amount of time [petitioner] would spend in prison").

- *Bauder v. Dep't of Corr.*, 619 F.3d 1272 (11th Cir. 2010) (per curiam) (counsel "misadvis[ed] Bauder regarding the possibility of being civilly committed as a result of pleading to a charge of aggravated stalking of a minor," erroneously telling client that "pleading to the criminal charge would not subject Bauder to civil commitment").

- *Dasher v. Attorney General*, 574 F.3d 1310 (11th Cir. 2009) ("Dasher's counsel gave plainly inadequate advice" in advising client to "plead guilty without an agreement and throw himself at the mercy of the judge" given that "Dasher was clearly risking a sentence of substantially more than … [plea agreement that had been offered] and there was certainly no reason to believe he would do better").

- *Julian v. Bartley*, 495 F.3d 487 (7th Cir. 2007) (counsel was ineffective "during plea negotiations when that counsel misinterpreted the Supreme Court decision in *Apprendi v. New Jersey* and [consequently] informed Julian that the maximum sentence he could receive would be thirty, rather than sixty years in prison").

- *Dando v. Yukins*, 461 F.3d 791 (6th Cir. 2006) (counsel was ineffective in advising petitioner to plead "no contest" without first consulting mental health expert to assess availability of evidence for duress defense based on Battered Woman Syndrome).

- *Satterlee v. Wolfenbarger*, 453 F. 3d 362 (6th Cir. 2006), cert, denied, 549 U.S. 1281 (2007) (counsel failed to inform petitioner of day-of-trial plea offer and petitioner consequently proceeded to trial and received sentence that was higher than plea offer).

- *Maples v. Stegall*, 427 F.3d 1020 (6th Cir. 2005) (counsel was ineffective in erroneously advising petitioner that guilty plea preserved speedy trial claim for appeal).

- *Burt v. Uchtman*, 422 F.3d 557 (7th Cir. 2005) (counsel was ineffective in failing to request renewed competency examination when client, who was of below-average intelligence and had "history of psychological problems" and was taking "large doses of psychotropic medications," abruptly decided midtrial to take guilty plea against advice of counsel).

- *United States v. Kwan*, 407 F.3d 1005 (9th Cir. 2005) (granting *coram nobis* relief to resident alien who challenged conviction – which was basis for pending deportation – on ground that "Kwan's counsel was constitutionally ineffective in affirmatively misleading him as to the immigration consequences of his conviction").

- *Nunes v. Mueller*, 350 F.3d 1045 (9th Cir. 2003), cert. denied, 543 U.S. 1038 (2004) (trial counsel was ineffective in "failing to inform [client] fully of the actual terms of the plea offer made by the prosecution").

- *Moore v. Bryant*, 348 F.3d 238 (7th Cir. 2003) ("Where erroneous advice is provided regarding the sentence likely to be served if the defendant chooses to proceed to trial, and that erroneous advice stems from the failure to review the statute or case law that the attorney knew to be relevant, the attorney has failed to engage in the type of good-faith analysis of the relevant facts and applicable legal principles" that effective assistance requires).

- *Lyons v. Jackson*, 299 F.3d 588 (6th Cir. 2002), cert, denied, 537 U.S. 1179 (2003) (same as *Miller v. Straub*, infra).

- *Miller v. Straub*, 299 F.3d 570 (6th Cir. 2002), cert, denied, 537 U.S. 1179 (2003) (counsel was ineffective in advising client to plead guilty in order to obtain juvenile sentence without informing client that state could appeal and seek alternate sentence of life imprisonment without possibility of parole. "[D]efense counsel's failure to consider a prosecutor's right to appeal is not a tactic or strategy").

- *Magana v. Hofbauer*, 263 F.3d 542 (6th Cir. 2001) (counsel was ineffective in advising client to reject plea offer, based on mistaken view that maximum possible sentence upon conviction at trial would be identical to sentence offered in plea deal).

- *Wanatee v. Ault*, 259 F.3d 700 (8th Cir. 2001) (counsel was ineffective in failing to advise client that going to trial exposed petitioner to potential sentence of life without parole, whereas plea offer would have ensured parole eligibility).

- *Mask v. McGinnis*, 233 F.3d 132 (2d Cir. 2000), cert, denied, 534 U.S. 943 (2001) (counsel failed to realize and to advise prosecutor that, contrary to her statement during plea bargaining, petitioner was not subject to harsh sentencing provisions for violent persistent offenders).

- *Phillips v. Mills*, 1999 U.S. App. LEXIS 20628 (6th Cir. Aug. 25, 1999) (counsel failed to conduct reasonably adequate investigation before advising petitioner to plead guilty).

- *Ivy v. Caspari*, 173 F.3d 1136 (8th Cir. 1999) (in advising petitioner about plea offer, counsel failed to give adequate explanation of elements of offense, did not alert petitioner to possible mental defense, and erroneously advised petitioner that he was eligible for death penalty if he did not plead guilty).

- *United States v. Alvarez-Tautimez*, 160 F.3d 573 (9th Cir. 1998) (counsel failed to move to withdraw guilty plea following grant of codefendant's motion to suppress, even though plea had not yet been accepted by the district court, giving section 2255 movant an absolute right to withdraw it).

- *United States v. Gordon*, 156 F.3d 376 (2d Cir. 1998) (in advising client about guilty plea, counsel grossly underestimated maximum sentencing exposure under Sentencing Guidelines if client opted for trial).

- *Meyers v. Gillis*, 142 F.3d 664 (3d Cir. 1998) (in advising capital murder defendant to plead guilty to second-degree murder with life sentence, counsel informed client that he would be eligible for parole, but sentence actually was "life imprisonment without parole" and parole was possible only in the event of Governor's commutation).

- *Boria v. Keane*, 99 F.3d 492 (2d Cir. 1996) (counsel was ineffective in failing to counsel client about wisdom of accepting plea bargain which would have substantially reduced sentence).

- *Dickerson v. Vaughn*, 90 F.3d 87 (3d Cir 1996) (petitioners pled nolo contendere based on counsel's erroneous advice that pretrial ruling on double jeopardy could be appealed after plea).

- *Agan v. Singletary*, 12 F.3d 1012 (11th Cir. 1994) (counsel, whose client pled guilty, was ineffective in failing to "make an independent examination of the facts and circumstance" in order to "offer an informed opinion as to the best course to follow," in that counsel "only spent seven (7) hours conducting any sort of external investigation of the case"; ignoring a potentially fruitful lead that would have "created substantial questions as to the identity of the actual perpetrator(s)"; and also ineffective in failing "to investigate [the] client's competency … to plead guilty" (in that counsel ignored indications of mental unfitness because client refused to submit to psychiatric examination)).

- *Osborn v. Shillinger*, 861 F.2d 612 (10th Cir. 1988) (counsel did nothing to assist petitioner in efforts to withdraw guilty plea before sentencing and made statements to media indication that motion to withdraw plea was meritless).

- *Holtan v. Paratt*, 683 F.2d 1163 (8th Cir. 1982), cert, denied, 459 U.S. 1225 (1983) (counsel failed to comply with petitioner's instruction to seek withdrawal of nolo contendere plea).

CHAPTER FIVE

CLAIMS AT TRIAL

Here we are on one of my favorite subjects: trial. I know that your reading of this chapter implies that you put the government's evidence to the test. I also know you likely had a lawyer representing you, leaving a plethora of likely errors. It is also near the turn of the year, as I write this installment to the series, meaning the new annual statistics are public. In 2016, it is estimated that 94% of all federal cases ended in guilty pleas, making you an anomaly.

Those of you who put the government to the test also put your lawyer to the test. Last year, the Department of Justice convicted (enslaved) almost 67,000 people in American courts. Based on that estimate, 62,980 people pled guilty, leaving 4,020 people who went to trial. The federal system is made up of 94 judicial districts, with an average of 30 federal criminal defense lawyers in each district. After doing the math, you discover that that leaves less than two clients for each lawyer to represent at trial.

It matters little what your occupation is; if you do not have practice doing it, you will not be any good at it. If your lawyer said he is a federal trial lawyer, he's lying. What I am telling you is that your trial lawyer made mistakes. However, where I see defendants fail in making a claim is their understanding of their rights and the procedure. Understand first that your rights concerning a criminal trial are established in the Fifth and Sixth Amendments to the U.S. Constitution. These rights are protected, in theory, by the practice of the laws passed in pursuance to the Constitution. What most people know little about, including your lawyer, is that the practice of criminal law is expedited by following the Federal Rules of Criminal Procedure.

Even for those of us who did not have a practicable understanding of the rules prior to trial, we can now follow them to identify potential claims. After reading all these potential trial claims, I strongly suggest that you read the Federal Rules of Criminal Procedure so that you may identify other meaningful claims. Do not miss a claim if you can help it, and it is less work if you get them all the first time.

- *Kimmelman v. Morrison*, 477 U.S. 365 (1986) (petitioner convicted after attorney failed to make obvious and meritorious objection to tainted evidence forming basis of state's case).

- *United States v. Freeman*, 818 F.3d 175 (5th Cir. 2016) (counsel was ineffective in failing to challenge count added by superseding indictment as barred by statute of limitations; "Although counsel's affidavit stated that he considered the issue, the record is silent as to the extent of counsel's research. … Even minimal research would have revealed a compelling argument" for dismissal of count).

- *United States v. Bankston*, 820 F.3d 215 (6th Cir. 2016) (counsel was ineffective in failing to move for dismissal of charge of false statements to judge that was inapplicable to case because "statute expressly exempts from criminal liability statements to a judge in the course of judicial proceedings").

- *Casiano-Jimenez v. United States*, 817 F.3d 816 (1st Cir. 2016) (defense counsel was ineffective in failing to tell defendant, "in words or substance, that he had a right to testify" and "to obtain his informed consent to remaining silent" at trial. "There must be a focused discussion between lawyer and client, and that discussion must – at a bare minimum – enable the defendant to make an informed decision about whether to take the stand").

- *Yun Hseng Liao v. Junious*, 817 F.3d 678 (9th Cir. 2016) (trial counsel, upon receiving court clerk's erroneous report that request for funding for essential medical examination of accused had been denied, did not "conduct [] any further inquiry into the status of his motion" and instead "proceeded to trial without the benefit of the medical examination").

- *Grueninger v. Director*, 813 F.3d 517 (4th Cir. 2016) (counsel's failure to move to suppress his [client's] confession under *Edwards v. Arizona*, 451 U.S. 477 (1981), which prohibits police interrogation after an invocation of Miranda rights, constituted ineffective assistance of counsel." State's claim of strategic judgment is rejected because "on this record, it is hard to discern any tactics at all. Clower did not, in fact, forgo an *Edwards* objection; he raised the *Edwards* issue on the first day of trial. The only thing forgone was the opportunity to make his *Edwards* argument in a timely manner and in writing, as required by local rules – or, once that opportunity was lost, to accept the invitation of the trial judge to object at trial when the confession was introduced.").

- *McShane v. Cate*, 636 Fed. Appx. 410 (9th Cir. 2016) (counsel was ineffective in "provid[ing] no evidence at trial of McShane's history of mental illness" to support counsel's trial strategy of "portray[ing] him as guilty only of either voluntary or involuntary manslaughter" rather than murder).

- *Crace v. Herzog*, 798 F.3d 840 (9th Cir. 2015) ("trial counsel was deficient for failing to request a jury instruction on 'unlawful display of a weapon,' a lesser included offense of second degree assault." If the "trial court would have been given [the instruction], there is a reasonable probability that the jury would have convicted Crace only of that [misdemeanor] offense," thereby avoiding third felony strike that resulted in Crace's being sentenced to life imprisonment without possibility of parole).

- *Gabaree v. Steele*, 792 F.3d 991 (8th Cir. 2015), cert, denied, 136 S. Ct. 1194 (2016) (trial counsel in child sexual abuse trial, in which "main evidence against Gabaree" was testimony of two child complainants, and "there was no medical evidence nor eyewitness accounts to support their testimony," was ineffective in failing to object to "inadmissible bolstering" by physician and "inadmissible propensity evidence" by child psychologist).

- *Thomas v. Clements*, 789 F.3d 760 (7th Cir. 2015), cert, denied, 136 S. Ct. 1454 (2016) (counsel was ineffective in failing to consult with or even consider forensic expert to support defense that accused unintentionally caused victim's death by strangulation, "especially when the state's expert testified that there was no evidence of external bruising").

- *Zapata v. Vasquez*, 788 F.3d 1106 (9th Cir. 2015) ("trial counsel's failure to object to egregious prosecutorial misconduct during closing argument constituted ineffective assistance of counsel").

- *Smith v. Jenkins*, 2015 U.S. App. LEXIS 6835 (6th Cir. April 23, 2015) (trial counsel was ineffective "for not investigating or presenting evidence that Biser's death resulted from a pre-existing medical condition, not Smith's punch").

- *Raether v. Meisner*, 2015 U.S. App. LEXIS 6107 (7th Cir. April 15, 2015)' (counsel's "fail[ure] to make use of the crucial [prosecution] witnesses' prior inconsistent statements" in cross-examination rendered counsel's representation deficient. Although counsel testified "that his choice was 'strategic,'" "counsel's preparation rendered this 'strategic' choice patently unreasonable").

- *Lee v. Clarke*, 781 F.3d 114 (4th Cir. 2015) (trial counsel in second-degree murder trial was deficient in failing to request "jury instruction defining heat of passion," which "competent attorney would have requested" given "testimony that arose during Lee's trial").

- *Rivas v. Fischer*, 780 F.3d 529 (2d Cir. 2015) (when chief medical examiner "changed his estimate as to the time of death six years after the fact, seemingly on the basis of no new evidence," to a time when defendant "had an incomplete alibi," "any reasonable attorney … [would have] conclude[d] that investigating the basis of [the medical examiner's] new findings was essential." The defense counsel's failure to investigate further violated "duty to make reasonable investigations or to make a reasonable decision that makes particular investigations unnecessary").

- *Drain v. Woods*, 595 Fed. Appx. 558 (6th Cir. 2014) ("defense counsel's failure to object to the manner in which the trial court dealt with the Batson violation … constitute[d] deficient counsel").

- *Grumbley v. Burt*, 591 Fed. Appx. 488 (6th Cir. 2015) (trial counsel was "ineffective for failing to move to suppress evidence illegally seized from Grumbley's home." "[W]e cannot know what Grumbley's trial counsel's reasons were for not filing a motion to suppress … [but] it is difficult to conceive of a legitimate trial strategy or tactical advantage to be gained by not filing a motion to suppress").

- *Mosley v. Butler*, 762 F.3d 579 (7th Cir. 2014) (defense counsel failed to investigate potential witness whose testimony "would have bolstered sole witness called by defense counsel, and so omitted witness from trial without making "informed decision").

- *Vega v. Ryan*, 757 F.3d 960 (9th Cir. 2014) (per curiam) ("trial counsel was constitutionally ineffective when he failed to review Vega's client file and, as a result, failed to call as a witness a Catholic priest to whom the victim had recanted her allegations of her stepfather's sexual abuse").

- *Peoples v. Lafler*, 734 F.3d 503 (6th Cir. 2013) ("trial counsel was constitutionally ineffective for failing to impeach the credibility of the two [key prosecution] witnesses based on known false testimony").

- *United States v. Liu*, 731 F.3d 982 (9th Cir. 2013) (granting section 2255 relief because trial counsel "fail[ed] to raise an obvious statute-of-limitations defense").

- *Griffin v. Harrington*, 727 F.3d 940 (9th Cir. 2013) (trial counsel was ineffective in failing to object to unsworn testimony by prosecution witness that opened door to prosecutions introduction of recorded witness statement by identifying accused as triggerman, "the only evidence that named him as Brook's killer").

- *Newman v. Harrington*, 726 F.3d 921 (7th Cir. 2013) (trial counsel's "failure to investigate Newman's fitness [for trial] and request a fitness hearing was constitutionally deficient, and based on the entire record, there is a reasonable probability that Newman would have been found unfit to stand trial").

- *Grant v. Lockett*, 709 F.3d 224 (3d Cir. 2013) (trial counsel did not "adequately investigate the criminal history and parole status of the Commonwealth's key witness," and this failed to learn information that could have been used to impeach witness).

- *Cannedy v. Adams*, 706 F.3d 1148 (9th Cir. 2013), cert, denied, 134 S. Ct. 1001 (2014) (trial counsel failed to interview witness who was "clearly identified" by petitioner as potential source of "information about [complainant's] motive for falsely accusing Petitioner").

- *McClellan v. Rapelje*, 703 F.3d 344 (6th Cir. 2013) (trial counsel "did not interview numerous eyewitnesses who would have testified that McClellan acted in self-defense").

- *Harris v. Thompson*, 698 F.3d 609 (7th Cir. 2012). cert, denied, 133 S. Ct. 2766 (2013) (trial counsel's ineffective handling of hearing on 6-year-old defense witness's competency to testify resulted in exclusion of witness's "critical exculpatory evidence," which probably would not have occurred "[i]f counsel had taken simple and obvious steps to prepare for the hearing").

- *Foster v. Wolfenbarger*, 687 F.3d 702 (6th Cir. 2012), cert, denied, 133 S. Ct. 1580 (2013) (trial counsel ineffectively failed to investigate and present alibi defense).

- *Toliver v. Pollard*, 688 F.3d 853 (7th Cir. 2012) (trial counsel failed to present two witnesses who could have corroborated accused's testimony that "he had not instructed [his brother] to shoot [decedent]").

- *Thomas v. Chappell*, 678 F.3d 1086 (9th Cir. 2012), cert, denied, 133 S. Ct. 1239 (2013) (trial counsel failed to investigate and present available evidence that would have corroborated defense theory that murder was committed by someone other than accused).

- *Cornell v. Kirkpatrick*, 665 F.3d 369 (2d Cir. 2011) (trial counsel ineffectively failed to object to venue under state law rule that would have prevented conviction on counts relating to one of two victims).

- *Elmore v. Ozmint*, 661 F.3d 783 (4th Cir. 2012) ("gross failure of Elmore's 1984 trial lawyers to investigate the State's forensic evidence … had a palpably adverse effect on the defense").

- *Tice v. Johnson*, 647 F.3d 87 (4th Cir. 2011) (counsel failed to investigate facts "already in the litigation file" and failed to file motion (to suppress a statement) which, if it had "been made, the trial court would have little choice but to grant").

- *Breakiron v. Horn*, 642 F.3d 126 (3d Cir. 2011) (counsel failed to take "corrective action" after venire member referred to accused's prior criminal history while in presence of another person who was later seated as juror; counsel also failed to request jury instruction on lesser included offense).

- *Sussman v. Jenkins*, 636 F.3d 329 (7th Cir.), cert, dismissed, 564 U.S. 1063 (2011) (trial counsel's errors resulted in loss of two important opportunities to impeach child complainant in sexual assault trial: (1) Counsel's failure to comply with rape shield law foreclosed showing that complainant had previously brought false allegation of sexual abuse against own father. (2) Counsel's misunderstanding of the judge's ruling caused counsel to forgo use of counseling that documented falseness of complainant's accusations against accused).

- *Couch v. Booker*, 632 F.3d 241 (6th Cir. 2011) ("counsel rendered ineffective assistance by failing to investigate a causation defense").

- *Showers v. Beard*, 635 (3d Cir. 2011) (counsel was ineffective in failing to enlist expert witness to rebut prosecutions' expert on key issue and relying instead on ill-informed cross-examination of prosecution's expert).

- *Hodgson v. Warren*, 622 F.3d 591 (6th Cir- 2010) (counsel was ineffective in failing to request adjournment in order to try to locate exculpatory eyewitness who was under subpoena but failed to appear).

- *Bellizia v. Florida Dep't of Corr.*, 614 F.3d 1326 (11th Cir. 2010) (per curiam) ("trial counsel was ineffective for failing to move for a judgment of acquittal based upon the insufficiency of the State's evidence" of element of crime that triggered twenty-five-year mandatory minimum sentence).

- *White v. Thaler*, 610 F.3d 890 (5th Cir. 2010) ("counsel rendered ineffective assistance by (1) [questioning petitioner on direct examination] … regarding his post-arrest silence, which allowed the prosecutor to impeach him with his failure to tell the police his exculpatory version of the events, and (2) failing to file a motion in time or object to evidence of the murder victim's pregnancy").

- *English v. Romanowski*, 602 F.3d 714 (6th Cir. 2010) (counsel "failed] to adequately investigate" before making subsequently unfulfilled promise to jury in opening statement to call accused's girlfriend to witness stand to corroborate self-defense claim).

- *Gentry v. Sevier*, 597 F.3d 838 (7th Cir. 2010) (counsel was ineffective in "failing to move to suppress or object to the admission … evidence" on 4th Amendment grounds).

- *Bigelow v. Haviland*, 576 F.3d 284 (6th Cir. 2009) (counsel "did not reasonably investigate his [client's] alibi defense." "An attorney's duty of investigation requires more than simply checking out the witnesses that the client himself identifies. And that is especially true here since Rost knew that Bigelow suffered from an 'untreated mental illness,' [and] that his 'recollection [was] not fully with him' regarding the June 1993 period because he was not 'taking his medication at the time.' … Rost had no reasonable basis for assuming that Bigelow's lack of information about still more witnesses meant that there were none to be found.").

- *DeShields v. Shannon*, 338 Fed. Appx. 120, 2009 U.S. App. LEXIS 15410 (3d Cir. July 10, 2009) ("cumulative effect of counsel's failures" amounted to ineffective assistance even if failures, "taken individually," would "perhaps be insufficient for us to conclude that his performance was constitutionally deficient." Counsel failed to confront eyewitness with "the clear contradiction between her trial testimony and the statement she made to [a police officer] … on the night of the incident." Counsel failed to "introduce evidence that [the accused's] … clothing was tested for shot residue and the results were inconclusive." And counsel failed to call potential defense witnesses "who would have testified that they were with or near DeShields during the altercation and that he neither possessed nor fired a gun").

- *Wilson v. Mazzuca*, 570 F.3d 490 (2d Cir. 2009) (defense counsel, who elicited testimony damaging to accused and opened door to introduction of other damaging evidence, "misinterpreted and misunderstood the law, failed to pay attention, acted recklessly, and did not appreciate the consequences of his decisions, even though in many cases he was explicitly warned of the risks by the trial court").

- *Richards v. Quarterman*, 566 F.3d 553 (5th Cir. 2009) (counsel "rendered ineffective assistance of counsel by failing to present – and, through hearsay objections, preventing the prosecution from presenting – crucial exculpatory evidence" and by failing to request instruction on lesser included offense, failing to make use of client's medical records, and failing to interview important witnesses before trial).

- *Hummel v. Rosemeyer*, 564 F.3d 290 (3d Cir.), cert, denied, 558 U.S. 1063 (2009) (counsel was ineffective in stipulating to accused's competency and failing to utilize state procedures for ascertaining competency).

- *Brown v. Smith*, 551 F.3d 424 (6th Cir. 2008 'I (counsel was ineffective in failing to investigate and obtain counseling records that could have been used to impeach complainant).

- *Avery v. Prelesnik*, 548 F.3d 434 (6th Cir. 2008), cert, denied, 558 U.S. 932 (2009) (counsel "failed to investigate and interview potential alibi witnesses").

- *Poindexter v. Booker*, 301 Fed. Appx. 522, 2008 U.S. App. LEXIS 24221 (6th Cir. Nov. 24, 2009) (counsel was ineffective in failing to investigate and present alibi, and in failing to exercise option under state law to reopen testimony when additional defense witnesses arrived in court during closing arguments).

- *Bell v. Miller*, 500 F.3d 149 (2d Cir. 2007) (trial counsel was ineffective in failing to "consult with a medical expert" to "ascertain the possible effects of trauma and pharmaceuticals" on "key prosecution witness" whose memory was "obviously impacted by medical trauma and prolonged impairment of consciousness" and whose "all-important identification … [was] unaccountably altered after the administration of medical drugs").

- *Richey v. Bradshaw*, 498 F.3d 344 (6th Cir. 2007) (trial counsel was ineffective in relying on defense export's opinion to forego defense without "consult[ing] with that expert to make an informed decision about whether [the] particular defense … [was] viable").

- *Ramonez v. Berghuis*, 490 F.3d 482 (6th Cir. 2007) (trial counsel's "decision to limit (or more accurately, not to pursue at all until it was too late) any investigation regarding … three potential [defense] witnesses were objectively unreasonable, leading to an uninformed and therefore unreasonable decision not to call those witnesses at trial")

- *Raygoza v. Hulick*, 474 F.3d 958 (7th Cir.), cert, denied, 552 U.S. 1033 (2007) (counsel was ineffective in failing to investigate and present alibi defense).

- *Higgins v. Renico*, 470 F.3d 624 (6th Cir. 2006) (counsel was ineffective in forgoing cross-examination of key prosecution witness; state's claim of tactical judgment is rejected as "too implausible to accept": "there was no conceivable tactical justification for … fail[ing] to cross-examine the key witness in the case").

- *Lankford v. Arave*, 468 F.3d 578 (9th Cir. 2006), cert, denied, 552 U.S. 943 (2007) (counsel proposed accomplice instructions based on federal law, thereby omitting more protective state law requirement of corroboration of accomplice testimony).

- *Stewart v. Wolfenbarger*, 468 F.3d 338 (6th Cir. 2006) (counsel was ineffective in failing to file proper alibi notice and failing to investigate potential witness).

- *Goodman v. Bertrand*, 467 F.3d 1022 (7th Cir. 2006) (counsel's failure to subpoena witness, along with inadequate objection and actions to preserve record, and opening of door to admission of petitioner's prior convictions constituted "pattern of … deficiencies" that were prejudicial when "considered in their totality").

- *Stanley v. Bartley*, 465 F.3d 810 (7th Cir. 2006) (counsel "prepared for the trial by reading the statements that prospective witnesses had given the police … [but] did not interview any of them").

- *Reynoso v. Giurbino*, 462 F.3d 1099 (9th Cir. 2006) (counsel was ineffective in failing to conduct investigative interviews of two alleged eyewitnesses and failing to cross-examine these witnesses. "Although trial counsel is typically afforded leeway in making tactical decisions regarding trial strategy, counsel cannot be said to have made a tactical decision without first procuring the information necessary to make such a decision").

- *Adams v. Bertrand*, 453 F.3d 428 (7th Cir. 2006) (counsel failed to find and present "pivotal witness" because counsel "committed to a predetermined strategy without a reasonable investigation").

- *Sanders v. Ryder*, 183 Fed. Appx. 666, 2006 U.S. App. LEXIS 16991 (9th Cir. June of 2006) (counsel was ineffective in child molestation case in "fail[ing] to consult or hire a child abuse interview expert regarding proper interview techniques or a DNA expert, [in] fail[ing] to interview state's DNA forensic expert," and in failing to use pretrial hearing on child's competency as witness to challenge admissibility of child's hearsay statements to parent).

- *Virgil v. Dretke*, 446 F.3d 598 (5th Cir. 2006) (counsel was ineffective in "failing to use a peremptory or for-cause challenge" to strike two jurors who "expressly state[ed] an inability to serve as fair and impartial jurors" and who "unequivocally expressed bias against Virgil").

- *Rolan v. Vaughn*, 445 F.3d 671 (3d Cir. 2006) (counsel was ineffective in failing to investigate witnesses named by accused as able to support self-defense claim).

- *Smith v. Lafler*, 175 Fed. Appx. 1, 2006 U.S. App. LEXIS 6667 (6th Cir. March 15, 2006) (counsel was ineffective in failing to investigate complainant's prior in-patient treatment in psychiatric facility which would have led to counsel's discovery of report containing prior inconsistent statements by complainant).

- *Nelson v. Washington*, 172 Fed. Appx. 748, 2006 U.S. App. LEXIS 5711 (9th Cir. March -6, 2006) (counsel was ineffective in failing to investigate whether complainant's claim of sexual abuse was fabricated or, even if crime had occurred, whether perpetrator was someone other than petitioner).

- *Cox v. Donnelly*, 432 F.3d 388 (2d Cir. 2005) (counsel was ineffective in "failing to object to an unconstitutional charge on the key issue of intent to kill").

- *Daniels v. Woodford*, 428 F.3d 1181 (9th Cir. 2005), cert, denied, 550 U.S. 968 (2007) (counsel failed to explain to client why client's testimony at guilt phase was essential to viable defense and failed to deal with breakdown in communications with client by notifying trial judge of problem or seeking assistance from private attorney whom petitioner trusted and who was available).

- *Thomas v. Varner*, 428 F.3d 491 (3d Cir. 2005), cert denied, 549 U.S. 1110 (2007) (counsel was ineffective in failing to file meritorious motion to suppress identification evidence).

- *Draughon v. Dretke*, 427 F.3d 286 (5th Cir. 2005), cert, denied, 547 U.S. 1019 (2006) (counsel failed to obtain forensic examination of physical evidence that would have contradicted state's theory of how fatal shooting occurred and would have countered state's argument that petitioner intended to kill victim).

- *Gersten v. Senkowski*, 426 F.3d 588 (2d Cir. 2005), cert, denied, 547 U.S. 1191 (2006) (counsel was ineffective in failing to investigate medical and psychological evidence that would have supported "strong affirmative case that the charged crime [of sexual abuse and endangering welfare of child] did not occur and [that] the alleged victim's story was incredible in its entirety"; state's claim of "'strategic decision' on the part of defense counsel" is rejected because "[d]efense counsel may not fail to conduct an investigation and then rely on the resulting ignorance to excuse his failure to explore a strategy that would have yielded exculpatory evidence").

- *Hodge v. Hurley*, 426 F.3d 368 (6th Cir. 2005) ("trial counsel's failure to object to any aspect of the prosecutor's egregiously improper closing argument was objectively unreasonable").

- *Martin v. Grosshans*, 424 F.3d 588 (7th Cir. 2005) ("defense counsel performed deficiently for failing to make the proper objections" to inadmissible, prejudicial testimony by prosecution witnesses and "for failing to move for a mistrial after the prosecution's [improper and prejudicial] closing argument").

- *Smith v. Dretke*, 417 F.3d 438 (5th Cir. 2005) (counsel was ineffective in failing to present testimony by witnesses who could have supported self-defense theory by corroborating accused's testimony about decedent's violent nature).

- *White v. Roper*, 416 F.3d 728 (8th Cir. 2005), cert, denied, 546 U.S. 1157 (2006) (counsel failed to investigate adequately, and this failed to call two witnesses who would have directly supported defense's theory of mistaken identification).

- *Termy v. Dretke*, 416 F.3d 404 (5th Cir. 2005) (counsel failed to investigate, and present self-defense claim adequately).

- *Henry v. Poole*, 409 F.3d 48 (2d Cir. 2005), cert, denied, 547 U.S. 1040 (2006) (counsel was ineffective in presenting witness who gave "alibi for the wrong date" and then "adher[ing] to the alibi defense and urg[ing] the jury to accept it").

- *United States v. Jones*, 403 F.3d 604 (8th Cir. 2005) (counsel was ineffective in "failing to challenge the indictment as multiplicitous").

- *Towns v. Smith*, 395 F.3d 251 (6th Cir. 2005) ("trial counsel rendered ineffective assistance … by failing to investigate a witness who had admitted to the police … that he had been involved in the crimes … and that [petitioner] had played no part").

- *Jacobs v. Horn*, 395 F.3d 92 (3d Cir.), cert, denied, 546 U.S. 962 (2005) ("trial counsel rendered ineffective assistance during the guilt phase by failing to adequately investigate, prepare, and present mental health evidence in support of his diminished capacity defense").

- *Owens v. United States*, 387 F.3d 607 (7th Cir. 2004) (counsel's motion to suppress tangible evidence erroneously forfeited meritorious claim).

- *Miller v. Webb*, 385 F.3d 666 (6th Cir. 2005) (counsel was ineffective in failing to challenge, for cause, juror who stated that she "thinks she can be fair, but immediately qualifi[ed] it with a statement of partiality"; "decision whether to seat a biased juror cannot be a discretionary or strategic decision").

- *Earls v. McCaughtry*, 379 F.3d 489 (7th Cir. 2004) (trial counsel was ineffective in failing to object to social worker's opinion that child complainant was truthful and failing to redact videotape of social worker's interview of complainant to remove prejudicial statements by social worker; "We can think of no strategic reason why Earl's counsel would not have objected").

- *Clinkscale v. Carter*, 375 F.3d 430, 443 (6th Cir. 2004), cert, denied, 543 U.S. 1177 (2005) (counsel was ineffective in failing to file notice of alibi defense until a few days before trial even though accused informed counsel of alibi promptly and defense investigator reported existence of at least three alibi witnesses: "even if Clinkscale's attorneys subjectively believed that failing to file an alibi notice on time was in some way strategic-which is doubtful … such a 'strategy' cannot, under the circumstances presented in this case, be considered objectively 'sound' … or 'reasonable'").

- *Soffar v. Dretke*, 368 F.3d 441 (5th Cir. 2004) ("defense counsel have offered no acceptable justification for their failure to take the most elementary step of attempting to interview the single known eyewitness to the crime"; counsel also failed to "consult a ballistics expert" for assistance in "making a strategic decision as to whether such information would have helped Soffar's defense").

- *Reagan v. Norris*, 365 F.3d 616 (8th Cir. 2004) (trial counsel failed to object to jury instruction that omitted essential men's rea element of charged offense).

- *Harris v. Cotton*, 365 F.3d 552 (7th Cir. 2004) (trial counsel was ineffective in failing to obtain toxicology report showing that decedent, who was shot by petitioner in altercation, "was under the influence of alcohol and cocaine" at time of death).

- *A.M. v. Butler*, 360 F.3d 787 (7th Cir. 2004) (trial counsel in juvenile delinquency proceeding was ineffective in failing to move for suppression of petitioner's confession, which could have been challenged under Miranda and due process doctrine of involuntariness and as fruit of unlawful arrest).

- *McFarland v. Yukins*, 356 F.3d 688 (6th Cir. 2014) (trial counsel, who represented both petitioner and her daughter at trial, was ineffective in opting to present "a common defense" that neither client "possessed the drugs, instead of contending that [daughter] was the owner").

- *Young v. Dretke*, 356 F.3d 616 (5th Cir 2004) ("constitutionally effective counsel would have moved to dismiss the [untimely] indictment [on state law grounds] and the state court would have been required to dismiss the persecution … with prejudice").

- *Riley v. Payne*, 352 F.3d 1313 (9th Cir. 2003), cert, denied, 543 U.S. 917 (2004) (counsel failed to interview eyewitness in order to "make an informed judgment about whether [witness's] testimony would help [accused's] claim of self-defense" and corroborate accused's claim that victim was initial aggressor).

- *Davis v. Secretary, Dep't of Corr.*, 341 F.3d 1310 (11th Cir. 2003) (per curiam) (trial "counsel performed deficiently in failing, as require by Florida's rule, to renew *Davis Batson [v. Kentucky]* challenge before accepting the jury").

- *Joshua v. DeWitt*, 341 F.3d 430 (6th Cir. 2003) (counsel was ineffective in failing to litigate 4th Amendment issue, which "reasonable trial attorney would have raised" based on applicable law and facts of case, given that "there is nothing in the record to reflect that … trial counsel considered and declined to raise [issue] … for strategic reasons").

- *Anderson v. Johnson*, 338 F.3d 382 (5th Cir. 2003) (counsel was ineffective in failing to interview eyewitness and instead "rely[ing] exclusively on the investigative work of the State and … assumptions divined from a review of the State's files"; "there is no evidence that council's decision to forego investigation was reasoned at all, and it is, in our opinion, far from reasonable").

- *Alcala v. Woodford*, 334 F.3d 862 (9th Cir. 2003) ("trial counsel made a sound strategic choice to present an alibi defense, but nonetheless failed in his duty to present that defense reasonably and competently" because counsel failed to present best alibi witness and records, which "competent attorney would have presented … unless the attorney was unaware of its existence").

- *Matthews v. Abramajtys*, 319 F.3d 780 (6th Cir. 2003) (counsel failed to capitalize on "flaws in the state's case" regarding identification of petitioner as perpetrator and failed to "present potential alibi witnesses, who testimony would have been quite useful, even if not conclusive]").

- *Holmes v. McKune*, 59 Fed. Appx. 239, 2003 U.S. App LEXIS 1769 (10th Cir. Jan. 31, 2003) (counsel's failure to investigate and present available alibi testimony violated even minimal, pre-Strickland standard of ineffective assistance).

- *Cargle v. Mullin*, 317 F.3d 1196 (10th Cir. 2003) (counsel failed to interview or call at least six witnesses who could have provided testimony undermining state's two star witnesses, erroneously agreed to forgo impeachment of immunized co-perpetrator with deferred sentence on unrelated charges that provided additional incentive to cooperate with prosecution, failed to challenge prosecution's bolstering of state's witness with incredible testimony of police detective, disparaged counsel's own client in course of attacking confession, and failed to object to instances or prosecutorial misconduct).

- *Catalan v. Cockrell*, 315 F.3d 491 (5th Cir. 2002) (counsel, who was appointed on day of trial to replace lawyer with potential conflict of interest, declined to seek statutorily available "ten-day preparation period" and relied instead on hour-long consultation with previous lawyer, thereby failing to learn of "facts and evidence helpful to [petitioner's] defense").

- *Pirtle v. Morgan*, 313 F.3d 1160 (9th Cir. 2002), cert, denied, 539 U.S. 916 (2003) (counsel, had presented expert testimony on accused's lack of capacity to premeditate due to seizures caused by chronic drug use, failed to request jury instruction on diminished capacity and instead merely requested instruction on intoxication).

- *Miller v. Dormire*, 310 F.3d 600 (8th Cir. 2002) (trial counsel waived right to jury trial without client's consent or understanding).

- *Luna v. Cambra*, 306 F.3d 954 (9th Cir.), amended, 311 F.3d 928 (9th Cir. 2002) (counsel failed to investigate, or present evidence corroborating petitioner's alibi defense and also failed to interview individual who ultimately confessed committing crime with which petitioner was charged).

- *Brown v. Stemes*, 304 F.3d 677 (7th Cir. 2002) (counsel's "failure to investigate adequately" resulted in failure to "discover [accused's] documented history of schizophrenia and treatment" and in counsel's consequent failure to "request a hearing to determine (accused's] competency to stand trial, and to consider seriously the question of whether to enter a plea of not guilty by reason of insanity"; public defenders' affidavits explaining and defending their representation are rejected by court of appeals as "post hoc, self-serving,... defensive and ... incomplete").

- *White v. Godinez*, 301 F.3d 796 (7th Cir. 2002) (lack of adequate consultation with client and investigation caused counsel to forgo potentially viable defense in favor of approach that was less likely to prevail).

- *Bios v. Rocha*, 299 F.3d 796 (9th Cir. 2002) (counsel was ineffective in presenting to unconsciousness defense before obtaining facts necessary to gauge whether to present alternative or additional defense of misidentification).

- *Avila v. Galaza*, 297 F.3d 911 (9th Cir. 2002), cert, denied, 538 U.S. 919 (2003) (counsel was ineffective in failing to investigate and present available evidence that shooting was committed by petitioner's brother, not petitioner; counsel's explanation that blaming brother would go against wishes of petitioner's family was "patently unreasonable basis not to investigate [brother's] involvement in the shooting").

- *Beltran v. Cockrell*, 294 F.3d 730 (5th Cir. 2002) ("[d]efense counsel's unreasonable strategic decisions and investigative failures," which led to failure to elicit evidence suggesting that codefendant was primary actor in capital murder, "amounted to ineffective assistance of counsel").

- *Ouber v. Guarino*, 293 F.3d 19 (1st Cir. 2002) (counsel committed unacceptable "error in professional judgment" in "advising the petitioner against testifying" after counsel had already given opening statement that repeatedly "promised … that the petitioner would testify and exhorted the jurors to draw their ultimate conclusions based on her credibility").

- *Jennings v. Woodford*, 290 F.3d 1006 (9th Cir. 2002), cert, denied, 539 U.S. 958 (2003) (counsel was ineffective in concentrating exclusively on alibi defense and thereby failing to investigate and present available mental health evidence that petitioner lacked capacity to form mens rea for first-degree murder).

- *Everett v. Beard*, 290 F.3d 500 (3d Cir. 2002), cert, denied, 537 U.S. 1107 (2003) (trial counsel was ineffective in failing to object to jury instructions permitting conviction of getaway driver without finding of intent to kill).

- *Fisher v. Gibson*, 282 F.3d 1283 (10th Cir. 2002) (trial counsel was ineffective in failing to conduct pretrial investigation and, at trial, failing to advance defense theory, forgoing opening a statement and closing argument, eliciting information damaging to defense, "mailing] no attempt whatsoever to draw the jury's attention to any gaps in the state's evidence," and engaging in behavior that revealed counsel's "animosity toward his client").

- *Dixon v. Snyder*, 266 F.3d 693 (7th Cir. 2001) (trial counsel, who assumed that conviction was precluded by eyewitness's recantation, failed to realize that state law permitted prosecution to introduce eyewitness's pretrial identification of accused as substantive evidence, then failed to respond to prosecution's introduction of statement by introducing eyewitness's recantations of earlier identification).

- *Northrop v. Trippett*, 265 F.3d 372 (6th Cir. 2001), cert, denied, 535 U.S. 955 (2002) (counsel failed to file meritorious motion to suppress physical evidence; counsel's claim of strategic judgment is rejected because "it is difficult to imagine what tactical advantage, cost, could justify [council's decision").

- *Bums v. Gammon*, 260 F.3d 892 (8th Cir. 2001) (trial counsel's failure to object to "prosecutor's closing argument derogating [petitioner's] constitutional right to a jury trial and to confront witnesses" "allowed, and in fact, invited the jury to punish [petitioner] for exercising his constitutional rights," and "[t]here was no reasonable basis for failing to make a constitutional objection to th[e] argument").

- *Pavel v. Hollins*, 2001 U.S. App. LEXIS 16809 (2d Cir. July 25, 2001) (counsel was ineffective in failing to: prepare defense because of assumption that weakness of prosecution's case would result in dismissal; failure to call witnesses who would have supported accused's account, although "'strategic' in some senses of the word, was not the   sort of conscious, reasonably informed decision made by an attorney with an eye to benefitting his client that the federal courts have denominated 'strategic' and have been especially reluctant to disturb"; counsel's failure to call expert could not be deemed strategic because counsel failed to consult with expert beforehand and lacked "education [and] experience necessary" to make a determination without advice from expert).

- *Hughes v. United States*, 258 F.3d 453 (6th Cir. 2001) (counsel failed to respond to venire person's expression of doubt about capacity for fairness by seeking removal for cause or exercising peremptory strike or even by asking follow-up questions; "no sound trial strategy could support counsel's effective waiver of Petitioner's basic Sixth Amendment right to trial by impartial jury").

- *Miller v. Anderson*, 255 F.3d 455 (7th Cir.), vac'd on other grounds, 268 F.3d 485 (7th Cir. 2001) (counsel was ineffective in calling witness whose testimony opened door to cross-examination about accused's prior convictions: "The fact that [this] was a tactic obviously does not immunize it from review in a challenge to the lawyer's effectiveness." ; counsel also was ineffective in failing to consult experts to prepare to challenge state's scientific and physical evidence).

- *Wilcox v. McGee*, 241 F.3d 1242 (9th Cir. 2001) (per curiam) (counsel failed to raise "obvious and meritorious" double jeopardy challenge to re-indictment).

- *Lindstadt v. Keana*, 239 F.3d 191 (2d Cir. 2001) (representation was rendered ineffective by cumulative effect of four errors: failure to exploit important discrepancy in prosecution witnesses' accounts; failure to raise available challenge to prosecution's physical evidence; comment in opening statement that amounted to concession that client's taking witness stand would signal that prosecution had satisfied burden of proving charges; failure to offer adequate arguments for relevance of important defense testimony).

- *Washington v. Hofbauer*, 228 F.3d 689 (6th Cir. 200) (trial counsel's failure to object to clear misconduct by prosecutor amounted to ineffective assistance of counsel: "One of defense counsel's most important roles is to ensure that the prosecutor does not transgress th[e] bounds [or proper conduct]").

- *Delgado v. Lewis*, 223 F.3d 976 (9th Cir. 2000) (trial counsel's repeated failure to appear at "important court proceeding[s]," inability to "make any representations to the court base on personal knowledge," and failure to advocate zealously on client's behalf amounted to "constructive withdrawal from the representation").

- *Washington v. Smith*, 219 F.3d 620 (7th Cir. 2000) (counsel failed to subpoena crucial but difficult-to-find alibi witness until second day of four-day trial and failed to interview and present testimony of other alibi witnesses).

- *Flores v. Demskie*, 215 F.3d 293 (2d Cir.), cert, denied, 531 U.S. 1029 (2000) (counsel incompetently waived potential challenge to state's failure to comply with statutory requirement for disclosure of witnesses' prior statements, which "would have entitled the petitioner to a new trial had it been raised before the trial … [and] would have constituted per se reversible error on direct appeal").

- *Stouffer v. Reynolds*, 214 F.3d 1231 (10th Cir. 2000) (counsel prejudiced petitioner because he "never made an opening statement," "exhibited ineptness at direct questioning without use of leading questions," was "unable to conduct effective cross-examination of the State's witnesses, "failed to lay proper grounds for prosecution witness," cross-examined four prosecutorial forensic experts without "attempt[ing] to interview these witnesses before trial," "failed to file an application for funds to hire experts to examine the opinions of the State's expert witnesses," failed to present testimony by defense investigator who "viewed the crime scene 'and discovered numerous [factual] inconsistencies with the State's theory of the case,'" and "presented closing arguments which were ineffective at proffering any semblance of a defense theory").

- *Combs v. Coyle*, 205 F.3d 269 (6th Cir.), cert, denied, 531 U.S. 1035 (2000) (counsel prejudicially failed to object to prosecution's use of petitioner's pretrial silence as substantive evidence of guilt and also failed to question defense expert sufficiently to anticipate that expert's answers on cross- examination could refute central defense theory).

- *Horton v. Massie*, 2000 U.S. App. LEXIS 1232 (10th Cir. Jan 31, 2000) (counsel failed to call witnesses who could have corroborated petitioner's account, failed to investigate and "present significant evidence that the State's key witnesses collaborated with one another and were lying about both their and petitioner's participation in the murder," and failed to request duress instruction).

- *Hernandez v. Cowan*, 200 F.3d 995 (7th Cir. 200) (counsel who moved for severance unsuccessfully on one ground, failed to recognize alternative, compelling ground for severance that would have been apparent if counsel had attended codefendant's suppression hearing or read transcript of hearing).

- *Maxwell v. Mahoney*, 1999 U.S. App. LEXIS 26592 (9th Cir. Oct. 20, 1999) (although prosecution's otherwise "weak" case relied heavily on police discovery of knife in petitioner's automobile, "defense counsel failed to do any investigation concerning the knife, failed to object to the admission of the knife into evidence the analysis by the State's Criminal Investigation Lab," which showed that blood on knife was rabbit blood and hair fragments were deer hair).

- *Hull v. Kyler*, 190 F.3d 88 (3d Cir. 1999) (petitioner was denied effective assistance at pretrial competency hearing because counsel failed to cross- examine psychiatrist who testified for state and also failed to present available evidence of incompetency).

- *Lord v. Wood*, 184 F.3d 1083 (9th Cir.), cert, denied, 528 U.S. 1198 (2000) (defense counsel failed to present testimony of three witnesses with highly exculpatory information and decided against calling than as witnesses without first personally interviewing them).

KELLY PATRICK RIGGS

32

CHAPTER SIX

INEFFECTIVE AT SENTENCING

Ineffective assistance of counsel during the sentencing stage of a criminal proceeding can be an elusive principle to pin down. First, realize that sentencing is an independent critical stage of the trial process. "Sentencing is a critical stage of the criminal proceeding at which [the defendant] is entitled to the effective assistance of counsel." *Gardner v. Florida*, 430 U.S. 349, 358, (1977). See also *United States v. Roy*, 855 F.3d at 1147 (11th Cir. 2017). As plain as this may appear, we must consider the different aspects of sentencing before we can get a clear picture.

In capital cases, sentencing issues are tried by a jury. Thus, the sentencing record should be examined for possible claims just as a trial would be. In essence, a capital case is broken down into two trials: one to determine guilt and the second to determine the penalty. In a capital case, you must consider the sentencing record as critically as you do the guilt and innocence trial record to achieve a proper evaluation.

With that said, let me make you painfully aware that what remains in noncapital sentencing is a wide range of variables. Regardless of whether your conviction stems from a state or federal conviction, a plea agreement, or a trial, you are facing what I believe to be a limitless list of possible sentencing errors. I have discovered that the most egregious sentencing errors are found in federal sentences, where errors are measured in decades rather than months or weeks. The upside to determining errors in a federal sentence is the United States Sentencing Guidelines.

The federal law in 18 U.S.C §3553 requires a sentencing judge to consider a long list of issues in determining an appropriate sentence. One of my personal favorites is §3553(a) (4) (A):

"The kind of sentence and sentencing range established for the applicable category of offense committed by the applicable category of defendant as set forth in the guidelines…"

Be aware also that the guidelines are only advisory. See *United States v. Booker*, 543 U.S. 220 (2005). But most importantly, "A district court should begin by correctly calculating the applicable guideline range. The guidelines are the starting point and initial benchmark, but they are not the only consideration." *Gall v. United States*, 552 U.S. 38 (2007).

When I say you'll find a multitude of possible sentencing errors, I refer largely to enhancement errors. For example, in reviewing *United States v. Tucker*, 404 U.S. 443 (1973), you find that the Supreme Court held that a convicted prisoner was due to be resentenced because the federal judge had given explicit attention to two previous felony convictions that were invalid under the Constitution. At the time of the previous convictions, the prisoner had no counsel, nor was he advised of his right to counsel.

In Mr. Tucker's case, it would have taken only minutes for his federal counsel to review the docket and find he was not represented in the previous cases. In most cases I review, defense counsel's apathy is often the cause of over-sentencing. Regardless of whether it is a failure to object to a P.S.R., a failure to investigate the case, or a failure to set straight the facts in the record, if the judge does not know about it then the judge cannot consider it. Review the cases that follow:

- *Porter v. McCollum*, 558 U.S. 30 (2009) (per curiam) (counsel at capital sentencing hearing "failed to uncover and present any evidence of Porter's mental health or mental impairment, his family background, or his military service. The decision not to investigate did not reflect reasonable professional judgment. … Porter may have been fatalistic or uncooperative, but that does not obviate the need for defense counsel to conduct same sort of mitigation investigation").

- *Rompilla v. Beard*, 545 U.S. 374 (2005) ("We hold that even when a capital defendant's family members and the defendant himself have suggested that no mitigating evidence is available, his lawyer is bound to make reasonable efforts to obtain and review material that counsel knows the prosecution will probably rely on as evidence of aggravation at the sentencing phase of trial." ; trial attorneys were "deficient in failing to examine the court file on Rompilla's prior conviction," given that "prosecution was going to use the dramatic facts of a similar prior offense, and [accordingly] Rompilla's counsel had a duty to make all reasonable efforts to learn what they could about the offense,] [which] certainly included obtaining the Commonwealth's own readily available file on the prior conviction to learn what the Commonwealth knew about the crime, to discover any mitigating evidence the Commonwealth would downplay and to anticipate the details of the aggravating evidence the Commonwealth would emphasize," and trial counsel's omission was prejudicial in that review of file would have revealed "range of mitigation leads that no other source had opened up").

- *Wiggins v. Smith*, 539 U.S. 510 (2003) (trial counsel's limited investigation of mitigating evidence violated petitioner's right to effective assistance of counsel at capital sentencing phase notwithstanding counsel's claim of "strategic decision" to curtail investigation and concentrate on other types of appeals to sentencing jury, because counsel's "decision to end their investigation when they did was neither consistent with the professional standards that prevailed … [at time of sentencing], nor reasonable in light of the evidence counsel uncovered in the social services records- evidence that would have led a reasonably competent attorney to investigate further").

- *(Terry) Williams v. Taylor*, 529 U.S. 362 (2000) ("counsel did not begin to prepare for th[e] [sentencing] phase until a week before the trial[,]…failed to conduct an investigation that would have uncovered extensive records graphically describing Williams' nightmarish childhood, … failed to introduce available evidence that Williams was 'borderline mentally retarded' and did not advance beyond sixth grade in school[,] … [and] failed to seek prison records recording Williams' commendations for [good conduct while in prison]").

- *Stephenson v. Neal*, 2017 U.S. App. LEXIS 14363 (7th Cir. Aug. 4, 2017) (counsel was ineffective at capital sentencing phase of trial in "failing to object to his client's having to wear a stun belt, given the absence of any reason to think his client would go berserk in the courtroom").

- *Phillips v. White*, 851 F.3d 567 (6th Cir. 2017) ("Phillips's counsel was ineffective … [i]n failing to mount a defense during a capital sentencing, [and] he [thereby] effectively deprived Phillips of counsel throughout a critical stage of trial").

- *United States v. Abney*, 812 F.3d 1079 (D.C. Cir 2016) (counsel in drug case was ineffective in failing to seek continuance of sentencing until after effective date of Fair Sentencing Act, which was passed by Congress five days before sentencing; although "it was an open question whether the reductions in the FSA would apply to pre-FSA conduct where the defendant was sentenced after the FSA took effect," "it was at least reasonably probable-if not more likely still- that courts would interpret the FSA's new [more defendant-favorable] mandatory minimums to apply to defendants sentenced after its effective date").

- *Hardwick v. Secretary*, 803 F.3d 541 (11th Cir. 2015), cert, denied, 137 S. Ct. 41 & 61 (2016) (counsel was ineffective in failing to "obtain any of Hardwick's life-history records or conduct a life-history investigation" even though "Hardwick's attorney had ample information signaling the existence of potential significant mitigation evidence": "He knew that Hardwick had been raised in an abusive environment and has been in and out of foster and boys' hones; and knew of Hardwick's particularly heavy usage of Quaaludes, marijuana, and alcohol immediately prior to the murder").

- *Saranchak v. Secretary*, 802 F.3d 579 (3d Cir. 2015), cert, denied, 136 S. Ct. 1494 (2016) ("Counsel's investigation here [for capital penalty phase of trial] fell woefully - short, under standards expressed both in clear Supreme Court precedent and as set forth by the ABA's professional guidelines. ... Even assuming the [state court] ... was correct that counsel learned nothing from Saranchak, his girlfriend, ... or his mother regarding Saranchak's mental health, his abusive upbringing, or his dysfunctional family, counsel nevertheless learned from Kruszewski ["neutral expert appointed to evaluate Saranchak's competency to stand trial"] about Saranchak's previous psychiatric hospitalization as well as his suicide attempt and depression. ... Yet counsel did not retain an expert on Saranchak's behalf or seek further medical evaluation. Instead, counsel was content with the court-appointed expert's investigation of only Saranchak's competency to stand trial. Counsel did not even obtain the records regarding the psychiatric hospitalization that was reflected in Kruszewski's report, much less Saranchak's school records or other hospitalization records").

- *Bemore v. Chappell*, 788 F.3d 1151 (9th Cir. 2015), cert, denied, 136 S. Ct. 1173 (2016) (counsel "decided to present her 'good guy' mitigation defense without first investigating appropriately the mental health alternative" and, when "mental health mitigation strategy become apparent," counsel "precipitously pushed that possibility aside as inconsistent with the 'sun child' aspect of her planned 'good guy' mitigation presentation").

- *Pruitt v. Neal*, 788 F.3d 248 (7th Cir. 2015), cert, denied, 136 S. Ct. 1161 (2016) ("trial counsel were ineffective in their investigation and presentation of evidence that Pruitt suffered from schizophrenia").

- *Doe v. Ayers*, 782 F.3d 425, 428-29 (9th Cir. 2015) (counsel's investigation for penalty phase of capital case was "facially inadequate": counsel failed to "obtain Doe's prison file, which contained readily apparent and powerful mitigating evidence," did not conduct "follow-up investigation to explore" indications that "Doe was beaten as a child" and may have "suffered more from mental health problems and substance abuse than he was willing to admit," and "did not retain an expert to conduct a penalty-phase investigation").

- *DeBruce v. Commissioner*, 758 F.3d 1263 (11th Cir. 2014) (counsel "failed] to investigate DeBruce's mental health and background" in search of mitigating evidence to present at capital sentencing phase of trial).

- *Cauthem v. Colson*, 736 F.3d 465 (6th Cir. 2013) (counsel failed to investigate possible mitigating evidence of childhood circumstances by interviewing "defendant's nearest relatives").

- *Gonzalez v. United States*, 722 F.3d 118 (2d Cir. 2013) (counsel "did not accompany Gonzalez when Gonzalez was interviewed by the Probation Department," did not provide client with a copy of presentence report, "spent no more than 15 minutes with Gonzalez discussing the [presentence report]," "failed to submit to the court a sentencing memorandum," and "failed to seek a downward departure" under federal sentencing guidelines).

- *Stankewitz v. Wong*, 698 F.3d 1163 (9th Cir. 2012) ("counsel failed to investigate and present readily available mitigation evidence").

- *Hooks v. Workman*, 689 F.3d 1148 (10th Cir. 2012) (counsel presented "woefully inadequate" mitigation presentation although "[e]ven the most minimal investigation would have uncovered a life story worth telling," failed to cross-examine prosecution's witness to show that prior conviction was not as aggravating as witness portrayed, and "bolstered the prosecution's case in aggravation by effectively conceding the continuing threat aggravator in his opening statement").

- *Winston v. Pearson*, 683 F.3d 489 (4th Cir. 2012), cert, denied, 133 S. Ct. 1458 (2013) ("trial attorneys were ineffective for failing to argue to the jury during sentencing that Winston is mentally retarded" so as to invoke *Atkins v. Virginia*s categorical prohibition of death penalty for mentally retarded offenders).

- *Blystone v. Horn*, 664 F.3d 397 (3d Cir. 2011) ("trial counsel was ineffective for failing to investigate, develop, or introduce expert mental health testimony and institutional records in mitigation").

- *Sowell v. Anderson*, 663 F.3d 783 (6th Cir. 2011) ("counsel did not conduct an investigation into Sowell's background or interview any of his family members" despite "reports of several court-appointed mental health experts, which hinted at Sowell's difficult upbringing," and thus counsel did not learn about "his severely impoverished and abusive childhood").

- *Foust v. Houk*, 655 F.3d 524 (6th Cir. 2011) ("Foust's attorneys did not interview any potential [mitigation] witnesses," "did not gather any records from Children's Services, despite [defense psychologist] Karpawich's repeated reminders," "did not prepare Foust's parents or Karpawich in advance of their testimony at the mitigation hearing," and "hired Karpawich in lieu of a trained mitigation specialist, even though Karpawish informed the attorneys that he was not a trained mitigation specialist").

- *Cooper v. Secretary*, 646 F.3d 1328 (11th Cir. 2011) ("Cooper's attorneys did not conduct an adequate background investigation and unreasonably decided to end the background investigation after only talking to Cooper, Cooper's mother and [clinical psychologist/ neuropsychologist] Dr. Merin").

- *Johnson v. Secretary*, 643 F.3d 907 (11th Cir. 2011) ("failure to adequately investigate Johnson's background and…resulting failure to present the non-statutory mitigating circumstances evidence").

- *Kindler v. Horn*, 642 F.3d 398 (3d Cir. 2011), cert, denied, 565 U.S. 1173 (2012) (reaffirming, in pertinent part, *Kindler v. Horn*, 542 F.3d 70 (3d Cir. 2008), vac'd, 558 U.S. 53 (2009)) (granting writ because, inter alia, "Kindler was denied effective assistance of counsel during the penalty phase").

- *Ferrell v. Hall*, 640 F.3d 1199 (11th Cir. 2011) ("[n]either the jury nor the sentencing judge was ever told, because defense counsel never discovered that Ferrell suffers from extensive, disabling mental health problems and diseases" and was subjected to physical abuse as child and grew up in conditions of extreme privation).

- *Goodwin v. Johnson*, 632 F.3d 301 (6th Cir. 2011) (trial counsel chose to "forgo presenting mitigation evidence [due to] incomplete, erroneous information and unsupported supposition").

- *Griffin v. Pierce*, 622 F.3d 831 (7th Cir. 2010), cert, denied, 562 U.S. 1250(2011) (counsel failed to "conduct any investigation into mitigation," presenting only testimony of defendant and "witness with whom Griffin's counsel had never spoken 'until just a few minutes' before she testified").

- *Theus v. United States*, 611 F.3d 441 (8th Cir. 2010) (counsel failed to object to "district court's error in imposing a ten-year mandatory minimum sentence for a quantity of cocaine that required only a five-year minimum sentence").

- *Rollins v. Horn*, 386 Fed. Appx. 267, 2010 U.S. App. LEXIS 13824 (3d Cir. July 7, 2010) (per curiam) ("Rollins' attorney performed deficiently by failing to adequately investigate and present evidence of mitigating circumstances").

- *Robinson v. Schriro*, 595 F.3d 1086 (9th Cir.), cert, denied, 562 U.S. 1037 (2010) (counsel did not conduct adequate investigation, thereby failing to "learn of aspects of Robinson's character and background that would have provided classic mitigation evidence").

- *Johnson v. Mitchell*, 585 F.3d 923 (6th Cir. 2009) (in retrial of case in which previous counsel had been found ineffective, new counsel "felt there was no need for any new investigation" and thus interviewed no witnesses and "did not request the assistance of an investigator"; "utter lack of meaningful mitigation investigation … compels the conclusion that the representation … was deficient").

- *Libberton v. Ryan*, 583 F.3d 1147 (9th Cir, 2009), cert, denied, 560 U.S. 979 (2010) (counsel, who "spent very little time preparing for sentencing" and "did not pursue [potentially mitigating] evidence," "called only two mitigating witnesses, both of whom were only tenuously related to Libberton"; "[n]o possible strategy could justify this lack of diligence in pursuing mitigating evidence").

- *Hamilton v. Ayers*, 583 F.3d 1100 (9th Cir. 2009) (counsel, who had never before tried capital case, failed to investigate and present available mitigating evidence; "Defense counsel did not even exhaust the few sources of information of which he was aware. Rather, he effectively abandoned his investigation after having acquired only rudimentary knowledge of [the defendant's] history from a narrow set of sources.

- *Mams v. Quarterman*, 324 Fed. Appx. 340, 2009 U.S. App. LEXIS 8693 (5th Cir. April 22, 2009) (per curiam) (counsel failed to develop and present available mitigating evidence. "Even if Adams had instructed [counsel] not to contact family members and presumably not to present mitigating evidence derived directly from them, [counsel] was not relieved of conducting a mitigation investigation." "When, as here, counsel does not conduct an investigation sufficient to enable him to reach an informed decision, we must reject the assertion that counsel made a strategic choice not to emphasize the defendant's background").

- *Walbey v. Quarterman*, 309 Fed. Appx 795, 2009 U.S. App. LEXIS 942 (5th Cir. Jen 19, 2009) (per curiam) (counsel was ineffective in failing to investigate and present available mitigating evidence: Supreme Court's decision in "*Williams* [*v. Taylor*] … stands for the proposition that counsel can be prejudicially ineffective even if some of the available mitigation evidence is presented and even if there is psychiatric testimony").

- *Sechrest v. Ignacio*, 549 F.3d 789 (9th Cir. 2008), cert, denied, 558 U.S. 938 (2009) (counsel was ineffective in permitting prosecution to review confidential report of mental health expert whom defense had decided not to call as witness, and by stipulating to prosecutor's calling expert as witness for prosecution at capital sentencing hearing, and by failing to prepare adequately to cross-examine expert).

- *Johnson v. Bagley*, 544 F.3d 592 (6th Cir. 2008) ("At a surface level, it appears that Johnson's counsel [followed "ABA guidelines on death-penalty representation" in] … consider[ing] all of the [] [Guidelines'] options [for "witnesses and evidence to introduce at the penalty phase of a capital case"]." But counsel "chose not to interview" petitioner's mother based on counsel's conclusion that mother would "be a 'bad mitigation witness,'" which "is no explanation for not interviewing her first." Counsel's failure to read extensive social services records on petitioner left counsel unaware of "different mitigation strategy" and led to counsel's submitting records to jury that "directly contradicted" counsel's mitigation argument. "[R]ecord suggests that these investigative blunders occurred because no one who participated in Johnson's penalty-phase defense made any deliberate decisions about the scope of the investigation, let alone the 'reasonable' ones Strickland requires").

- *Mason v. Mitchell*, 543 F.3d 766 (6th Cir. 2008), cert, denied, 558 U.S. 1007 (2009) ("trial counsel provided ineffective assistance by failing to interview Mason's family members and investigate the obvious red flags contained in state records suggesting that Mason's childhood was pervaded by violence and exposure to drugs in the home from an early age").

- *Williams v. Allen*, 542 F.3d 1326 (11th Cir. 2008), cert, denied, 556 U.S. 1253 (2009) (counsel's investigation was constitutionally inadequate: "despite the availability of several of Williams' family members, trial counsel sought mitigating evidence" exclusively from petitioner's mother and thereby "obtained an incomplete and misleading understanding of Williams' life history"; "counsel's failure to pursue this additional evidence cannot be characterized as the product of a reasonable strategic decision. Counsel uncovered nothing in their limited inquiry into Williams' background to suggest that 'further investigation would have been fruitless'").

- *Bond v. Beard*, 539 F.3d 256 (3d Cir. 2008), cert, denied, 558 U.S. 835 (2009) (counsel waited "until the eve of the penalty phase to begin their preparations," causing "them to fail to inquire meaningfully into Bond's childhood and mental health," and depriving defense's mental health expert of "sufficient information to evaluate Bond accurately"; "We will not excuse this conduct on the ground that Bond and his family members did not tell counsel that his background provided fertile territory for mitigation arguments. Neither Bond nor his family had a duty to instruct counsel how to perform such a basic element of competent representation as the inquiry into a defendant's background").

- *Jells v. Mitchell*, 538 F.3d 478 (6th Cir. 2008) (trial counsel was ineffective in "(1) failing to prepare for the mitigation phase of the case until after [petitioner] was convicted; [and] (2) failing to utilize a mitigation specialist to gather information and [petitioner's] background, including his educational, medical, psychological, and social history").

- *Burdge v. Belleque*, 290 Fed. Appx. 73, 2008 U.S. App. LEXIS 17889 (9th Cir. Aug. 15, 2008) (counsel was ineffective in failing to object to trial court's application of habitual offender statute that was inapplicable to petitioner's situation; "counsel's failure to object" cannot be "characterized as the product of sound strategy" since "[n]othing in the record indicates that counsel carefully considered whether to object but ultimately decided against it").

- *Correll v. Ryan*, 539 F.3d 938 (9th Cir. 2008), cert, denied, 555 U.S. 1098 (2009) (counsel was ineffective in failing to investigate and present mitigating evidence: "To the extent that there was any strategy involved in the penalty phase presentation, it cannot be considered a reasonable strategy by any objective measure").

- *Gray v. Branker*, 529 F.3d 220 (4th Cir. 2008), cert, denied, 556 U.S. 1106 (2009) ("[c]ounsel rendered ineffective assistance by failing to investigate and develop, for sentencing purposes, evidence that Gray suffered from a severe mental illness").

- *Duncan v. Omoski*, 528 F.3d 1222 (9th Cir. 2008), cert, denied, 556 U.S. 1131 (2009) ("counsel's failure to investigate and present ... potentially exculpatory serological evidence ... prejudiced Duncan with respect to the jury's special circumstance finding" and requires vacating of capital sentence).

- *Lawhom v. Allen*, 519 F.3d 1272 (11th Cir. 2008) (counsel was ineffective in waiving closing argument in capital sentencing hearing; although counsel claimed strategic reason for waiver, counsel "failed to adequately investigate or research the law and was thus unable to make a strategic decision as to whether to waive argument").

- *Morales v. Mitchell*, 507 F.3d 916 (6th Cir. 2007) ("trial counsel conducted an inadequate investigation in preparation for the penalty phase": "defense counsel failed to interview key witnesses for both the prosecution and the defense. ... Moreover, defense counsel did not hire a mitigation specialist or investigator and did not himself contact any of Morales's family members other than Morales's father, ... even though numerous other family members were willing to testify").

- *Haliym v. Mitchell*, 492 F.3d 680 (6th Cir. 2007) ("counsel failed to follow up with obvious avenues of investigation that would have produced valuable mitigating evidence").

- *Lairibright v. Schriro*, 490 F.3d 1103 (9th Cir. 2007), cert, denied, 552 U.S. 1097 (2008) (counsel "failed to do even a minimal investigation of 'classic mitigation evidence,' notwithstanding the fact that he knew such evidence potentially existed").

- *Stevens v. McBride*, 489 F.3d 883 (7th Cir. 2007), cert, denied, 553 U.S. 1034, 1048 (2008) (counsel were ineffective in failing to "investigate and present mitigation evidence on [petitioner's] mental state," relying exclusively on psychologist whom counsel had come to regard as "a 'quack,'" and calling psychologist to witness stand without knowing anything "about the content of [psychologist's] planned testimony," thereby activating duty to provide prosecutor with psychologist's "extremely detrimental written report").

- *Miller v. Martin*, 481 F.3d 468 (7th Cir. 2007) (counsel was ineffective in standing mute at sentencing based on counsel's assumption that conviction would be overturned on appeal).

- *Anderson v. Sirmons*, 476 F.3d 1131 (10th Cir. 2007) ("trial counsel's failure to investigate and obtain ... readily available evidence in mitigation ... fell well below the prevailing professional norms and amounted to deficient performance"; "Trial counsel did not undertake a strategic decision in this case to omit the mitigation evidence identified above; counsel simply did not investigate and therefore did not know such evidence was available").

- *Outten v. Kearney*, 464 F.3d 401 (3d Cir. 2006) (counsel was ineffective in failing to investigate and present mitigating evidence: counsel's "effort fell well short of the national prevailing professional standards articulated by the American Bar Association and was, therefore, unreasonable").

- *Frierson v. Woodford*, 463 F.3d 982 (9th Cir. 2006), cert, denied, 551 U.S. 1134 (2007) (counsel was ineffective in failing to investigate and present mitigating evidence and in "inducing and failing to challenge [defense witness's] ... invocation of his Fifth Amendment right to self-incrimination" and thereby losing best opportunity to refute prosecution's argument that petitioner committed another, prior murder).

- *Williams v. Anderson*, 460 F.3d 789 (6th Cir. 2006) ("[d]efense counsel's complete failure to investigate before deciding not to present mitigating evidence is deficient performance as a matter of law under Strickland"; "council's decision to focus on residual doubt alone could not constitute a reasonable trial strategy because defense counsel never conducted an investigation into mitigation before deciding to pursue residual doubt").

- *Hovey v. Ayers*, 458 F.3d 892 (9th Cir. 2006) (counsel was ineffective in failing to "adequately prepare Hovey's penalty-phase expert witness sufficiently" by providing hospital records and other documentation supporting the diagnosis and information about petitioner's conduct during months leading up to commission of crime: "Regardless of whether a defense expert requests specific information relevant to a defendant's background, it is defense counsel's 'duty to seek out such evidence and bring it to the attention of the experts'").

- *Poindexter v. Mitchell*, 454 F.3d 564 (6th Cir. 2006) (counsel was ineffective in failing to investigate and present available mitigating evidence: counsel's allegedly strategic decision to limit mitigation to certain family members, friends, and petitioner himself "was unreasonable since {it] was the product of an incomplete investigation").

- *Dickerson v. Bagley*, 453 F.3d 690 (6th Cir. 2006) (counsel "did not properly conduct a mitigation investigation" and consequently did not learn of client's borderline IQ and other mitigating aspects of "family, educational, social and medical history").

- *Daniels v. Woodford*, 428 F.3d 1181 (9th Cir. 2005), cert, denied, 550 U.S. 968 (2007) (counsel failed to prepare adequately for sentencing phase, including failing to follow up on psychological screening that showed mental disorder, "fail[ing] to review ... family and social history which described a history of mental illness," and failing to investigate effects of prescribed medication and illegal substances on client's state of mind at time of crime).

- *Marshall v. Cathel*, 428 F.3d 452 (3d Cir. 2005), cert, denied, 547 U.S. 1035 (2006) ("numerous failures in investigating and preparing for the penalty phase of the case, and in putting on and arguing a case for life").

- *Miller v. Dretke*, 420 F.3d 356 (5th Cir. 2005) (counsel failed to investigate potential mitigating evidence by interviewing physicians who had treated petitioner for "mental and emotional injuries" stemming from earlier car accident, and counsel "made his decision not to call ... physicians as witnesses without speaking to them").

- *Harries v. Bell*, 417 F.3d 631 (6th Cir. 2005) (counsel was ineffective in failing to "conduct a thorough investigation of Harries's mental health" or to consult mental health expert even though "Harries's mother alerted them that Harries suffered from mental illness" and in failing to "adequately investigate Harries's family background, despite indications of Harries's troubled childhood"; counsel's explanation that failure to investigate stemmed from client's opposition and from counsel's doubts about persuasiveness of such mitigating evidence is rejected by court of appeals based on prior circuit case law rejecting such rationales).

- *Canaan v. McBride*, 395 F.3d 376 (7th Cir. 2005) ("counsel was ineffective in failing to consult with [petitioner] regarding his right to testify at the penalty phase of the trial").

- *Smith v. Mullin*, 379 F.3d 919 (10th Cir. 2004) (counsel was ineffective in failing to present mitigating evidence of petitioner's brain damage, mental retardation and troubled background at capital sentencing hearing: "While the same constitutional principles that guide[] our examination of [counsel's] guilt stage performance apply to his performance at sentencing, we are particularly vigilant in guarding th[e] right [to effective assistance of counsel] when the faces a sentence of death. ... Our heightened attention parallels the heightened demands on counsel in a capital case." (citing ABA Standards for Criminal Justice)).

- *Lewis v. Dretke*, 355 F.3d 364 (5th Cir. 2003) (per curiam) (counsel was ineffective in failing to "investigate mitigating evidence of [client's] abusive childhood"; counsel's claim of strategy is rejected because "[n]othing in counsel's testimony … supports the theory of their decision having been tactical": "It is axiomatic – particularly since Wiggins – that such a decision [to forgo pursuit of mitigating evidence] cannot be credited as calculated tactics or strategy unless it is grounded in sufficient facts, resulting in turn from an investigation that is at least adequate for that purpose").

- *Hamblin v. Mitchell*, 354 F.3d 482 (6th Cir. 2002), cert, denied, 543 U.S. 925 (2004) ("counsel's failure to investigate and prepare for the sentencing phase of the ABA standards [which, under *Wiggins v. Smith*, "provide the guiding rules and standards to be used in defining the 'prevailing professional norms' in ineffective assistance cases"] and applicable case law"; trial counsel's claim of strategic reasons for failing to investigate "does not make sense," and trial counsel's claim that he followed his client's wishes cannot excuse failure, including because ABA Guidelines state that "'investigation regarding penalty should be conducted regardless of any statement by the client that evidence bearing upon penalty is not to be collected or presented'").

- *United States v. Conley*, 349 F.3d 837 (5th Cir. 2003) (trial counsel was "ineffective in failing to object" to sentence that exceeded statutory maximum).

- *Frazier v. Huffman*, 343 F.3d 780 (6th Cir. 2003), supplemented, 348 F.3d 174 (6th Cir. 2003), cert, denied, 541 U.S. 1095 (2004) (trial counsel was ineffective in railing to "investigate amd present evidence of [petitioner's] brain impairment": "We can conceive of no rational trial strategy that would justify the failure…to investigate and present evidence of [petitioner's] brain impairment, and to instead rely exclusively on the hope that the jury would spare his life due to any 'residual doubt' about his guilt").

- *United States v. Horey*, 333 F.3d 1185 (10th Cir. 2003) (counsel in federal sentencing hearing was ineffective in failing to "object to an indisputably inapplicable career offender enhancement that increased both Mr. Horey's total offense level and his criminal history category…, increasing the applicable guideline range minimums").

- *Powell v. Collins*, 332 F.3d 376 (6th Cir. 2003) (attorney who "spent less than two full business days preparing [for capital sentencing stage of trial], waiting until after the conclusion of the guilt phase to do so," was ineffective in failing to develop and present mitigating evidence, and deficiencies could not could not be justified as "strategic" decisions because counsel had not conducted sufficient investigation to assess strategy reasonably).

- *Cargle v. Mullin*, 317 F.3d 1196 (10th Cir. 2003) (counsel performed no investigation in preparation for capital sentencing phase and consequently failed to present available evidence of petitioner's difficult childhood and good personal traits, with result that "jury heard only brief, personally remote, and fairly generic testimony from testimony from petitioner's pastor, who simply could not relate the individualized, humanizing facts that other potential witnesses could have provided"; counsel also failed to call petitioner to witness stand "to express remorse or to otherwise suggest why he should not be defined solely by the terrible act of which he stood convicted").

- *Douglas v. Woodford*, 316 F.3d 1079 (9th Cir.), cert, denied, 540 U.S. 810 (2003) (counsel was ineffective in presenting only "minimal" mitigating evidence and suggesting "in very general terms" that petitioner had difficult childhood; counsel's failure to develop and present mitigating evidence could not be justified by petitioner's refusal to cooperate with counsel's investigation and could not be attributed to strategic decision given counsel's lack of information needed for evaluating strategy).

- *Hooper v. Mullin*, 314 F.3d 1162. (10th Cir. 2002), cert, denied, 540 U.S. 838 (2003) (trial counsel's presentation of psychologists at sentencing hearing was "disastrous" and undermined defense's theory of mitigation because counsel presented mental health evidence without adequate "investigation, in an unprepared and ill-informed manner").

- *Brownlee v. Haley*, 306 F.3d 1043 (11th Cir. 2002) (counsel failed to "investigate, obtain, or present" mitigating evidence, despite availability of "powerful mitigating evidence of [petitioner]'s borderline mental retardation, psychiatric disorders, and history of drug and alcohol abuse").

- *Simmons v. Luebbers*, 299 F.3d 929 (8th Cir. 2002), cert, denied, 538 U.S. 923 (2003) (counsel was ineffective in "fail[ing] to present any meaningful mitigating evidence" despite availability of mental health evidence; state supreme court's view of "attorney's penalty phase actions [as] part of a sound trial strategy" is rejected because "there was no justifiable reason to prevent the jury from learning about Simmon's [mitigating] childhood experiences").

- *Carpenter v. Vaughn*, 296 F.3d 138 (3d Cir. 2002) (counsel was ineffective in failing to object to "highly misleading answer given by the trial judge in response to a jury question about the availability of parole if Carpenter was sentenced to life imprisonment").

- *Karis v. Calderon*, 283 F.3d 1117 (9th Cir. 2002), cert, denied, 539 U.S. 958 (2003) (counsel was ineffective in failing to investigate and present mitigating evidence: "a substantial mitigating case may be impossible without a life-history investigation").

- *Silva v. Woodford*, 279 F.3d 825 (9th Cir.), cert, denied, 537 U.S. 942 (2002) (counsel ineffectively elected to "abandon []…the investigation into [petitioner's] background – including his family, criminal, substance abuse, and mental health history –" "base entirely on an overboard acquiescence in his client's demand that he refrain from calling his parents as witnesses." "[I]f a client forecloses certain avenues of investigation, it arguably becomes even more incumbent upon trial counsel to seek out and find alternative sources of information and evidence, especially in the context of a capital murder trial… [and] a concomitant duty to try to educate or dissuade [petitioner] about the consequences of his actions").

- *Mayfield v. Woodford*, 270 F.3d 915 (9th Cir. 2001) (en banc) (counsel "neither adequately investigated and prepared for the penalty phase [counsel "billed only 40 hours in preparation for both the guilt and penalty phases of trial … [,] had only one substantive meeting with his client, the morning the trial began, and did not discuss with him possible witnesses or trial strategies[,] … [and] spent less than half the defense investigation budget authorized"] nor presented and explained the significance of all the available mitigating evidence to the jury").

- *Ainsworth v. Woodford*, 268 F.3d 868 (9th Cir. 2001) ("counsel engaged in minimal preparation,…interview[ing] one defense witness for only ten minutes on the morning she was scheduled to testify"; "failed to examine [petitioner]'s ["readily available"] employment records, medical records, prison records, past probation reports, and military records" "abdicated the investigation of [petitioner]'s psychosocial history to one of [his] female relatives"; "failed to present…evidence of [petitioner]'s positive adjustment to prison life during his previous incarcerations"; and, due to lack of preparation, conducted direct examination of witness that opened door to damaging cross-examination about petitioner's intention to commit other crime).

- *Coleman v. Mitchell*, 268 F.3d 417 (6th Cir. 2001), cert, denied, 535 U.S. 1031 (2002) (counsel "failed to [develop and] present … any aspects of Petitioner's personal history," which included extensive physical and psychological abuse in childhood, prior hospitalizations for head injuries, and possible psychological and organic brain disorders; counsel's claim that mitigating evidence was omitted in order to "honor Petitioner's wishes" is rejected as "baseless").

- *Jermyn v. Horn*, 266 F.3d 257 (3d Cir. 2001) (counsel, who had been out of law school for less than two years, "failed to investigate the circumstances surrounding [petitioner]'s childhood," even though counsel was informed by defense expert prior to trial that petitioner "had been abused as a child, and … that the abuse was a critical component to understanding [his] mental illness"; counsel "practically concedes that his course of conduct was not based on his exercise of sound professional judgment[,]…[and] that he had no tactical reason for failing to investigate").

- *Battenfield v. Gibson*, 236 F.3d 1215 (10th Cir. 2001) (counsel's failure to investigate available mitigating evidence could not be excused either by claim of strategic judgment to rely on appeal to jurors' sympathy and mercy or by accused's statement at trial that he did not want to present any mitigating evidence).

- *Skaggs v. Parker*, 235 F.3d 261 (6th Cir. 2000), cert, denied, 534 U.S. 943 (2001) (counsel chose to call psychiatric expert at sentencing, notwithstanding expert's "bizarre and eccentric testimony" at trial, rather than seeking different expert, because counsel assumed that court would not grant motion for new expert; consequent failure to present available mitigating evidence "could not be considered a strategic decision, but rather, an abdication of advocacy").

- *United States v. Frank*, 230 F.3d 811 (5th Cir. 2000) (counsel failed to raise available challenge to application of Federal Sentencing Guidelines to enhance sentence).

- *Lockett v. Anderson*, 230 F.3d 696 (5th Cir. 2000) (counsel failed to conduct adequate investigation into available mitigating evidence).

- *Carter v. Bell*, 218 F.3d 581 (6th Cir. 2000) (counsel prejudicially failed to investigate mitigating evidence and relied exclusively on possibility of a residual doubt at sentencing; although "counsel advanced several reasons for adopting their strategy, their reasons do not excuse their deficiency"; nor does client's unwillingness to rely on mental health problems justify n counsel's failure to investigate potentially mitigating psychological evidence).

- *Jackson v. Calderon*, 211 F.3d 1148 (9th Cir. 2000), cert, denied, 531 U.S. 1072 (2001) (counsel's "total investigation for purposes of the penalty phase took less than two hours some weeks before the trial began" and consisted of interviews of petitioner's mother and estranged wife and review of his juvenile and military records; "[n]o attempt was made to compile a social history of Jackson, to indicate the conditions in which he had been brought up and lived").

CHAPTER SEVEN

CLAIMS CONCERNING APPEAL

Repeatedly I have been asked if ineffective assistance of counsel claims can be raised against appellate counsel. The answer is yes. For those of you who require a bit more explanation, read the following:

- The Sixth Amendment to the United States Constitution, which states in pertinent part: "In all criminal prosecutions, the accused shall enjoy the right to…have the assistance of counsel for his defense."

- 18 U.S.C. §3006A states in pertinent part that, "The district shall establish a method of providing adequate representation for those qualified… through appeal."

- *Harrington v. Gillis*, 456 F.3d 118, 132 (3d Cir. 2006) (noting that "an appeal is a critical stage of the criminal proceedings").

What is unimaginable is that a defendant's appellate counsel would act ineffectively at his client's first forum of review. The facts of today's legal trend are self-evident. In my own personal case, my last trial lawyer volunteered to perform as appellate counsel to conceal his own deficient performance. See *United States v. Kelly Patrick Riggs*. Case No.: 14-11917 (11th Cir. 2015). In my case, the Eleventh Circuit went on to refuse publication, thus concealing that an actually innocent citizen was convicted without counsel and due process, in violation of the Thirteenth Amendment.

The point here is that when a defendant suffers a "Rush to Judgment" and/or otherwise suffers a miscarriage of justice, he depends on direct appeal to redress his grievances. Most commonly, though, in cases of appointed counsel or pre-paid retained counsel, counsel files a motion to withdraw under *Anders v. California*, regardless of meritorious issues, leaving a defendant to remain in prison regardless of actual justice.

Most commonly, an underprivileged or minority federal defendant suffers because the courts, the government, and defense/appellate counsel deprive the defendant of their honest service. When this happens, a defendant may raise a claim that his appellate counsel provided ineffective assistance of counsel. The appellant may seek redress in a motion to vacate under 28 U.S.C. §2255, the statute that restates clarifies, and/or simplifies the procedure in the nature of the ancient writ of error *coram nobis*. §2255 was enacted to provide an expeditious remedy for correcting erroneous sentences and/or convictions without resorting to *habeas corpus*. See the examples that follow:

- *Evitts v. Lucey*, 469 U.S. 387 (1985) (ineffective assistance of counsel on appeal).

- *Loher v. Thomas*, 2016 U.S. App. LEXIS 10971 (9th Cir. June 17, 2016) (appellate counsel was ineffective in failing to raise claim that trial court violated *Brooks v. Tennessee*, 406 U.S. 605 (1972) by directing defendant to testify as first defense witness because other defense witnesses were not yet present).

- *Overstreet v. Warden*, 811 F.3d 1283 (11th Cir. 2016) (appellate counsel's failure to challenge sufficiency of kidnapping convictions by invoking state supreme court decision, which was issued between dates of conviction and direct appeal. This changed the aspiration element of kidnapping, "can be explained in one of two ways: he either failed to recognize or elected not to raise this strong basis for reversal of four criminal convictions. … Either way, counsel's performance is patently deficient.").

- *Hawes v. Perry*, 633 Fed. Appx. 720 (11th Cir. 2015) (per curiam) (appellate counsel was ineffective in "fail[ing] to raise an ineffective-assistance-of-trial-counsel claim" based on trial counsel's failure to authenticate email by complainant that would have "undermine[d] the truthfulness of … [her] testimony").

- *Lynch v. Dolce*, 789 F.3d 303 (2d Cir. 2015) ("[a]ppellate counsel's failure to raise… [meritorious] issue [on trial court's refusal to grant defense counsel's request for jury instruction defining element of crime] and [appellate counsel's] decision instead to raise weaker issues that were unlikely to succeed fell below prevailing norms of professional conduct").

- *Sullivan v. United States*, 587 Fed. Appx. 935 (6th Cir. 2014) (appellate counsel was ineffective in failing to raise claim that mandatory guidelines sentencing system was unconstitutional under *United States v. Booker*, 543 U.S. 220(2005), which was issued "while Sullivan's case was pending on direct appeal").

- *Payne v. Stansberry*, 760 F.3d 10 (D.C. Cir. 2014) ("appellate counsel failed to seek plain error review" of "erroneous jury instruction [that] reduced the government's burden of proof").

- *Vance v. Scutt*, 573 Fed. Appx. 415 (6th Cir. 2014) ("appellate counsel was ineffective for failing to file an appeal of right, filing instead an application for leave to appeal").

- *Norris v. Lester*, 545 Fed. Appx. 320 (6th Cir. 2013) ("appellate counsel was ineffective for failing to argue that [Norris'] confession was obtained after the violation of his constitutional right to a prompt probable-cause determination").

- *Farina v. Secretary*, 536 Fed. Appx. 966 (11th Cir. 2013) (pier curiam) (appellate counsel was ineffective in failing to assert, as "fundamental error," unpreserved claim that "prosecutor's injection of religious authority into a capital sentencing proceeding" – in *voir dire*, cross-examination of defense witness, and closing argument – "diminished the jury's sense of responsibility in a way that undermined the reliability of its death recommendation").

- *United States v. Cong Van Pham*, 722 F.3d 320 (5th Cir. 2013) (granting section 2255 relief because trial counsel "fail[ed] to consult with [client] about filing a direct appeal of his sentence … [even though] Pham reasonably expressed an interest in an appeal immediately after he was sentenced").

- *Shaw v. Wilson*, 721 F.3d 908 (7th Cir. 2013), cert, denied, 134 S. Ct. 2818 (2014) ("On direct appeal, Shaw's new lawyer abandoned trial counsel's [potentially meritorious] contention that the information was amended too late and instead pressed a futile claim that the evidence against Shaw was insufficient to support his conviction").

- *Glover v. Birkett*, 679 F.3d 936 (6th Cir. 2012) (counsel "failed to timely file a notice of appeal," thereby depriv[ing] Glover of his appeal of right").

- *Hardaway v. Robinson*, 655 F.3d 445 (6th Cir. 2011) (counsel "failed to file an appellate brief and thereby deprived Hardaway of a direct appeal").

- *Showers v. Beard*, 635 F.3d 625 (3d Cir. 2011) (appellate counsel failed to raise meritorious challenge to trial counsel's ineffectiveness, thereby "ignor[ing] an argument going directly to the issue of guilt that is 'clearly stronger than those presented'").

- *Theus v. United States*, 611 F.3d 441 (8th Cir. 2010) (counsel failed to "raise … on direct appeal the district court's error in imposing a ten-year mandatory minimum sentence for a quantity of cocaine that require only a five-year minimum sentence").

- *Goff v. Bagley*, 601 F.3d 445 (6th Cir. 2010), cert, denied, 131 S. Ct. 1045 (2011) (appellate counsel was ineffective in failing to raise claim that trial judge violated state law rule establishing accused's "right to allocate before sentencing").

- *Ramchair v. Conway*, 601 F.3d 66 (2d Cir. 2010) ("Appellate counsel's failure to raise the mistrial claim was not a sound strategic decision, but a mistake based on counsel's misunderstanding that the mistrial claim, which trial counsel explicitly made, had not been preserved").

- *Bostick v. Stevenson*, 589 F.3d 160 (4th Cir. 2009) (applying *Roe v. Flores-Ortega*, 528 U.S. 470 (2000) to find that counsel was ineffective in "fail[ing] to consult with Bostick about filing an appeal": "trial counsel had a duty to consult with Bostick because he went to trial, there were non-frivolous grounds to pursue, and, most importantly, Bostick unequivocally demonstrated his interest in an appeal post-verdict").

- *Hodge v. United States*, 554 F.3d 372 (3d Cir. 2009) (trial counsel was ineffective in failing to file timely notice of appeal based on counsel's mistaken belief that "his motions practice had out of the pertinent deadline"; even if government is correct that "record contains insufficient evidence to establish what, if anything, Hodge told his counsel regarding an appeal before the filing period expires," "[w]e need not resolve" issue because "[nobody contends that Hodge told his lawyer that he did not want to appeal" and "we cannot envision a scenario, aside from following a client's thoroughly informed and perfectly explicit direction, where it would be reasonable for an attorney not to appeal the life sentence of a client with a nonfrivolous argument … as to why the sentence is unlawful").

- *Carmell v. Quarterman*, 292 Fed. Appx. 317, 2008 U.S. App. LEXIS 19261 (5th Cir. Sept. 8, 2008) (per curiam), cert, denied, 557 U.S. 922 (2009) (appellate counsel was inadequate in failing to seek extension of time for filing tried failing: to file brief before court issued decision affirming conviction, and failing to discuss case with petitioner).

- *Thompson v. United States*, 504 F.3d 1203 (11th Cir. 2007) (trial counsel violated "duty to consult with the defendant about an appeal" by responding to client's question about appeal by "[s]imply asserting the view that an appeal would not be successful": "No information was provided to Thompson from which he could have intelligently and knowingly either asserted or waived his right to an appeal … [and] no reasonable effort was made to discover Thompson's informed wishes regarding an appeal").

- *Franklin v. Anderson*, 434 F.3d 412 (6th Cir. 2006), cert, denied, 549 U.S. 1156 (2007) (appellate counsel was ineffective in failing to challenge judge's impaneling of juror whose "statements indicat[ed] that she did not understand that [accused] was not required to prove himself not guilty").

- *Frazer v. South Carolina*, 430 F.3d 696 (4th Cir. 2005) (applying *Roe v. Flores-Ortega*, 528 U.S. 470 (2000), to find trial counsel ineffective for failing to consult with client regarding direct appeal).

- *Cirilo-Munoz v. United States*, 404 F.3d 527 (1st Cir. 2005) (appellate counsel was ineffective in failing to raise meritorious challenge to applicability of sentencing enhancement factor; "[a]ssuming that the omission of the argument was deliberate … [to] increase the chance of prevailing … [with] a more far-reaching [claim] … such a calculation would have been manifestly unreasonable").

- *Ballard v. United States*, 400 F.3d 404 (6th Cir. 2005) (appellate counsel was ineffective in "fail[ing] to raise certain legal issues relevant to vacating [section 2255 movant's] sentence on appeal").

- *Sanders v. Cotton*, 398 F.3d 572 (7th Cir. 2005) (appellate counsel was ineffective in failing to "challeng[e] the trial court's refusal to properly instruct the jury" on State's burden to prove element of charged crimes).

- *United States v. Hilliard*, 392 F.3d 981 (8th Cir. 2004) (trial counsel was ineffective in failing to file timely post-trial motion for new trial, particularly given that district court reminded counsel at conclusion of trial to check rules on timing of post-trial motions).

- *Mapes v. Tate*, 388 F.3d 187 (6th Cir. 2004) (appellate counsel was ineffective in failing to raise meritorious claim of instructional error at capital sentencing hearing that had been preserved by trial counsel).

- *Lewis v. Johnson*, 359 F.3d 646 (3d Cir. 2004) (applying *Roe v. Flores-Ortega*, 528 U.S. 470 (2000) to find trial counsel ineffective for failing to consult client before deciding not to file notice of appeal).

- *United States v. Reinhart*, 357 F.3d 521 (5th Cir. 2004) (appellate counsel was ineffective in failing to raise meritorious challenge to district court's reliance on certain factors to raise offense level under Sentencing Guidelines).

- *McFarland v. Yukins*, 356 F.3d 688 (6th Cir. 2004) ("appellate counsel's failure to raise … argument [that "would likely have prevailed"] was sufficiently unreasonable to violate McFarland's right to counsel").

- *United States v. Conley*, 349 F.3d 837 (5th Cir. 2003) (appellate counsel was ineffective in failing to raise appellate challenge to sentence that exceeded statutory maximum).

- *Caver v. Straub*, 349 F.3d 340 (6th Cir. 2003) (appellate counsel was ineffective in failing to present claim that "was much stronger than the issues" counsel did raise).

- *Joshua v. DeWitt*, 341 F.3d 430 (6th Cir. 2003) (appellate counsel was ineffective in failing to raise 4th Amendment issue which, although not litigate at trial level, could have been raised on appeal as plain error).

- *United States v. Bass*, 310 F.3d 321 (5th Cir. 2002) (appellate counsel was ineffective in failing to raise meritorious claim of insufficiency of evidence).

- *Eagle v. Linahan*, 279 F.3d 926 (11th Cir. 2001) (direct appeal counsel failed to raise preserved, meritorious *Batson v. Kentucky* challenge to prosecutor's racially based use of peremptory challenges).

- *Fields v. Bagley*, 275 F.3d 478 (6th Cir. 2001) (per curiam) (trial counsel failed to oppose prosecutor's interlocutory appeal of grant of pretrial suppression motion, due to counsel's erroneous belief that representation had terminated with suppression of evidence and petitioner's release on bond).

- *Carter v. Bowersox*, 265 F.3d 705 (8th Cir. 2001), cert, denied, 535 U.S. 999 (2002) (direct appeal counsel failed to raise plain error resulting from trial court's omission of sentencing-instruction on effect of lack of unanimity on capital-sentencing verdict).

- *Harris v. Day*, 226 F.3d 361 (5th Cir. 2000) (appellate counsel's "Anders brief" failed to identify arguable issues for appeal).

- *Delgado v. Lewis*, 223 F.3d 976 (9th Cir. 2000) (appellate counsel filed "Anders brief" claiming absence of non-frivolous appellate issues even though state trial court had certified that probable cause to appeal existed with regard to two issues).

SECTION TWO
CHAPTER EIGHT

DUE PROCESS CLAIMS

In this section, I am going to be addressing the Constitutional foundation of a sound claim. In the event you have been diligent in your study, you will have discovered that all *habeas* claims – i.e., post-conviction – rely on some claim of a Violation of Constitutional rights. One of the most important rights, and the sole focus of this section, is the rights of Americans to the "Due Process of Law" (see 28 U.S.C. §2253; §2254, and §2255).

As you study the cases in this book, you are likely to discover that "Due Process of Law" is the one reverberating phrase of the Constitution and the Supreme Court of the United States. Although you are likely to assume that "Due Process" refers to proper court procedure alone – like whether or not you have a right to a jury trial – you will learn that the phrase means so much more. The Supreme Court has expanded the meaning of due process over the years. Take, for example, the Sixth Amendment guarantees a defendant "the assistance of counsel for his defense," but the Supreme Court declared that a criminal defendant in a felony case has a right to the "effective assistance of counsel" (see *Strickland v. United States*, 404 U.S. 668 (1984)). Thus, the Supreme Court has expanded its interpretation of "Due process" to include "substantive due process." In other words, the rights the Constitution actually provides or protects.

In a more basic sense, "Due process of Law" bears the simple definition that a defendant has a right to present his case. The Supreme Court said in 1914, "The fundamental requisite of due process of law is the opportunity to be heard," yet subject to substantive due process, or the court's interpretation of the right to be heard. It is important to possess your own understanding of "Due process." You can reach your own interpretation by reading the Amendments to the Constitution for yourself. "Due process" is specifically referenced in the negative in the Fifth and Fourteenth Amendments as "without due process of law." The right is explained, as to criminal accusations, further in the Sixth Amendment, beginning with the phrase, "the accused shall enjoy the right…" Punishment is the subject of the Thirteenth Amendment, stating, "except as a punishment for crime whereof the party shall have been duly convicted …"

CHAPTER NINE

RIGHT TO SELF-REPRESENTATION

The right to represent yourself in a federal trial is a foreign concept to most people, including judges and lawyers. This right, however, has been a bedrock principle since 1789. The right to self-representation in a federal trial has been guaranteed by a provision of the Judiciary Act of 1789, the same year the Constitution of the United States was enacted by its ratification. In 1942, the High Court declared the right was naturally related to the right to the assistance of counsel guaranteed by the Sixth Amendment to the Constitution. The court's declaration was later codified in 1948 with 28 U.S.C. §1654 which states:

> *In all courts of the United States, the parties may plea and conduct their own cases personally or by counsel as, by the rules of such courts, respectively, are permitted to manage and conduct causes therein.*

The next significant change occurred in 1963 with the Supreme Court's decision in *Gideon v. Wainwright*, 372 U.S. 335. In that decision, the High Court decided that a criminal defendant could not be deprived of counsel because he or she was unable to pay for a lawyer. Thus, responsibility was laid upon the court to provide counsel to those who could not afford counsel. Under 18 U.S.C. §3006A the law required adequate representation, resulting in the United States Courts bearing the burden of the quality of counsel for the poor. These changes all but denied a poor defendant any right to represent himself. Finally, in 1975 the question of this prejudice was brought before the Supreme Court in *Faretta v. California*, 422 U.S. 806. In that case, the High Court held that the Sixth and Fourteenth Amendments to the United States Constitution guarantee that any person brought to trial in any state or federal court must be afforded the right to assistance of counsel before they can be validly convicted and punished by imprisonment. A defendant in state criminal trial also has a constitutional right to proceed without counsel when he voluntarily and intelligently elects to do so. This right to self-representation being supported by structure of the Sixth Amendment, which necessarily implies right of self-representation, and by English and Colonial jurisprudence, from which the Sixth Amendment emerged (see *Faretta v. California*, 422 U.S. 806, 45 L. Ed 2d 562, 95 S. Ct. 2525).

Because of all these factors, a court must take steps to secure other rights of a criminal defendant when the right to self-representation is invoked. Such as when a criminal defendant chooses to represent himself or herself at trial, has discretion to, and may wish to, determine whether the defendant has the mental capacity to present a clear and thoughtful defense. Among other things, the court may also find it productive to appoint standby counsel, especially if the case is likely to be long or complicated or where other defendants are involved in the case.

Keeping in balance with the district court's broad discretion to limit self-representation, the Supreme Court has held that someone accused of a crime has a federal Constitutional right of self-representation at trial, which includes other related and specific rights concerning the presentation of his or her defense.

In *McKaskle v. Wiggins*, 465 U.S. 168 (1984), the Supreme Court expressed the view that (1) in determining whether the defendants Sixth Amendment right to conduct his own defense has been respected, the primary focus must be on whether the defendant had a fair chance to present the case in the defendant's own way; and (2) the right to self-representation plainly encompasses certain specific rights, such as the right to (a) control the organization and content of defense, (b) make motions, (c) argue points of law, (d) participate in *voir dire*, (e) question witnesses, and (f) address the court and the jury at appropriate points in the trial.

Authors Note: Please do not misunderstand this chapter as advice to proceed in pro se *or to represent yourself. My opinion on this matter is equivalent to the age-old adage, "A lawyer who represents himself at trial has a fool for a client." Due to the emotional side of a trial, I believe that there exists no replacement for the effective assistance of counsel if that can be found. I also know that if you are appointed counsel, it is very unlikely that you will have adequate representation. But, after you are convicted, and you lose at appeal, at least you will have ineffective assistance of counsel claim.*

Now allow me to be clear. This chapter will help you understand the right to self-representation so those of you who invoked the right can understand how that right was likely violated. See the following examples for a better understanding.

- *Tatum v. Foster*, 847 F.3d 459 (7th Cir. 2017) (trial court improperly "refused to allow Robert Tatum to represent himself" based on colloquy in which "[n]othing … suggest[ed] that Tatum suffered from deficient mental functioning, as opposed to a limited education," and court "inappropriately placed the burden on Tatum to convince it that he understood, and accepted, the challenges of self-representation")

- *Imani v. Pollard*, 826 F.3d 939 (7th Cir. 2016) (trial court violated *Faretta v. California* by ruling that "Imani could not represent himself, treating the matter as a request that required the judge's permission," and concluding that "Imani did not have a 'sufficiently rational basis' to justify his decision").

- *Burton v. Davis*, 816 F.3d 1132 (9th Cir. 2016) ("Twice before trial and another two times during trial. Burton invoked his constitutional right to represent himself under *Faretta v. California*," tut "[e]ach time, the judge denied the request because Burton needed time to prepare and asked that the trial be continued"; "Faretta motion made before the jury is empaneled must be granted unless it is shown that the motion was made for the purpose of securing delay").

- *Robinson v. Louisiana*, 606 Fed. Appx. 199 (5th Cir. 2015) (per curiam) ("judge did not warn Robinson about the dangers of proceeding to trial *pro se* before allowing Robinson to represent himself"; "trial court's reliance on standby counsel's representations was insufficient to establish a knowing and intelligent waiver of Robinson's right to counsel").

- *Batchelor v. Cain*, 682 F.3d 400 (5th Cir. 2012) (trial court violated Faretta by denying accused's "clear and unequivocal invocation of his Sixth Amendment right to represent himself").

- *Alongi v. Ricci*, 367 Fed. Appx. 341, 2010 U.S. App. LEXIS 3933 (3d Cir. Feb. 25, 2010) (per curiam) ("trial court's handling of Alongi's request to represent himself was woefully inadequate under Faretta": "trial court entirely misstated the applicable standard, and incorrectly asserted that the decision to permit a defendant to proceed *pro se* fell within the court's discretion"; "In addition, the court did nothing to appraise Alongi of the risks of self-representation ").

- *Gross v. Cooper*, 312 Fed. Appx. 671, 2009 U.S. App. LEXIS 4247 (5th Cir. March 3, 2009) (per curiam) (trial judge violated *Faretta v. California* by accepting accused's waiver of counsel without adequately "wam[ing] Gross about the dangers of self-representation" and adequately "evaluat[ing] the defendant's background")

- *Moore v. Haviland*, 531 F.3d 393 (6th Cir. 2008), cert, denied, 558 U.S. 933 (2009) (trial court violated *Faretta v. California* by rejecting accused's mid-trial requests to proceed *pro se* without engaging in "Faretta-compliant colloquy").

- *Pruitt v. Pliler*, 178 Fed. Appx. 752, 2006 U.S. App. LEXIS 12279 (9th Cir. May 8, 2006) (trial court's denial of request for self-representation on ground of untimeliness of request was improper given that "request appears to have been asserted in good faith," "delay in the trial proceedings would not have prejudiced the court or the prosecution," and "request could not have reasonably been made earlier in the proceedings").

- *Hirschfield v. Payne*, 420 F.3d 922 (9th Cir. 2005) (trial court improperly denied "request for self-representation on the ground that the defendant lacks sufficient knowledge of legal procedure").

- *Bribiesca v. Galaza*, 215 F.3d 1015 (9th Cir. 2000) (accused was improperly denied right to self-representation!; although state courts "noted that Bribiesca would not have had access to the law library and therefore could not have represented himself effectively," state courts based ultimate ruling on view of accused's conduct as "obstructionist," which was "not supported by the factual record in this case").

- *Myers v. Johnson*, 76 F.3d 1330 (5th Cir. 1996) (percuriam) (state appellate court's appointment of appellate counsel instead of standby counsel for *pro se* appeal, and counsel's refusal to provide client with transcript, violated appellant's right to self-representation on appeal).

- *Williams v. Bartlett*, 44 F.3d 95 (2d Cir. 1995) (trial court improperly denied petitioner's timely and unequivocal assertion of right of self-representation).

- *Peters v. Gunn*, 33 F.3d 1190 (9th Cir. 1994) (trial court improperly denied petitioner's right to self-representation on ground that petitioner lacked adequate legal acumen).

CHAPTER TEN

CLAIMS IN PRELIMINARY PROCEEDINGS

Now that we have reviewed all aspects of cause – in Section One – it is time to reach into the basis of your claim, the denial of a constitutional right. Also, remember to go a step further by explaining how the constitutional violation hurt your case. A prime example is what is called a fundamental miscarriage of justice or the conviction of an innocent person in layman's terms.

This is what we call the 'prejudice' part, the part in which you suffered. For example: My lawyer slept through my trial and did not call any witnesses. Because my lawyer was asleep, I was deprived of my Sixth Amendment right to a compulsory process for obtaining witnesses. Because my witnesses were not called to testify, I was not able to show my alibi defense, nor was I able to show my actual innocence.

This sounds silly, right? Unfortunately, this actually happened in a United States district court in Alabama. This is a perfect example of the good-ole-boy justice system for minorities at work in the Deep South.

In this chapter and the chapters that follow, I am going to be identifying the basic claims at each stage of the trial process. Remember, this is the section that will start the identification of the prejudice in your case, the denial of a constitutional right.

You must also go one step further by showing what damage you suffered because of the denial. I will also discuss 'error' during the preliminary stage of a criminal proceeding. Most often, you will find that defense lawyers fail to investigate the case prior to the indictment being issued. Although the case can be brought to an end in the preliminary hearing, that usually will not happen because the lawyer knows if they do, the pay stops then.

The following cases all include errors of different types in the preliminary phase of a criminal proceeding:

Claims related to police misconduct:

- *Withrow v. Williams*, 507 U.S. 680 (1993) (affirming grant of *habeas corpus* relief because police used trickery in securing confession from petitioner).

- *Miller v. Fenton*, 474 U.S. 104 (1985) (petitioner convicted on basis of involuntary confession that police extracted by intensively interrogating him while he was in state of physical shock and by telling petitioner he would not be punished if he confessed).

- *United States v. Henry*, 447 U.S. 264 (1980) (police violated 6th Amendment right to counsel by using paid informant to extract statement from already-indicted, incarcerated section 2255 movant).

Claims related to the prosecutors and charging papers:

- Claims arising under *Bailey v. United States*, 516 U.S. 137 (1995) that conduct of section 2255 movant did not satisfy definition of "use" of firearm for purposes of federal criminal statute:

- *United States v. Guess*, 230 F.3d 1143 (9th Cir. 2000)

- *United States v. Romero*, 183 F.3d 1145 (9th Cir. 1999)

- *United States v. Ponce*, 168 F.3d 584, (2nd Cir. 1999)

- *United States v. Pearce*, 146 F.3d 771 (10th Cir. 1998)

- *United States v. Gobert,* 139 F.3d 436 (5th Cir. 1998)

- *United States v. Carter,* 117 F.3d 262 (5th Cir. 1997)

- *Stanback v. United States*, 113 F.3d 651 (7th Cir. 1997)

- *Lee v. United. States*, 113 F.3d 73 (7th Cir. 1997)

- *United States v. McPhail*, 112 F.3d 197 (5th Cir. 1997)

- *United States v. Morrison*, 98 F.3d 619 (D.C. Cir.), cert, denied, 520 U.S. 1131 (1997)

- *United States v. Garcia,* 77 F.3d 274 (9th Cir. 1996)

- *United States v. Bruno*, 903 F.2d 393 (5th Cir. 1990)

- *Callanan v. United States*, 881 F.2d 229 (6th Cir. 1989)

- *Toulabi v. United States*, 875 F.2d 122 (7th Cir. 1989)

- *United States v. Mitchell*, 867 F.2d 1232 (9th Cir. 1989)

- *Magnuson v. United States*, 861 F.2d 166 (7th Cir. 1988)

- *United States v. Shelton*, 848 F.2d 1485 (10th Cir. 1988)

- *Ward v. United States*, 845 F.2d 1459 (7th Cir. 1988)

- *Vasquez v. Hillery*, 474 U.S. 254 (1986) (grand jury selection process systematically excluded blacks).

- *Crist v. Bretz*, 437 U.S. 28 (1978) (double jeopardy violation).

- *Castaneda v. Partida*, 430 U.S. 482 (1977) (Mexican-American petitioner suffered intentional discrimination in grand jury selection process; only 39 percent of those summoned for grand jury service were Mexican-American although that group accounted for 79 percent of county population).

- *Smith v. Goguen*, 415 U.S. 566 (1974) (petitioner convicted under Massachusetts' vague flag-misuse statute).

- *Wilkinson v. Gingrich*, 806 F.3d 511 (9th Cir. 2015) (Double Jeopardy Causes collateral principle precluded perjury prosecution of petitioner for allegedly testifying falsely in prior traffic court trial that ended in acquittal; "traffic court necessarily decided, in Wilkinson's favor, an issue that was critical to both the traffic court and perjury proceedings—that Wilkinson was not the driver of the speeding car").

- *Wood v. Milyard*, 721 F.3d 1190 (10th Cir. 2013) (double jeopardy violation).

- *Magnan v. Trammell*, 719 F.3d 1159 (10th Cir. 2013) (Oklahoma state courts lacked jurisdiction because crimes occurred on Indian land and thus "exclusive jurisdiction over th[e] crimes rests with the United States").

- *Brazzel v. Washington*, 491 F.3d 976 (9th Cir. 2007) (conviction on lesser alternative offense in first trial amounted to "implied acquittal" of more serious charge in indictment and barred retrial on latter charge).

- *Walck v. Edmondson*, 472 F.3d 1227 (10th Cir. 2007) (joining "several of our sister circuits" in holding that section 2241, not section 2254, "is the proper avenue by which to challenge pretrial detention, including when such challenges are based on double jeopardy grounds," and granting writ on double jeopardy grounds because prior trial ended in judge's granting prosecution's request for mistrial over defense counsel's objections with "manifest necessity" and without considering reasonable alternatives).

- *Damian v. Vaughn*, 186 Fed. Appx. 775, 2006 U.S. App. LEXIS 15869 (9th Cir. June 21, 2006) (retrial on indictment that included two counts that had resulted in acquittal in previous trial violated Double Jeopardy Clause).

- *Stow v. Murashige*, 389 F.3d 880 (9th Cir. 2004) (reclassifying state prisoner's section 2254 petition "which raised a double jeopardy challenge to his pending retrial" as section 2241 petition because petitioner's "status was that of a pretrial detainee" and not state prisoner, finding AEDPA inapplicable because petition is governed by section 2241, and granting writ "[b]ecause Stow's impending retrial on the charges of attempted second degree murder would violate double jeopardy").

- *Dye v. Frank*, 355 F.3d 1102 (7th Cir. 2004) (charge of possession with intent to deliver cocaine was barred by Double Jeopardy Clause because petitioner was previously subjected to seizure of assets under "Wisconsin Controlled Substance Tax," which was civil penalty "so punitive in purpose and effect that it constituted a criminal punishment").

- *McCoy v. Stewart*, 282 F.3d 626 (9th Cir.), cert denied, 537 U.S. 993 (2002) (conviction of "participating in a criminal street gang," based on petitioner's having advised gang members about how to operate organization, violated First Amendment).

- *Morris v. Reynolds*, 264 F.3d 38 (2d Cir. 2001), cert denied, 536 U.S. 915 (2002) (state trial court violated Double Jeopardy Clause by reinstating dismissed felony charge after having already accepted petitioner's guilty plea to lesser included misdemeanor charge).

- *Huss v. Graves*, 252 F.3d 952 (8th Cir. 2001), cert, denied, 535 U.S.

- 951 (2002) (Double Jeopardy Clause precluded prosecution following bench trial on stipulated record that ended in trial judge's de facto declaration of mistrial).

- *Prou v. United States*, 199 F.3d 37 (1st Cir. 1999) (untimeliness of government's filing of charging paper alleging grounds for sentencing enhancement requires that section 2255 movant's sentence be vacated, and that movant be "remand[ed] for resentencing without the statutory enhancement").

- *Johnson v. Karnes*, 198 F.3d 589 (6th Cir.) (Double Jeopardy Clause barred prosecution because prior trial ended in declaration of mistrial, over defense objection, without manifest necessity).

Claims relating to official misconduct:

- *Banks v. Dretke*, 540 U.S. 668 (2004) ("State persisted in in hiding [prosecution witness's] informant status and misleadingly represented that it had complied in full with its Brady disclosure obligations" and prosecutors failed to correct witness's "misrepresent[ations] [of] his dealings with police" in testimony at guilt and penalty phases of trial: "When police or prosecutors conceal significant exculpatory or impeaching material in the State's possession, it is ordinarily incumbent on the State to set the record straight").

- *Kyles v. Whitley*, 514 U.S. 419 (1995) ("Because the net effect of the evidence withheld by the State in this case raises a reasonable probability that its disclosure would have produced a different result, Kyles is entitled to a new trial").

- *Fuentes v. Griffin*, 2016 U.S. App. LEXIS 12993 (2d Cir. July 15, 2016) (prosecutor violated Brady by suppressing psychiatric report about complainant that "would have, inter alia, provided a way [for defense counsel] to cross-examine [complainant] G.C. as to her mental state, and potentially corroborated Fuentes' account … [,] [and, importantly, timely disclosure of the [report] … would have provided defense counsel with an opportunity to seek an expert opinion with regard to the [report's] … indication of other significant symptoms, in order to establish reasonable doubt in the minds of the jurors").

- *McCormick v. Parker*, 821 F.3d 1240 (10th Cir. 2016) (prosecution witness "Ridling examined [complainant] M.K. at the behest of law enforcement as part of a criminal investigation into M.K.s allegation that McCormick sexually abused her" and later "testified falsely that she [Ridling] was a certified sexual assault nurse examiner (SANE nurse) at the time of trial." Under these circumstances, "Ridling was part of the prosecution team for Brady purposes … [and] we must impute her knowledge of her own lack of certification to the prosecutor," even though petitioner "doesn't point to any evidence that indicates the prosecutor actually knew about Ridling's lapsed credentials").

- *Shelton v. Marshall*, 796 F.3d 1075 (9th Cir.), amended, 806 F.3d 1011 (9th Cir. 2015) ("prosecution committed Brady error by concealing from the defense and the jury its deal precluding an examination of the mental competency of its star witness," whose "mental competence" prosecution had "serious doubts" about, and whose "testimony was central to the prosecution's case that Shelton premeditated and deliberated regarding Thorpe's murder").

- *Barton v. Warden*, 786 F.3d 450 (6th Cir. 2015) (per curiam), cert. denied, 136 S. Ct. 1449 (2016) (prosecution, which "presented an unsupported, shifting, and somewhat fantastical story at trial," failed to disclose to defense counsel "evidence that would have impeached the sole witness against [accused]").

- *Lewis v. Connecticut Comm'r of Correction*, 790 F.3d 109 (2d Cir. 2015) ("State failed to disclose to the defense that Ruiz ["key witness" on whom "government's case against Lewis depended almost entirely"] had repeatedly denied having any knowledge of the murders and only implicated Lewis after a police detective promised to let Ruiz go if he gave a statement in which he admitted to being the getaway driver and incriminated Lewis and another individual").

- *Comstock v. Humphries*, 786 F.3d 701 (9th Cir. 2015) (prosecutor in burglary case involving theft of ring withheld from defense counsel that complainant "had serious doubts about whether his ring was actually stolen" and said that "ring might have been lost outside, not stolen, just as Comstock's lawyer … argued to the jury.

- *Bies v. Sheldon*, 775 F.3d 386 (6th Cir. 2014) (state violated

- *Brady v. Maryland* by "fail[ing] to turn over hundreds of pages of evidence gathered during the murder investigation," "includ[ing] a substantial collection of tips, leads and witness statements relating to other individuals who had been investigated for the murder—two of whom had apparently confessed to the crime, and neither of whom was ever ruled out as the perpetrator," and "State also withheld witness statements that undermine the State's theory of the case and information that could have been used to further impeach two of State's witnesses").

- *Gumm v. Mitchell*, 775 F.3d 345 (6th Cir. 2014) (same as *Bies v. Sheldon*, supra, involving Gumm's co-defendant).

- *Amado v. Gonzalez*, 758 F.3d 1119 (9th Cir. 2014) (prosecution failed to disclose that primary witness for prosecution had pled guilty and was on probation for robbery and that witness was former member of gang whose members were targets of gang-related homicide for which petitioner was being prosecuted).

- *Lambert v. Beard*, 537 Fed. Appx. 78 (3d Cir. 2013), cert denied, 134 S. Ct. 1938 (2014) (prosecutor failed to disclose that witness, upon whom "Commonwealth's case against Lambert rested almost entirely" and who testified in exchange for "open guilty plea," naming Lambert as co-perpetrator in crime, had previously "identified not Lambert, but another man").

- *Dow v. Virga*, 729 F.3d 1041 (9th Cir. 2013) (prosecutor "knowingly elicited and then failed to correct false testimony" by police detective, who falsely testified that accused – rather than defense counsel – was source of request that "each of the participants in a lineup wear a bandage under his right eye at location at which [accused] had a small scar under his," and prosecutor thereafter "told the jury during closing argument that accused] had demonstrated consciousness of guilt by trying to hide his scar in order to prevent the sole eyewitness from identifying him").

- *Aguilar v. Woodford*, 725 F.3d 970 (9th Cir. 2013), cert denied, 134 S. Ct. 1869 (2014) (prosecutor suppressed information that police dog – whose "scent evidence was the only evidence at trial linking Aguilar to the getaway car, as well as the only evidence corroborating strikingly weak eyewitness identifications" – "had a history of mistaken identifications").

- *Browning v. Trammell*, 717 F.3d 1092 (10th Cir. 2013) (prosecution withheld psychiatric records of "most important [prosecutorial] witness at trial," showing that witness "blurs reality and fantasy, projects blame onto others, and is perhaps even homicidal," all of which would have supported accused's ability "to impeach [witness's] credibility and portray her as a participant in the crime").

- *Mike v. Ryan*, 711 F.3d 998 (9th Cir. 2013) ("state knew about … but did not disclose" police detective's "long history of lying under oath and other misconduct," even though "trial was, essentially, a swearing contest" between detective's claim that accused had confessed and accused's denial that unrecorded confession ever took place).

- *Munchinski v. Wilson*, 694 F.3d 308 (3d Cir. 2012) (prosecutors withheld "almost a dozen articles of exculpatory evidence"; "[t]he scopes of the Brady violations here is staggering").

- *Wolfe v. Clarke*, 691 F.3d 410 (4th Cir. 2012) (prosecution suppressed "plainly momentous … written police report reflecting that – before [state's key witness] ever asserted that [accused] hired him to murder [decedent] – [police detective] advised [state's key witness] that he could avoid the death penalty by implicating [accused]").

- *Phillips v. Ornoski*, 673 F.3d 1168 (9th Cir. 2012), cert, denied, 133 S. Ct. 2020 (2013) ("prosecution's failure to reveal that a key prosecution witness received significant benefits in exchange for her testimony after the witness falsely testified she had been promised no such benefits, coupled with the prosecutor's false representation of, and "willfully misl[ed] the jury as to, critical evidence that was material to the special circumstance finding that the murder was committed during the course of a robbery (rather than vice versa)").

- *Guzman v. Secretary*, 663 F.3d 1336 (11th Cir. 2011) (testimony by state's key witness and lead investigator about state's deal with witness omitted payment of $500 reward shortly before witness's grand jury testimony, and prosecutor failed to correct omission).

- *Sivak v. Hardison*, 658 F.3d 898 (9th Cir. 2011) (prosecution failed to correct perjurious testimony by jailhouse informant, who claimed that cooperation with state was motivated solely by desire to protect wife and children, thereby concealing that prosecution had arranged dismissal of informant's charges in neighboring county and had assisted in arranging parole• and that informant had previously received cash payment for providing information in another case in another State).

- *LaCaze v. Leger*, 645 F.3d 728 (5th Cir. 2011), amended on denial of rehearing en banc, 647 F.3d 1175 (5th Cir. 2011), cert denied, 132 S. Ct. 1137 (2012) (prosecution failed to disclose that plea deal given to state's key witness went beyond reduction of charges and included assurance that witness's son would not be prosecuted as accessory).

- *Breakiron v. Horn*, 642 F.3d 126 (3d Cir. 2011) (prosecution failed to disclose that jailhouse informant "had sought a deal … in exchange for his testimony and was a suspect in an investigation pending when he testified" and "had been convicted of an impeachable *crimen falsi*").

- *Maxwell v. Roe*, 628 F.3d 486 (9th Cir. 2010), cert, denied, 132 S. Ct. 611 (2012) (prosecution failed to disclose "multiple pieces of critical impeachment information that could have been used to undermine the credibility of [jailhouse informant]").

- *Goudy v. Basinger*, 604 F.3d 394 (7th Cir. 2010) (prosecution failed to "disclose three eyewitness statements that implicated one of its main witnesses").

- *Robinson v. Mills*, 592 F.3d 730 (6th Cir. 2010) (prosecution suppressed evidence of key witness's status as paid police informant, which could have "supported the assertion that … [witness] was biased in favor of the local authorities" and caused jury to be "suspicious of [witness] … and cautious about her testimony").

- *Simmons v. Beard*, 590 F.3d 223 (3d Cir. 2009), cert dismissed, 559 U.S. 965 (2010) (prosecution suppressed evidence of (i) police pressure on accused's girlfriend, who changed account that previously had been favorable to accused, (ii) grounds for impeaching credibility of key prosecution eyewitness, (iii) lab reports that could have been used to raise questions about eyewitness's credibility, and (iv) eyewitness's failure to identify accused in "mug book" prior to witness's subsequent lineup identification).

Claims relating to the denial of expert services:

- *Powell v. Collins*, 332 F.3d 376 (6th Cir. 2003) (denial of request for independent mental health expert and continuance for purpose of conducting psychological testing violated *Ake v. Oklahoma*, 470 U.S. 68 (1985): "an indigent criminal defendant's constitutional right to psychiatric assistance in preparing an insanity defense is not satisfied by court appointment of a 'neutral' psychiatrist – i.e., one whose report is available to both the defense and prosecution").

- *Schultz v. Page*, 313 F.3d 1010 (7th Cir. 2002), cert, denied, 538 U.S. 1057 (2003) (denial of request for evaluation of accused's sanity at time of offense violated *Ake v. Oklahoma* notwithstanding that competency evaluation ordered by court near the time of trial did not suggest basis for raising insanity defense: "it is difficult to understand why the [state] appellate court considered a fitness examination sufficient for purposes of determining Schultz's sanity at the time of the crime" (emphasis in original)).

- *Brown v. Champion*, 1998 U.S. App. LEXIS 30723 (10th Cir. Dec. 2, 1998) (trial court violated *Ake v. Oklahoma*, 470 U.S. 68 (1985) by denying request for funding for independent psychiatrist to assist with insanity defense).

- *Starr v. Lockhart*, 23 F.3d 1280 (8th Cir. 1994) (indigent petitioner denied expert needed to prove diminished capacity mitigating circumstance).

- *Liles v. Saffle*, 945 F.2d 333 (10th Cir. 1991), cert, denied, 502 U.S. 1066 (1992) (due process violated by denial of motion for psychiatric assistance in preparing and presenting insanity defense at trial and in refuting claim of future dangerousness at capital sentencing hearing).

- *Smith v. McCormick*, 914 F.2d 1153 (9th Cir. 1990) (trial judge violated rule of *Ake v. Oklahoma*, 470 U.S. 68 (1985), by denying request for defense expert and instead appointing court expert who would report directly to judge).

- *Buttrum v. Black*, 908 F.2d 695 (11th Cir. 1990) (trial court's limited grant of psychiatric assistance deprived petitioner of psychiatric testing and testimony needed to present adequate defense at capital sentencing hearing).

- *Christy v. Horn*, 28 F. Supp. 2d 307 (W.D. Pa. 1998) (trial court violated *Ake v. Oklahoma*, 470 U.S. 68 (1985) by denying defense request for independent psychiatrists who could not perform functions of experts employed by defense, namely, (i) "marshaling the facts to assist in developing" mental defenses for use at trial, and (ii) testifying at sentencing phase to "impact of Christy's mental impairments on his conduct throughout his lifetime and particularly on the night in question").

Claims related to the defendant's capacity to stand trial:

- *McManus v. Neal*, 779 F.3d 634 (7th Cir. 2015) ("regimen of mind-altering medications" administered during trial to petitioner, who "decompensated soon after the trial testimony got underway," "alone created substantial doubt about McManus's mental fitness for trial, but the judge never ordered a competency evaluation" and instead "focused on getting McManus 'fixed up' enough to complete the trial").

- *Maxwell v. Roe*, 606 F.3d 561 (9th Cir. 2010) (trial court violated Due Process Clause by failing to conduct competency hearing *sua sponte* under circumstances that would have caused "reasonable trial judge" to have "bona fide doubt" about accused's ability to "'consult with his lawyer with a reasonable degree of rational understanding'").

- *McMurtrey v. Ryan*, 539 F.3d 1112 (9th Cir. 2008) ("McMurtrey's due process rights were violated when the state trial court failed to hold a hearing to determine whether he was competent to stand trial and be sentenced," given that "bona fide doubt existed as to McMurtrey's competence to stand trial and be sentenced").

- *Johnson v. Norton*, 249 F.3d 20 (1st Cir. 2001) (trial court failed to hold competency hearing sua sponte despite knowledge that petitioner had been struck on head morning of jury selection and subsequently lost consciousness and had to be hospitalized).

- *McGregor v. Gibson*, 248 F.3d 946 (10th Cir. 2001) (en banc) (state court employed unconstitutional standard to determine competency to stand trial and "meaningful retrospective competency determination cannot be made").

- *Torres v. Prunty*, 223 F.3d 1103 (9th Cir. 2000) (trial court denied hearing on competency to stand trial despite accused's "unusual and self-defeating behavior in the courtroom and defense counsel's report that accused believed that counsel and judge were involved in conspiracy against him).

- *Barnett v. Hargett*, 174 F.3d 1128 (10th Cir. 1999) (trial court apparently failed to hold pretrial competency hearing; even if hearing had been held, competency standard employed by state courts at time was unconstitutional).

- *Blazak v. Ricketts*. 1 F.3d 891 (9th Cir. 1993), cert, denied, 511 U.S. 1097 (1994) (trial court failed to conduct competency hearing despite petitioner's history of mental illness and finding of incompetency to stand trial at prior trial on unrelated charges).

- *Laffery v. Cook*, 949 F.2d 1546 (10th Cir. 1991), cert, denied, 504 U.S. 911 (1992) (state trial court's finding of competency to stand trial relied on legal standard inconsistent with due process; because record contained evidence that would have permitted finding of incompetency under proper standard, court grants writ and vacates conviction and death sentence).

- *Wallace v. Kemp*, 757 F.2d 1102 (11th Cir. 1985) (capitally sentenced petitioner found to have been incompetent to assist attorney at trial; on retrial after being restored to sanity, petitioner was acquitted).

- *Strickland v. Francis*, 738 F.2d 1542 (11th Cir. 1984) (evidence did not support special jury's finding that petitioner was competent to stand trial; state violated due process by subjecting incompetent petitioner to trial).

Claims challenging denial of a change of venue, jury – selection procedures, other jury – related practices, or neutrality of judge:

- *Miller-El v. Dretke*, 545 U.S. 231 (2005) (granting *habeas corpus* relief under 28 U.S.C. §2254(d) (2) on claim of racial discrimination in jury selection in violation of *Batson v. Kentucky*, 476 U.S. 79 (1986), because "state court's conclusion that the prosecutors' [peremptory] strikes of [two African American venirepersons were not really determined is shown up as wrong to a clear and convincing degree").

- *Bracy v. Gramley*, 520 U.S. 899 (1997) (because judge who presided at trial at which petitioner was convicted and sentenced to die took bribes in return for leniency in many cases besides petitioner's, sometimes exhibited bias against defendants like petitioner who did not pay bribes, and had incentive to compensate for leniency in cases in which bribes were paid by being excessively harsh in other cases, district court abused discretion in denying petitioner discovery of documents in government's control that might show that judge was biased in favor of state in petitioner's case).

- *Amadeo v. Zant*, 486 U.S. 214 (1988) (jury selection pursuant to deliberate scheme devised by district attorney and jury commissioners to underrepresent African Americans and women; scheme memorialized in handwritten note found after trial and appeal in office of clerk of court.).

- *Turner v. Murray*, 476 U.S. 28 (1986) (capital defendant charged with interracial Crime entitled to have prospective jurors informed of victim's race and questioned on subject of racial bias).

- *Sheppard v. Maxwell*, 384 U.S. 333 (1966) (massive, pervasive, and prejudicial pretrial publicity and circus-style atmosphere at trial).

- *Irvin v. Dowd*, 386 U.S. 717 (1961) (failure to grant second change of venue despite widespread and inflammatory publicity; 8 of 12 jurors seated admitted to belief that defendant was guilty).

- *Currie v. McDowell*, 2016 U.S. App. LEXIS 10362 (9th Cir. June 8, 2016) (prosecutor "removed one African American juror via peremptory strike," stating "reasons for striking this juror [that] were all flawed – each reason was either unreasonable, demonstrably false, or applied just as well to the non-black jurors [whom prosecutor] … allowed to remain on the jury").

- *Shirley v. Yates*, 807 F.3d 1090 (9th Cir. 2015) (petitioner's prima facie showing that prosecutor's peremptory strike of African-American venire person "was motivated in substantial part by race" was adequately rebutted by prosecutor, who could not "recall his actual reason for striking the juror in question," and who could do no more than express "vague, general preference" for "jurors with highly indefinite attributes or qualities" "as opposed to a regular practice of striking venire members for a specific reason").

- *Crittenden v. Chappell*, 804 F.3d 998 (9th Cir. 2015) (prosecutor's peremptory strike of sole African-American prospective juror, which was "substantially motivated by race," violated *Batson v. Kentucky*).

- *Garcia-Dorantes v. Warren*, 801 F.3d 584 (6th Cir. 2015), cert, denied, 136 S. Ct. 1823 (2016) ("computer glitch … that had systematically excluded African-Americans from the jury pool" resulted in violation of 6th Amendment "fair-cross-section right": "absolute disparity for African-Americans of 3.45% and corresponding 42% comparative disparity are sufficient to satisfy the *Duren* [*v. Missouri*, 439 U.S. 357 (1979)] second prong").

- *Drain v. Woods*, 595 Fed. Appx. 558 (6th Cir. 2014) (trial judge's response to "acknowledged Batson violations"—"allow[ing] *voir dire* to proceed with the sole requirement that the prosecutor request permission from the court before using any more peremptory challenges against black jurors"—was "plainly inadequate to cure the Batson violation"; if "improperly struck jurors" were not "available to be reinstated on the jury," "only remaining remedy for the Batson violation would be to discharge the entire venire and state the process anew").

- *Woodfox v. Cain*, 772 F.3d 358 (5th Cir. 2014), cert, denied, 136 S. Ct. 38 (2015) (petitioner "successfully made out a prima facie case of discrimination in the selection of the grand jury foreperson," which State failed to rebut "by demonstrating the use of race-neutral criteria in the selection of grand jury forepersons").

- *Castellanos v. Small*, 766 F.3d 1137 (9th Cir. 2014) (Batson violation is found because, although prosecutor claimed that peremptory strike of Hispanic female venireperson was due to venire woman's not "hav[ing] any children…[and] [t]he victim here is going to be a child testifying,' " prosecutor's assertion was " 'belied by the record,' " which showed that that venire woman responded that " 'she had two adult children' " and prosecutor even " 'asked about the occupations of her adult children, and she answered,' " and was further refuted by "side-by-side comparison" of venire woman with three others who had no children but "were ultimately permitted to serve on the jury," as was venireperson who "did not even answer the question about whether he had adult children").

- *Lark v. Secretary*, 556 Fed. Appx. 161 (3d Cir. 2014) (mem.), cert. denied, 135 S. Ct. 945 (2015) (petitioner "established by a preponderance of the evidence that the Commonwealth had struck five Black potential jurors because of their race").

- *Sampson v. United States*, 724 F.3d 150 (1st Cir. 2013) (granting new capital sentencing hearing because "juror dishonesty during the *voir dire* process antecedent to the penalty-phase hearing deprived [section 2255 movant] of an impartial jury").

- *Adkins v. Holman*, 710 F.3d 1241 (11th Cir.), cert, denied, 134 S. Ct. 268 (2013) (petitioner "has met his burden at Batson's third step and shown purposeful discrimination" by prosecutor in using peremptory strike: "record of the *voir dire* and the Batson hearing … support the conclusion that [venireperson] … was not excused for any legitimate reason" and "was removed because of his race").

- *Harris v. Hardy*, 680 F.3d 942 (7th Cir. 2012) (prosecutor violated *Batson v. Kentucky* by "exercis[ing] 17 of its 20 peremptory challenges on African Americans," and "State's proffered reasons are simply unbelievable" given that "comparative juror analysis shows that the purported reasons for striking certain African-Americans were not equally applied to non-African-Americans").

- *Rice v. White*, 660 F.3d 242 (6th Cir. 2011), cert, denied, 132 S. Ct. 2751 (2012) ("trial court breached its constitutional duty at step three of Batson 'to determine if the defendant has established purposeful discrimination,' " and "[c]ompound[ed]" this error by acting on "apparent[] belief] that any Batson violation could be 'cured' by seating proportionate share of African-Americans).

- *Love v. Cate*, 449 Fed. Appx. 570, 2011 13. S. App. LEXIS 18445 (9th Cir. Aug. 31, 2011) (prosecutor violated Batson by using peremptory strike in "race motivated" manner to remove "only black venire-member": although prosecutor "did not dismiss non-black venire-members within this category" and prosecutor's claimed practice of more thoroughly questioning teachers and social workers was not supported by record).

- *Hayes v. Thaler*, 361 Fed. Appx. 563, 2010 U.S. App. LEXIS 1152 (5th Cir. Jan. 19, 2010) (prosecutor's explanations for use of peremptory challenges to strike African American prospective jurors "were implausible or invalid and, therefore, were pretexts for discrimination").

CHAPTER ELEVEN

CLAIMS CONCERNING PLEA AGREEMENTS

The due process claims concerning guilty pleas are quite plentiful, yet most often go unexplored. If you are unfamiliar with the process, it is defined in Federal Rules of Criminal Procedure, rules ten and eleven. Be mindful that no constitutional provision exists that allows a criminal defendant to plea guilty. Thus, a guilty plea requires your agreement, and unless you enter into either a verbal or written contract to plead guilty, the plea itself is illegal.

Another important factor is that there is no legal provision, constitutional or statutory, that allows you to plead guilty to the government's factual basis. Rule and law require that you actually admit facts that constitute an offense under the criminal statute: Yes and no answers do not satisfy the law in this area.

One of the most common claims is that the defendant did not plead knowingly or intelligently. But, to succeed with this claim requires a showing that you would have proceeded to trial had you been properly advised so. See *Lee v. United States*, 582 U.S. The misadvise that I find so troubling is the advice of defense counsel behind closed doors. When in front of the sentencing judge, the attorney will have or already has claimed that he advised his client concerning the laws and facts of the case. Unfortunately, in most cases, this is just flat-out untrue. I have discovered that in most cases, the attorney has failed to mention the binding plea agreement provision of Fed. R. Crim. P., Rule 11(c) (1) (C). This is the part of the rule that will set a fixed sentence as a condition for the plea agreement. All other pleas allow the probation office to suggest and the sentencing court to impose a sentence based solely on the financial needs of the judicial district, which are explained in detail in the first three installments of this series.

In the ordinary case, a plea is entered into the record at arraignment, which is subject to withdraw with leave of the court at a later date. In theory, three types of pleas are available to the defendant: a plea of *not guilty*, a plea of *guilty*, and *nolo contendere*.

A plea of not guilty to the indictment or information is a plea that preserves all of the defendants' rights and requires proof beyond a reasonable doubt to find guilt. Unfortunately, in most cases, the defendant is not advised of his rights and is told to plead not guilty, although defense counsel fully intends to coerce his client into changing their plea at a later time.

A plea of guilty means that the defendant admits that he or she did, in fact, commit the prohibited act as accused. With this type of plea, the defendant waives most—nearly all—defenses against the conviction. However, there are a few claims that remain after the sentencing stage that will be covered later in this chapter.

In some courts, a defendant has a third option. In this case, a defendant may enter a plea of nolo contendere. Under this plea, the defendant does not contest the charge, thereby accepting the court's sentence to imprisonment just as though they had pleaded guilty. The difference from a guilty plea is that a nolo plea may not be used against a defendant as an admission in a later proceeding, either civil or criminal. A similar plea that most courts disapprove of is one that the Supreme Court upheld in *North Carolina v. Alford*. In that case, the Supreme Court upheld a guilty plea that contained an assertion of innocence. A court is not prohibited from accepting an Alford plea if a strong factual basis is established, but the Alford court made it clear that a trial court is not required to accept this type of plea.

I cannot express to you how many choices are before a defense lawyer in this stage of a trial process in only one book. I could probably write an entire series of books on this one subject alone. What I strongly suggest is that you study Federal Rules of Criminal Procedure, rules ten and eleven, before going any further.

Withdrawal of a plea agreement is an important factor in post-conviction proceedings. As I said earlier, the only way to gain relief is to show that you would have gone to trial had you been properly advised. A motion to withdraw your guilty plea before sentencing is proof that you desired a trial.

- *United States v. Vonn.* 535 U.S. 55, 72. 122 S. Ct. 1043, 1053. 152 L. Ed. 2d 90, 107-08 (2002) ("a defendant who fails to move "for withdrawal before sentencing has no further recourse except 'direct appeal or … motion under 28 U.S.C. §2255'….Whatever the 'fair and just standard may require on presentence motions; the Advisory Committee Notes confirm the textual suggestion that the Rule creates a 'near-presumption' against granting motions filed after sentencing.") (discussing Rule 32).

- *United States v. Vonn,* 535 U.S. 55, 64, 122 S. Ct. 1043, 1049, 152 L. Ed. 2d 90, 102 (2002) ("a defendant cannot overturn a guilty plea on collateral review absent a showing that the Rule 11 proceeding was 'inconsistent with the rudimentary demands of fair procedure' or constituted a 'complete miscarriage of justice.' ").

- *United States v. Gobert,* 139 F.3d 436, 438-39 (5th Cir. 1998) (permitted withdrawal of guilty plea because of injustice due to lack of factual basis for offense).

- *Hicks v. Franklin,* 546 F.3d 1279 (10th Cir. 2008) (guilty plea was constitutionally inadequate because petitioner "did not receive true notice" of essential element of crime and "in fact received misleading instruction from the court").

- *Jamison v. Klem,* 544 F.3d 266 (3d Cir. 2008) (guilty plea was not adequately knowing and intelligent because accused was never advised of mandatory minimum sentence).

- *Nara v. Frank,* 488 F.3d 187 (3d Cir. 2007), cert, denied, 552 U.S. 1309 (2008) (petitioner was mentally incompetent to enter guilty plea).

- *Davis v. Woodford,* 446 F.3d 957 (9th Cir. 2006) (sentencing that treated prior robbery conviction to which petitioner had pled guilty as "eight 'strikes'" under California's Three Strikes Law because eight robberies had been involved violated plea agreement and Due Process Clause because "state [had] expressly agreed [at time of plea] to treat the robbery conviction as only 'strike' for purposes of later recidivist sentencing").

- *Hanson v. Phillips,* 442, F.3d 789 (2d Cir. 2006) ("record does not affirmatively disclose that Hanson intelligently and voluntarily pleaded guilty, as required under *Boykin* [*v. Alabama*, 395 U.S. 238 (1969)]").

- *Buckley v. Terhune,* 441 F.3d 688 (9th Cir. 2006) (en banc), cert, denied, 550 U.S. 913 (2007) (sentence of "indeterminate prison term of fifteen years to life" violated petitioner's "due process right to enforce the provisions of his plea agreement" because "bargained – for sentence, to which he was constitutionally entitled, was a maximum of fifteen years").

- *Burt v. Uchtman,* 422, F.3d 557 (7th Cir. 2005) (trial court violated Due Process Clause by accepting petitioner's mid-trial guilty plea without sua sponte ordering renewed competency hearing given that trial judge was aware of petitioner's below-average intelligence, "history of psychological problems," and treatment with "large doses of psychotropic medications," and given that plea was "sudden unexplained … [and] against the advice of counsel").

- *Brown v. Poole*, 337 F.3d 1155 (9th Cir. 2003) (granting writ and ordering "released from custody forthwith" because state breached oral plea agreement that petitioner would only have to serve half of 15-year minimum if petitioner maintains clean prison record).

- *Ivy v. Caspari*, 173 F.3d 1136 (8th Cir. 1999) (guilty plea was not voluntary, knowing and intelligent because petitioner was 16 years old, had no prior experience with criminal justice system, had been diagnosed by psychiatrist as having mental illness, "was not advised [by judge] that intent was an element of the underlying offense," was not adequately aware of mental defense that could have been based on psychiatrist's finding, and erroneously believed at time he pleaded guilty that he was eligible for death penalty).

- *Wilkins v. Bowersox*, 145 F.3d 1006 (8th Cir. 1998), cert, denied, 525 U.S. 1094 (1999) (guilty plea, waiver of counsel, and waiver of right to present mitigating evidence at capital sentencing hearing were not voluntary, knowing, and intelligent because petitioner was 16 years old, had limited education, and was mentally disturbed).

- *United States v. Wolff*, 127 F.3d 84 (D.C. Cir. 1997), cert, denied, 524 U.S. 929 (1998) (government conceded that it breached the plea agreement).

- *United States v. Brown*, 117 F.3d 471 (11th Cir. 1997) (guilty plea was rendered invalid by holding in *Ratzlaf v. United States*, 510 U.S. 135 (1994) that crime of currency structuring requires knowledge of illegality).

- *United States v. Guerra*, 94 F.3d 989 (5th Cir. 1996) (guilty plea was not knowing and voluntary because district court misinformed section 2255 movant as to possible maximum sentence).

- *United States v. Taylor*, 77 F.3d 368 (11th Cir. 1996) (government breached plea agreement by expressing agreement with presentence report's recommended sentence which was higher than bargained-for sentence).

- *United States v. Neely*, 38 F.3d 458 (9th Cir. 1994) (guilty plea was not voluntary because district court failed to inform section 2255 movant that federal sentence could be served consecutively to any state sentence subsequently imposed).

- *United States v. De la Fuente*, 8 F.3d 1333 (9th Cir. 1993) (government breached plea agreement by failing to recommend sentence below mandatory minimum).

- *United States v. Roberts*, 5 F.3d 365 (9th Cir. 1993) (district court violated Fed. R. Crim. P. 11 by failing to advise movant of term of supervised release).

- *United States v. Garfield*, 987 F.2d 1424 (9th Cir. 1993) (district court improperly participated in plea negotiations in violation of Fed. R. Crim. P. 11(e) (1) and failed to make adequate findings regarding disputed information in the presentence report, as required by Fed. R. Crim. P. 32(c) (3) (D)).

- *United States v. Garcia*, 956 F. 2d 41 (4th Cir. 1992) (government breached plea agreement, which had specified that section 2255 movant not be required to cooperate with law enforcement, by subpoenaing movant to testify before grand jury).

- *United States v. Fuller*, 941 F.2d 993 (9th Cir. 1991) (guilty plea was involuntary because section 2255 movant was denied right to counsel during plea negotiations and consequently was unable to understand charges and consequences).

- *Nevarez-Diaz v. United States*, 870 F.2d 417 (7th Cir. 1989) (guilty plea hearing was defective because section 2255 movant did not understand nature of charges).

- *Brunelle v. United States*, 864 F.2d 64 (8th Cir. 1988) (government breached plea agreement).
- *Montgomery v. United States*, 853 F.2d 83 (2d Cir. 1988) (section 2255 movant's guilty plea was accepted by district court without adequate basis, in violation of Fed. R. Crim. P. 11(f)).

CHAPTER TWELVE

DUE PROCESS VIOLATIONS AT TRIAL

When it comes to due process, the most fundamental right to a criminal defendant is the right to a fair trial. This right is most often unknown to criminal defendants and avoided by all the Bar members involved: judge, defense, and prosecution. Fair trial is defined in the Bill of Rights by the Sixth Amendment. When reading the Sixth Amendment, three trial rights can be easily recognized: the right to a speedy trial, the right to a public trial, and the right to a trial by an impartial jury from the district where the crime was committed.

Although these rights are fairly straightforward and the subject of many television shows, they are also the most commonly trampled upon by the court and the government, with the help of your very own defense lawyer. The lawyers who conspire together to conduct business in the American criminal justice system avoid fair trials for two very obvious yet misunderstood reasons. The first is the limitations of federal jurisdiction. A focused study of Supreme Court decisions over the last thirty years will show how the high court has routinely defined federal jurisdiction. The second reason is the cost of fair trials. Make no mistake, lawyers, judges, and courthouse owners are paid and paid very well at that. That pay depends on the number of months handed down at sentencing in relation with the cost of doing so. Considering the obvious cost of a lengthy trial, it is no surprise why those in charge of the system will avoid extra trial expenditures at all cost, even with the conviction of the innocent.

To deprive a defendant of his right to a fair trial is a violation of his constitutional right to due process. To successfully deny a defendant a fair trial, the court must be willing to do two things: (1) break the law and (2) cover it up by reducing the avenues of review after the defendant realizes he has been deceived.

Recognize also that your attempt to get due process of law in a federal court is like trying to herd a pig down the road in a straight line with a stick. With that thought in mind, know that the errors that separate a defendant from a fair trial are quite plentiful indeed. Read the following winning post-conviction cases that follow:

- *Wainwright v. Greenfield*, 474 U.S. 284 (1985) (state permitted to use, as evidence of petitioner's guilt, fact that petitioner exercised right to silence after police officers thrice told him he could refuse to talk to them without suffering adverse consequences).

- *Miller v. Pate*, 386 U.S. 1 (1967) (prosecutor claimed at trial that principal item of evidence, a pair of shorts, was stained with blood when he knew that substance on shorts was in fact paint).

- *Kubsch v. Neal*, 838 F.3d 845 (7th Cir. 2016) (en banc), cert. denied, 137 S. Ct. 2161 (2017) (trial court's exclusion of evidence "that was vital to the defense" based on "state's hearsay rule … [and] the state's [evidentiary] rule requiring vouching [by witness] before recorded recollections may be introduced" violated *Chambers v. Mississippi* and follow-up Supreme Court decisions "requiring state evidentiary rules to yield to the defendant's fundamental due-process right to present a defense").

- *Alvarez v. Lopez*, 835 F.3d 1024 (9th Cir. 2016) (Indian "Community denied Alvarez his right under ICRA [Indian Civil Rights Act] to be tried by a jury" by "failing to inform him that he could receive a jury trial only by requesting one").

- *Ardoin v. Arnold*, 653 Fed. Appx. 532 (9th Cir. 2016) (trial court "violated Ardoin's Sixth Amendment right to counsel during closing argument" by refusing to reopen closing arguments after authorizing jury, during deliberations, to consider felony murder theory that previously had applied only to co-defendant, thereby depriving petitioner's counsel of any "opportunity whatsoever to argue felony murder after learning that the jury could convict on that theory').

- *Brown v. Superintendent*, 834 F.3d 506 (3d Cir. 2016), cert, denied, 137 S. Ct. 1581 (2017) (prosecutor violated *Bruton v. United States* by disclosing to jury in closing argument that sanitized references in co-defendant's confession to " 'the other guy' " actually referred to petitioner' although "[t]here are some circumstances when the prosecution can commit what otherwise would be a constitutional violation but nonetheless escape a mistrial through limiting instructions^] ... in cases falling within the ambit of Bruton and its progeny, limiting instructions cannot cure the error").

- *Colon v. Rozum*, 649 Fed. Appx. 259 (3d Cir. 2016), cert, denied, 137 S. Ct. 1579 (2017) (introduction into evidence non-testifying co-defendant's statement violated Confrontation Clause, even though statement had been redacted to "replace Colon's name with the words 'another person' and 'other person,' " because "jury knew that" there were only three people in the car at the time of the crime" and, "[b]y a process of elimination, it was easy for the jury to infer that Colon was the person referenced when Gonzales was asked if the 'other person' heard Betancourt say that 'he was gonna rob somebody's purse and stuff like that' ").

- *Deck v. Jenkins*, 814 F.3d 954 (9th Cir. 2016) ("prosecutor's uncorrected misstatements" during closing argument about state law of attempt violated due process).

- *McCarley v. Kelly*, 801 F.3d 652 (6th Cir. 2015), cert, denied, 136 S. Ct. 2508 (2016) (trial court violated Confrontation Clause by allowing prosecution to present out-of-court statements of murder victim's three-year-old son through testimony of child psychologist who obtained statements in clinical interviews).

- *Washington v. Secretary*, 801 F.3d 160 (3d Cir. 2015), cert, denied, 136 S. Ct. 1713 (2016) ("'admission into evidence of a confession by a non-testifying codefendant that redacted James Washington's name and replaced it with ... generic terms describing Washington and his role in the charged crimes" violated Confrontation Clause because "there were two obvious alterations that notified the jury that Washington's name was deleted").

- *Nappi v. Yelich*, 793 F.3d 246 (2d Cir. 2015) (trial judge violated Confrontation Clause by precluding defense counsel from cross-examining accused's wife about her romantic relationship with another man to show that wife had "motive to implicate Nappi in the illegal possession of a weapon—which she knew was a violation of his parole").

- *Camp v. Neven*, 606 Fed. Appx. 322 (9th Cir. 2015) (by "allowing the State to present unnoticed expert rebuttal testimony when Camp was required to disclose his own expert testimony on the same issues," pursuant to statutory requirement of discovery that applied to State's case in chief and defense case but not to State's rebuttal case, trial judge created "non-reciprocal disclosure obligation" that violated accused's due process rights under *Wardius v. Oregon*, 412 U.S. 470 (1973)).

- *Blackston v. Rapelje*, 780 F.3d 340 (6th Cir.), cert, denied, 136 S. Ct. 388 (2015) (trial court violated Confrontation Clause by permitting readback of two unavailable witnesses' testimony, from previous trial of petitioner on same charges "while at the same time denying Blackston the right to impeach their testimony with evidence of their subsequent recantations").

- *Gumm v. Mitchell*, 775 F.3d 345 (6th Cir. 2014) (prosecutor "relentlessly pressed ... witnesses to obtain ... highly inflammatory and unreliable" testimony and "then used the inflammatory information ... in the rebuttal closing arguments to the jury to argue that Petitioner is a sexual deviant who likely committed the crimes").

- *Alvarez v. Ercole*, 763 F.3d 223 (2d Cir. 2014) (trial court violated 6th Amendment and due process right to present defense by misapplying hearsay rule to prohibit defense cross-examination of "lead detective to show that the police had not investigated leads provided by a witness ... whose tips were memorialized in a detective's notes and an investigative ... report").

- *Eley v. Erickson*, 712 F.3d 837 (3d Cir.), cert, denied, 134 S. Ct. 254 (2013) (trial court violated Confrontation Clause by denying severance and allowing admission of jailhouse informant's account that non-testifying co-defendant confessed to committing charged crime with " 'other two' " individuals, which jury doubtless would have understood to refer to petitioner and third co-defendant).

- *Gongora v. Thaler*, 710 F.3d 267 (5th Cir. 2013) (per curiam), cert, denied, 134 S. Ct. 941 (2014) (prosecutor's closing argument contained "extraordinarily extensive comments on Gongora's failure to testify").

- *Ortiz v. Yates*, 704 F.3d 1026 (9th Cir. 2012), (trial court violated "Sixth Amendment right to confront adverse witnesses" by precluding defense counsel from asking state's central witness whether "she was afraid to deviate from her initial incriminating statement to the police because of threats allegedly made against her by the prosecutor").

- *Cudjo v. Ayers*, 698 F.3d 752 (9th Cir. 2012), cert, denied, 133 S. Ct. 2735 (2013) (trial court violated due process doctrine of *Chambers v. Mississippi* by excluding defense witness who would have testified to hearing actual perpetrator confess to crime that petitioner was charged with committing).

- *Harris v. Thompson*, 698 F.3d 609 (7th Cir. 2012), cert, denied, 133 S. Ct. 2766 (2013) (trial court violated 6th Amendment right to present defense by excluding "critical exculpatory evidence" of 6-year-old based on finding that witness was incompetent to testify).

- *Simpson v. Warren*, 475 Fed. Appx. 51, 2012 U.S. App. LEXIS 7184 (6th Cir. April 10, 2012) ("cumulative effect of the prosecutor's improper and flagrant questioning ... and his prejudicial comments during closing arguments deprived Petitioner of a fair trial").

- *Merolillo v. Yates*, 663 F.3d 444 (9th Cir. 2011), cert, denied, 568 U.S. 927 (2012) ("admission at trial of the non-testifying autopsy pathologist's opinion" violated "Sixth Amendment right to confront witnesses").

- *Ocampo v. Vail*, 649 F.3d 1098 (9th Cir. 2011), cert, denied, 567 U.S. 952 (2012) (Confrontation Clause was violated by detectives' references to non-testifying witness's out-of-court statements corroborating other witnesses' identifications of accused as shooter).

- *Jones v. Basinger*, 635 F.3d 1030 (7th Cir. 2011) (trial judge violated Confrontation Clause by permitting "two police detectives [to] testif[y] in detail about an informant's double-hearsay statement ... [claiming] Jones [w]as the leader of the robbery and murders," which judge "allowed on the theory that it was offered not to show the truth of the informant's statement but for the purpose of showing the course of the police investigation that led to Jones' arrest" but which "was in fact used as substantive evidence to prove Jones' guilt, in violation of his Sixth Amendment rights").

- *Adamson v. Cathel*, 633 F.3d 248 (3d Cir. 2011) (trial court violated *Tennessee v. Street*, 471 U.S. 409 (1985) by admitting statements of non-testifying accomplices—which prosecution introduced for "purpose of impeaching Adamson's testimony that his own confession had been fabricated by a police officer"— without limiting instruction that statements could only be considered for impeachment and not as substantive evidence of guilt).

- *Secretary, Fla. Dep't of Corr. v. Baker*, 406 Fed. Appx. 416, 2010 U.S. App. LEXIS 26216 (11th Cir. Dec. 27, 2010) (per curiam) (trial court violated Confrontation Clause and due process by precluding impeachment of child complainant in sex offense with prior allegations of sexual assault, none of which was prosecuted, and three of which complainant admitted having been false).

- *Maxwell v. Roe*, 628 F.3d 486 (9th Cir. 2010), cert, denied, 565 U.S. 1138 (2012) ("conviction based on false material evidence violated ... due process").

- *Hurd v. Terhune*, 619 F.3d 1080 (9th Cir. 2010) (trial court * violated *Doyle v. Ohio*, 426 U.S. 610 (1976) by allowing prosecution to introduce evidence of accused's post-Miranda silence and to refer to it in closing argument).

- *Miller v. Stovall*, 608 F.3d 913 (6th Cir. 2010) (trial court violated Confrontation Clause by admitting suicide note of defendant's dead lover which implicated defendant in lover's killing of defendant's spouse).

- *Lunbery v. Hornbeak*, 605 F.3d 754 (9th Cir.), cert, denied, 562 U.S. 1102 (2010) (trial judge violated *Chambers v. Mississippi*, 410 U.S. 284 (1973) by applying hearsay rule strictly to exclude exculpatory statement that "bore substantial guarantees of trustworthiness and was critical to [accused's] defense").

- *Jones v. Cain*, 600 F.3d 527 (5th Cir. 2010) (admission of "recorded testimony from a deceased witness" violated Confrontation Clause).

- *Ward v. Hall*, 592 F.3d 1144 (11th Cir.), cert, denied, 562 U.S. 1082 (2010) ("constitutional right to a fair trial and a reliable sentence were violated when a bailiff improperly responded to a juror's question about parole during the penalty phase of trial").

- *Jensen v. Romanowski*, 590 F.3d 373 (6th Cir. 2009) (trial judge violated Confrontation Clause in child sexual assault trial by admitting police officer's account of interview of child complainant in prior case in which petitioner was accused of sexual assault).

- *Earhart v. Konteh*, 589 F.3d 337 (6th Cir. 2009), cert, denied, 562 U.S. 874 (2010) ("admission of the videotape deposition [of child complainant] without a proper finding that the witness was constitutionally unavailable violated Earhart's ... right to confrontation").

- *Bobadilla v. Carlson*, 575 F.3d 785 (8th Cir. 2009), cert, denied, 558 U.S. 1137 (2010) (trial judge violated Confrontation Clause in child sexual assault trial by admitting videotaped interview of 3-year-old complainant and testimony by social worker who conducted the interview).

- *Holley v. Yarborough*, 568 F.3d 1091 (9th Cir. 2009) (trial court violated Confrontation Clause in sex offense trial by "preclud[ing] the introduction of impeachment evidence and preventing] ... [defense counsel's] cross-examination of the alleged victim about her prior statements, including statements about sex and indications that others had made sexual advances toward her").

- *Slovik v. Yates*, 556 F.3d 747 (9th Cir. 2009) (trial court violated Confrontation Clause by preventing defense counsel from impeaching prosecution witness with extrinsic evidence refuting witness's denial that "he was currently on probation").

- *Vazquez v. Wilson*, 550 F.3d 270 (3d Cir. 2008) (trial court violated Confrontation Clause by permitting prosecution to introduce statement of non-testifying codefendant which, although redacted to remove express references to petitioner, "almost certain[ly]" would have been construed by jury as inculpating petitioner).

- *Brinson v. Walker*, 547 F.3d 387 (2d Cir. 2008) (trial judge violated Confrontation Clause by precluding defense cross-examination of complainant with prior bad act that defense counsel sought to elicit to show complainant's racial animus and to support defense theory that complainant fabricated charges against accused).

- *Taylor v. Cain*, 545 F.3d 327 (5th Cir. 2008) (trial court violated Confrontation Clause by permitting prosecution to elicit from detective that "unidentified, nontestifying witness identified the defendant as * the perpetrator' ").

- *Fratta v. Quarterman*, 536 F.3d 485 (5th Cir. 2008) (trial court violated Confrontation Clause by permitting prosecution to introduce custodial statements by petitioner's co-defendants and heresay account of co-defendant's statement to girlfriend).

- *Barbe v. McBride*, 521 F.3d 443 (4th Cir. 2008) ("Sixth Amendment confrontation [clause] … was indisputably contravened … by the state circuit court's application of a per se rule restricting cross-examination of the prosecution's expert [licensed clinical counselor who had met with victim on several occasions] under the state rape shield law").

- *Gray v. Moore*, 520 F.3d 616 (6th Cir.), cert, denied, 555 U.S. 894 (2008) (trial court violated petitioner's "constitutional rights to due process, to be present at his trial, and to confront the witnesses against him, when it removed him from the courtroom without warning him of the consequences of his actions").

- *Parle v. Runnels*, 505 F.3d 922 (9th Cir. 2007) ("cumulative effect of multiple evidentiary errors" violated due process).

- *Girts v. Yanai*, 501 F.3d 743 (6th Cir. 2007), cert, denied, 555 U.S. 819 (2008) (prosecutor's closing argument, which referred three times to accused's constitutionally protected silence, constituted "flagrant prosecutorial misconduct").

- *Ferensic v. Birkett*, 501 F.3d 469 (6th Cir. 2007) (trial court's exclusion of defense expert on eyewitness identifications and lay witness whom defense sought to call violated 6th Amendment right to present defense).

- *Vasquez v. Jones*, 496 F.3d 564 (6th Cir. 2007) (trial court violated Confrontation Clause by preventing defense counsel from responding to prosecution's introduction of preliminary hearing transcript of unavailable prosecution witness by introducing impeaching evidence of witness's prior convictions).

- *Winzer v. Hall*, 494 F.3d 1192 (9th Cir. 2007) (trial court violated Confrontation Clause by "finding that [alleged victim's] report [to police officer] was [admissible as] a spontaneous declaration or excited utterance").

- *Lyell v. Renico*, 470 F.3d 1177 (6th Cir. 2006) (trial judge "made a fair trial impossible" by "sua sponte interrupting] the prosecution to assist it, sua sponte interrupting] [defense counsel's] questioning in a way that undermined his presentation of the case (frequently during the cross-examination of the central witness in the case), fail[ing] to interrupt in a like manner during the prosecution's questioning (at least in a way that undermined its case), stating] or impl[ying] her disapproval of [petitioner's] theory of the case[,] … and ma[king] clear her disapproval of defense counsel … [and] issu[ing] a contempt order against Lyell's counsel in front of the jury").

- *Gaston v. Brigano*, 208 Fed. Appx. 376, 2006 U.S. App. LEXIS 30219 (6th Cir. Dec. 7, 2006) (admission of audiotape of child witness's statements violated Confrontation Clause).

- *Stevens v. Ortiz*, 465 F.3d 1229 (10th Cir. 2006), cert, denied, 549 U.S. 1281 (2007) (trial court violated Confrontation Clause by permitting prosecution to introduce, at trial, co-defendant's custodial statement implicating petitioner).

- *Stallings v. Bobby*, 464 F.3d 576 (6th Cir. 2006) (trial court violated Confrontation Clause by allowing prosecution to introduce co-arrestee's statement implicating petitioner).

- *Fulcher v. Motley*, 444 F.3d 791 (6th Cir. 2006) (admission, at trial, of tape-recorded statements by accused's girlfriend in police station interview violated Confrontation Clause).

- *Ben-Yisrayl v. Davis*, 431 F.3d 1043 (7th Cir. 2005) (prosecutor's

- closing argument violated Fifth Amendment by encouraging jury to infer guilt from accused's failure to testify).

- *Kittelson v. Dretke*, 426 F.3d 306 (5th Cir. 2005) (per curiam) (trial court violated Confrontation Clause and Due Process Clauses by curtailing defense's cross-examination of two key prosecution witnesses and preventing defense counsel from eliciting favorable evidence from defense witnesses).

- *Fowler v. Sacramento County Sheriff's Dep't*, 421 F.3d 1027 (9th Cir. 2005) (trial court violated Confrontation Clause by preventing defense counsel in sexual molestation trial from cross-examining complainant about two prior unfounded complaints).

- *Christie v. Hollins*, 409 F.3d 120 (2d Cir. 2005) (trial court violated due process right to present defense by preventing petitioner from introducing prior testimony of unavailable defense witness, based on trial court's unsupported view that defense counsel had not been adequately diligent in trying to secure witness's attendance).

- *Howard v. Walker*, 406 F.3d 114 (2d Cir. 2005) (trial court violated 6th Amendment by curtailing defense cross-examination of state's expert and by impeding defense from presenting expert of its own).

- *Ruimveld v. Birkett*, 404 F.3d 1006 (6th Cir. 2005) (during trial, petitioner was unconstitutionally "shackled in view of the jury, despite the fact that he did not pose any special risk of flight or violence").

- *Murillo v. Frank*, 402 F.3d 786 (7th Cir. 2005) (admission of hearsay statement made by another suspect during custodial interrogation violated Confrontation Clause).

- *White v. Coplan*, 399 F.3d 18 (1st Cir.), cert, denied, 546 U.S. 972 (2005) (trial court violated Confrontation Clause by preventing defense counsel from cross-examining complainants in sexual assault trial about prior false accusations of sexual assault by other individuals).

- *Dorchy v. Jones*, 398 F.3d 783 (6th Cir. 2005) (admission of unavailable eyewitness's testimony given at co-defendant's trial violated Confrontation Clause).

- *Guidry v. Dretke*, 397 F.3d 306 (5th Cir. 2005), cert, denied, 547 U.S. 1035 (2006) (admission of hearsay statement violated Confrontation Clause).

- *Chia v. Cambra*, 360 F.3d 997 (9th Cir. 2004), cert, denied, 544 U.S. 919 (2005) (trial court violated *Chambers v. Mississippi*, 410 U.S. 284 (1973) by excluding four statements of codefendant, which exculpated petitioner while inculpating declarant).

- *Brown v. Keane*, 355 F.3d 82 (2d Cir. 2004) (admission of anonymous 911 call under state hearsay law exception for "present sense impression" violated Confrontation Clause).

- *Hall v. Director of Corr.*, 343 F.3d 976 (9th Cir. 2003) (per curiam) ("false and material evidence was admitted at Hall's trial in violation of his due process rights").

- *Hill v. Hofbauer*, 337 F.3d 706 (6th Cir. 2003) (admission of nontestifying codefendant's confession, which inculpated petitioner, violated Confrontation Clause).

- *Alcala v. Woodford*, 334 F.3d 862 (9th Cir. 2003) (trial court's exclusion of testimony of defense psychologist that prosecution's key witness "had been hypnotically influenced in various interviews with police investigators" violated petitioner's "due process right to a fundamentally fair trial and to present crucial witnesses in his defense").

- *Ward v. Sternes*, 334 F.3d 696 (7th Cir. 2003) (trial court failed to conduct adequate colloquy to ensure that defendant with brain damage was knowingly and intelligently waiving right to testify on advice of counsel).

- *Cotto v. Herbert*, 331 F.3d 217 (2d Cir. 2003) (trial court violated Confrontation Clause by barring defense from cross-examining prosecution witness whom defendant had allegedly intimidated into altering account of events).

- *Ellis v. Mullin*, 326 F.3d 1122 (10th Cir. 2002), cert, denied, 540 U.S. 977 (2003) (trial court violated *Chambers v. Mississippi*, 410 U.S. 284 (1973) by excluding psychiatrist's report, which, although addressed to issue of competency to stand trial, contained mental health evidence supporting adducer's insanity defense).

- *Cook v. McKune*, 323 F.3d 825 (10th Cir. 2003) (prosecutor's introduction of preliminary hearing testimony of absent witness violated Confrontation Clause because state had not made adequate efforts to secure witness's presence at trial).

- *Cargle v. Mullin*, 317 F.3d 1196 (10th Cir. 2003) (prosecutor's argument at guilt-innocence stage of capital case that "his office prosecutes only those who are guilty" " 'infringe[d] upon the role of the jury as fact finder and determiner of guilt and innocence,' " and prosecutor also improperly used co-perpetrator's immunity agreement to "vouch for the truthfulness " of co-perpetrator's account and to suggest that "information available to the prosecution but not presented to the jury supports the witness's testimony").

- *Lewis v. Wilkinson*, 307 F.3d 413 (6th Cir. 2002) (trial judge violated Confrontation Clause by applying rape shield law to bar defense counsel from cross-examining complainant with diary passages supporting consent defense).

- *Ryan v. Miller*, 303 F.3d 231 (2d Cir. 2002) (prosecution violated Confrontation Clause by using direct examination questions to "create the impression for the jury" that co-perpetrator's statements "led the police to focus on [petitioner] as a suspect," thereby "'plain[ly] impl[ying]' … that [co-perpetrator] accused [petitioner]").

- *Little v. Kern Cnty. Super. Ct.*, 294 F.3d 1075 (9th Cir. 2002) (per curiam) (summary hearing for criminal contempt violated Due Process Clause because of lack of "specific notice of the contempt charges and the time of the hearing" and because of judge's "bias and personal embroilment").

- *Greene v. Lambert*, 288 F.3d 1081 (9th Cir. 2002) (trial court violated right to present defense by wholly excluding testimony, either from accused or from victim—who was accused's therapist—about accused's Dissociative Identity Disorder).

- *Stapleton v. Wolfe*, 288 F.3d 863 (6th Cir. 2002) (trial court violated Confrontation Clause by admitting audiotaped custodial statements of codefendant).

- *Calvert v. Wilson*, 288 F.3d 823 (6th Cir. 2002) (admission of audiotaped confession of accused's codefendant violated Confrontation Clause).

- *Killian v. Poole*, 282 F.3d 1204 (9th Cir. 2002), cert, denied, 537 U.S. 1179 (2003) (prosecution's star witness testified perjuriously at trial, prosecution failed to provide defense with letters in which witness admitted perjury to gain sentencing concessions, and prosecution improperly referred to accused's post-arrest silence in cross-examination and closing argument).

- *Riley v. Taylor*, 277 F.3d 261 (3d Cir. 2001) (en banc) (prosecutor's opening statement, which was misleading as to the scope of appellate review," violated *Caldwell v. Mississippi*, 472 U.S. 320 (1985)).

- *Thomas v. Hubbard*, 273 F.3d 1164 (9th Cir. 2001), overruled in part on other grounds, *Payton v. Woodford*, 299 F.3d 815 (9th Cir. 2002) (en banc), vac'd & remanded, 538 U.S. 975 (2003) (cumulative effect of three trial errors—admission of triple hearsay, prosecutorial misconduct in eliciting defendant's prior conviction in violation of pretrial ruling, and improper limitation of defense's cross-examination of investigating officer—produced trial that was ,"so infected … with unfairness as to make the resulting conviction a denial of due process ").

- *Brumley v. Wingard*, 269 F.3d 629 (6th Cir. 2001) (trial court's admission of videotaped deposition of out-of-state incarcerated witness, "without first determining that the deponent was unavailable in the constitutional sense," violated Confrontation Clause).

- *Moore v. Morton*, 255 F.3d 95 (3d Cir. 2001) ("prosecutor's inflammatory and highly prejudicial argument" was designed to play on racial prejudice and "sympathy for the victim").

- *Heliums v. Williams*, 16 Fed. Appx. 905, 2011 U.S. App. LEXIS 17697 (10th Cir. Aug. 8, 2001) (prosecution's expert witnesses, who had examined child complainant in sexual abuse case, "impermissibly vouched for the victim's credibility by indicating that they believed her testimony").

- *Agnew v. Leibach*, 250 F.3d 1123 (7th Cir. 2001) (trial court refused to grant mistrial when deputy, who had served as bailiff for first day of two-day trial, was called to witness stand by prosecution).

- *Newman v. Hopkins*, 247 F.3d 848 (8th Cir. 2001), cert, denied, 536 U.S. 915 (2002) (state courts' application of per se rule to exclude voice exemplar, proffered by petitioner to support misidentification defense by showing that petitioner did not have accent, violated right to present defense).

- *Noble v. Kelly*, 246 F.3d 93 (2d Cir.) (per curiam), cert, denied, 534 U.S. 886 (2001) (trial court violated 6th Amendment's Compulsory Process Clause by excluding defense alibi witness on ground that defense counsel failed to comply with alibi notice rule).

- *DePetris v. Kuykendall*, 239 F.3d 1057 (9th Cir. 2001) (trial court's exclusion of victim's handwritten journal and preclusion of testimony by accused about journal's effect on perceived need for self-defense unconstitutionally inhibited right to present defense).

- *Vincent v. Seabold*, 226 F.3d 681 (6th Cir. 2000), cert, denied, 532 U.S. 1063 (2001) (trial court violated Confrontation Clause by relying on "statement against penal interest" principle to introduce hearsay statements by co-perpetrator who "attempt[ed] to distance [himself] from the murder and minimize his participation in the crime" by blaming petitioner).

- *Smith v. Groose*, 205 F.3d 1045 (8th Cir.) cert, denied, 531 U.S. 985 (2000) (prosecutor violated due process by using "inherently factually contradictory theories" of case at separate trials of petitioner and alleged co-perpetrator).

- *Gordon v. Kelly*, 2000 U.S. App. LEXIS 1507 (6th Cir. 2000) (prosecutor violated due process right to fair trial by using witness examinations and closing arguments to suggest that witnesses feared petitioner and that he was responsible for death of crucial eyewitness).

- *Conde v. Henry*, 198 F.3d 734 (9th Cir. 2000) (trial judge precluded defense counsel from arguing theory of case to jury in closing argument).

- *Henry v. Kernan*, 197 F.3d 1021 (9th Cir. 1999), cert, denied, 528 U.S. 1198 (2000) (trial court improperly allowed prosecutor to use petitioner's unconstitutionally coerced confession to impeach him at trial).

- *Rhoden v. Rowland*, 172 F.3d 633 (9th Cir. 1999) (petitioner was shackled throughout trial, in view of jurors, even though no compelling security need for shackles was established).

- *Gonzales v. Lyttle*, 167 F.3d 1318 (10th Cir. 1999) (trial was fundamentally unfair because judge allowed prosecution to present preliminary hearing testimony of unavailable witness linking petitioner to crime but did not permit defense to inform jury that witness subsequently recanted under oath).

- *English v. Artuz*, 164 F.3d 105 (2d Cir. 1998) (trial court violated right to public trial by closing proceedings during testimony of undercover officer).

- *Harrison v. Chandler*, 1998 U.S. App. LEXIS 27744 (6th Cir. Oct. 26, 1998) (per curiam) (trial court violated confrontation clause by introducing police officer's hearsay account of statement by petitioner's non-testifying co-perpetrator).

- *Eslaminia v. White*, 136 F.3d 1234 (9th Cir. 1998) (jury's exposure to unadmitted, prejudicial statement of petitioner's brother, which was on reverse side of police audiotape introduced into evidence, deprived petitioner of rights to confrontation, cross-examination, and assistance of counsel).

- *Hill v. Turpin*, 135 F.3d 1411 (11th Cir. 1998) (prosecutor repeatedly referred to petitioner's post-Miranda silence and requests for counsel).

- *Snowden v. Singletary*, 135 F.3d 732 (11th Cir.), cert, denied, 525 U.S. 963 (1998) (trial on charges of sexual abuse of child violated due process right to fair trial because prosecutor presented and relied heavily on inaccurate expert testimony that "99.5% of children tell the truth" when making accusations of abuse).

- *Jones v. Vacco*, 126 F.3d 408 (2d Cir. 1997) (trial judge improperly barred petitioner from conferring with counsel during overnight recess in midst of petitioner's cross-examination).

- *Lindh v. Murphy*, 124 F.3d 899 (7th Cir. 1997), cert, denied, 522 U.S. 1069 (1998) (at insanity phase of trial, judge violated Confrontation Clause by forbidding petitioner's counsel to cross-examine state's psychiatrist on biases created by threatened prosecution of psychiatrist for sexually abusing patients).

- *Lyons v. Johnson*, 99 F.3d 499 (2d Cir. 1996) (denial of defense request that jury view person whom defense claimed was actual perpetrator violated due process right to fair trial).

- *United States v. Cheek*, 94 F.3d 136 (4th Cir. 1996) (codefendant attempted to bribe juror during joint trial).

- *Justice v. Hoke*, 90 F.3d 43 (2d Cir. 1996) (exclusion of defense witnesses' testimony casting doubt on complainant's credibility and supporting defense theory of fabrication violated 6th Amendment right to present defense).

- *Ayala v. Speckard*, 89 F.3d 91 (2d Cir. 1996) (closure of courtroom to protect identity of undercover officer violated petitioner's right to public trial).

- *Gravley v. Mills*, 87 F.3d 779 (6th Cir. 1996) (prosecutor violated due process by repeatedly making improper references to petitioner's post-arrest silence in cross-examination and closing argument).

- *Delguidice v. Singletary*, 84 F.3d 1359 (11th Cir. 1996) (introduction at trial of uncounseled statements petitioner made to psychiatrist during competency evaluation in another case, without notification or waiver of right to silence, violated rule of *Estelle v. Smith*, 451 U.S. 454 (1981)).

- *Yohn v. Love*, 76 F.3d 508 (3d Cir. 1996) (ex parte communication between prosecutor and state supreme court justice, resulting in ruling that had originally favored defense, violated Due Process Clause and 6th Amendment right to counsel).

- *Offor v. Scott*, 72 F.3d 30 (5th Cir. 1995) (introduction of videotaped interview of child complainant violated Confrontation Clause).

- *Franklin v. Duncan*, 70 F.3d 75 (9th Cir. 1995) (per curiam), (prosecutor's reference in closing argument to post-Miranda silence, coupled with jury instruction informing jury that silence could be construed as adoptive admission, violated 5th Amendment right to remain silent).

- *Riley v. Deeds*, 56 F.3d 1117 (9th Cir. 1995) (read back of complainant's direct examination testimony, authorized by judge's law clerk in response to jurors' request and conducted in judge's absence, violated Due Process Clause).

- *Wigglesworth v. Oregon*, 49 F.3d 578 (9th Cir. 1995) (statutorily authorized procedure of admitting certified copy of drug analysis report, subject to defendant's subpoenaing and cross-examining chemist who prepared report, violated Due Process Clause by "reliev[ing] the state of its burden of proof on an essential element of its case").

- *Webb v. Lewis*, 44 F.3d 1387 (9th Cir. 1994), cert, denied, 514 U.S. 1128;(1995) (introduction of videotaped interview of child victim of sexual abuse violated Confrontation Clause).

- *United States v. Ross*, 40 F.3d 144 (7th Cir. 1994) (per curiam) (granting section 2255 relief because post trial decision in *Staples v. United States*, 511 U.S. 600 (1994), established that instruction on men's rea element of offense was erroneous).

- *Davis v. Zant*, 36 F.3d 1538 (11th Cir. 1994) (prosecutor's "repeated and clearly intentional misrepresentations" in objection and closing argument rendered trial fundamentally unfair in violation of Due Process Clause).

- *Maurer v. Department of Corrections*, 32 F.3d 1286 (8th Cir. 1994) (admission of testimony by prosecution witnesses that "complainant seemed sincere when she said she was raped" rendered trial "fundamentally unfair" in violation of Due Process Clause).

- *Vidal v. Williams*, 31 F.3d 67 (2d Cir. 1994), cert, denied, 513 U.S. 1102 (1995) (trial court violated petitioner's Sixth Amendment right to public trial by closing courtroom, and excluding petitioner's parents, during undercover officer's testimony).

- *Pelaez v. United States*, 27 F.3d 219 (6th Cir. 1994) (retroactively applying *Crosby v. United States*, 506 U.S. 255 (1993), which precludes trial in absentia if accused was not present at commencement of trial).

- *Bonner v. Holt*, 26 F.3d 1081 (11th Cir. 1994), cert, denied, 514 U.S. 1010 (1995) (jury was improperly exposed to inadmissible extra-record evidence when prosecutor stated to judge in jury's presence that petitioner was habitual offender).

- *Martin v. Parker*, 11 F.3d 613 (6th Cir. 1993) (per curiam) (due process right to fair trial violated by prosecutor's references to petitioner's prior bad acts and closing argument comparing petitioner to Hitler).

- *Carter v. Sowders*, 5 F.3d 975 (6th Cir. 1993), cert, denied, 511 U.S. 1097 (1994) (admission, at trial, of pretrial deposition of paid police informant violated petitioner's 6th Amendment right to confrontation because, contrary to findings of state court and district court, neither petitioner nor counsel validly waived petitioner's 6th Amendment right to attend deposition).

- *Shaw v. Collins*, 5 F.3d 128 (5th Cir. 1993) (Confrontation Clause violated by introduction of videotaped testimony of prosecution witness who did not testify at trial).

- *Lowery v. Collins*, 988 F.2d 1364 (5th Cir.), supplemented on reh'g, 996 F.2d 770 (5th Cir. 1993) (introduction of videotaped interview of child complainant violated petitioner's right to confrontation).

- *Derden v. McNeel*, 938 F.2d 605 (5th Cir. 1991) (petitioner denied fair trial by combination of judge's repeated admonitions to defense counsel and accused (thereby "encourag[ing] a predisposition of guilt by the jury"), prosecutor's failure to disclose impeachment evidence in violation of *Brady v. Maryland*, 373 U.S. 83 (1963), and prosecutor's violations of state law standards for *voir dire* questions and introduction of other crimes evidence).

- *Gaines v. Thieret*, 846 F.2d 402 (7th Cir. 1988) (per curiam) (introduction of hearsay statement of petitioner's brother, implicating petitioner as triggerman, violated Confrontation Clause).

- *Brown v. Lynaugh*, 843 F.2d 849 (5th Cir. 1988) (presiding judge took witness stand and provided prosecution's principal evidence against petitioner).

- *Walker v. Lockhart*, 763 F.2d 942 (8th Cir. 1985) (en banc), cert. denied, 478 U.S. 1020 (1986) (trial before biased judge).

- *Albert v. Montgomery*, 732 F.2d 865 (11th Cir. 1984) (petitioner convicted based on evidence of prior offense of which petitioner previously had been acquitted).

- *Anderson v. Warden*, 696 F.2d 296 (4th Cir. 1982) (en banc), cert, denied, 462 U.S. 1111 (1983) (judge took witnesses to chambers and pressed them to change their testimony).

- *Chavis v. North Carolina*, 637 F.2d 213 (4th Cir. 1980) (petitioner denied opportunity to cross-examine critical prosecution witnesses about special treatment witnesses received).

- *Smith v. Smith*, 454 F.2d 572 (5th Cir. 1971), cert, denied, 409 U.S. 885 (1972) (state law shifted burden of proving alibi defense to petitioner).

CHAPTER THIRTEEN

DUE PROCESS ERRORS CONCERNING JURY ERRORS

Although jury errors are so plentiful that an entire chapter is dedicated to them, this does not signify that errors before a jury are viewed as constituting a separate or independent critical stage of the trial process. The fact is that the trial jury is "the spinal column of American democracy," quoted in honor of the late Supreme Court Justice Antonin Scalia.

The role of the jury is to be the finder of fact. You should never dismiss the importance of your trial jury's authority or how those in front of the jury conduct themselves. One example of the jury's authority being greater than any judge and the United States Congress, which makes the law, is made apparent by the jury's authority of jury nullification. In a criminal trial, it is the parties or their counsel who is responsible for presenting the facts of the case to the jury; the judge is tasked with instructing the jury on the law, and the jury is responsible for making findings of fact based on the law as provided to them by the judge. Simply put, it is the jury's verdict that decides whether the defendant is guilty or not guilty. But even with all the instructions about the law, it is the jury that has the right to ignore said law and to act according to their collective conscious.

The act of ignoring the law is called jury nullification. One of the most compelling examples of jury nullification in the United States occurred during the period of prohibition (1920-1933). On January 16, 1919, the Eighteenth Amendment was ratified, which criminalized "the manufacture, sale, or transportation of intoxicating liquors." But, even after an amendment to the Constitution of the United States, juries often refused to convict defendants charged under the laws that governed alcohol control. On December 5, 1933, the Twenty-First Amendment was ratified, which repealed the Eighteenth.

Judges, however, are quite displeased with juries that exercise their authority to ignore the law. When in a 1988 case, a judge whom I won't name here was asked about jury nullification by the jury, they replied, "There is no such thing as valid jury nullification." In 1997, the Second Circuit Court of Appeals decided that a juror who intended to nullify the law could be dismissed from a jury.

Needless to say, there are hundreds of possible jury errors. The following list is not all-inclusive, but it is a good place to begin. I challenge you to study the authority of your jury and, of course, adding your winning case to this long list of winners.

- *Sandstrom v. Montana*, 442 U.S. 510 (1979), (that jury instructions on malice or intent violated due process by relieving state of proving every element beyond reasonable doubt).

- *Yates v. Evatt*, 500 U.S. 391 (1991) (jury instructions on malice violated due process by relieving state of burden of proving every element of crime beyond reasonable doubt).

- *Francis v. Franklin*, 471 U.S. 307 (1985) (instruction that person "is presumed to intend the natural and probable consequences of his acts" unconstitutionally gave defendant burden of proof on element of intent to kill).

- *Chambers v. McDaniel*, 549 F.3d 1191 (9th Cir. 2008) (instructions "permitted the jury to convict [petitioner] without a finding of the essential element of deliberation").

- *Medley v. Runnels*, 506 F.3d 857 (9th Cir. 2007) (en banc), cert. denied, 552 U.S. 1316 (2008) ("state trial court violated … due process by instructing the jury that a flare gun is a firearm, thus taking from the jury the determination of an element of the offense").

- *Polk v. Sandoval*, 503 F.3d 903 (9th Cir. 2007) (jury instruction in first-degree murder case violated due process by dictating finding of deliberateness if jury found premeditation).

- *Stark v. Hickman*, 455 F.3d 1070 (9th Cir. 2006) ("trial court's instruction during the guilt phase of the trial that the jury was to conclusively presume petitioner was sane" unconstitutionally^ "shifted the burden of proof to the defendant").

- *Powell v. Galaza*, 328 F.3d 558 (9th Cir. 2002) (jury instruction "improperly removed the element of specific intent … —the only contested issue—from the jury's consideration and in effect commanded a directed verdict for the state").

- *Robertson v. Cain*, 324 F.3d 297 (5th Cir. 2003) ("jury instruction on the law of principals … improperly reliev[ed] the prosecution of the burden of proving an essential element of the crime (namely, the defendant's specific intent to kill)").

- *Caldwell v. Bell*, 288 F.3d 838 (6th Cir. 2002) ("there is a reasonable likelihood that jurors concluded that use of a deadly weapon raised a presumption of malice for first-degree murder as well as second-degree murder").

- *Gall v. Parker*, 231 F.3d 265 (6th Cir. 2000), cert, denied, 533 U.S. 941 (2001) (although jury instructions correctly stated that prosecution bore burden of proving absence of "extreme emotional disturbance" beyond reasonable doubt, state supreme court's review of sufficiency of evidence unconstitutionally shifted burden on element to accused).

- *O'Neal v. McAninch*, 513 U.S. 432 (1995) (accepting court of appeals' assumption that combination of invalid instruction and improper argument by counsel misstating mental element of offense warranted *habeas corpus* relief).

- *Riley v. McDaniel*, 786 F.3d 719 (9th Cir. 2015), cert, denied, 136 S. Ct. 1450 (2016) (jury instruction "relieved the state of its burden to prove element of the offense," thereby violating Due Process Clause, by "advising the jury that if it finds 'premeditation,' it has necessarily found 'deliberation' ").

- *Williams v. Trammel*, 539 Fed. Appx. 844 (10th Cir. 2013), cert, denied, 134 S. Ct. 1492 (2014) (trial court violated *Beck v. Alabama*, 447 U.S. 625 (1980) by failing to instruct jury on lesser-included offense of second-degree depraved-mind murder).

- *Dixon v. Williams*, 750 F.3d 1027 (9th Cir. 2014) (self-defense instruction's misstatement of applicable standard violated due process by "reduc[eing] the State's burden for convicting Dixon of murder instead of voluntary manslaughter").

- *Doe v. Busby*, 661 F.3d 1001 (9th Cir. 2011) (jury instruction impermissibly lowered prosecution's burden of proof, thereby violating Due Process Clause, by "permitt[ing] a murder conviction based on a preponderance of the evidence that prior uncharged crimes occurred."

- *Hooks v. Workman*, 606 F.3d 715 (10th Cir. 2010) ("Allen charge given by the trial court in the midst of penalty-phase deliberations, when considered in the context of all surrounding circumstances, coerced the jury into returning death sentences").

- *Phillips v. Workman*, 604 F.3d 1202 (10th Cir. 2010) (trial court's refusal to give instruction on lesser included noncapital offense violated rule of *Beck v. Alabama*, 447 U.S. 625 (1980)).

- *Richie v. Workman*, 599 F.3d 1131 (10th Cir. 2010) (trial judge violated *Beck v. Alabama*, 447 U.S. 625 (1980) by refusing to give instruction on lesser included noncapital offense).

- *Smith v. Curry*, 580 F.3d 1071 (9th Cir. 2009), cert, denied, 131 S. Ct. 10 (2010) (trial judge coerced guilty verdict by responding to holdout juror's known concerns but giving supplemental instruction that "effectively highlighted the specific evidence the court thought supported the guilty verdict favored by the majority of jurors"). 554 F.3d 879 (10th Cir. 2009) (denial of jury lesser included noncapital offense violated Due

- *Harris v. Alexander*, 548 F.3d 200 (2d Cir. 2008) (trial court violated due process by refusing to instruct jury on accused's theory of case).

- *Clark v. Brown*, 450 F.3d 898 (9th Cir.), cert, denied, 549 U.S. 1027 (2006) ("state trial court's failure to give a felony-murder special circumstance jury instruction … violated Clark's due process right to present a complete defense").

- *Laird v. Horn*, 414 F.3d 419 (3d Cir. 2005), cert, denied, 546 U.S. 1146 (2006) (jury instruction on accomplice liability violated Due Process Cause by relieving prosecution of burden of establishing that petitioner had specific intent to kill).

- *Jackson v. Edwards*, 404 F.3d 612 (2d Cir. 2005) (trial court's denial of defense's request for instruction on justification violated Due Process Clause).

- *Gibson v. Ortiz*, 387 F.3d 812 (9th Cir. 2004), overruled in part on other grounds by *Byrd v. Lewis*, 566 F.3d 855, 866 (9th Cir. (2009) (instruction on prior sexual offenses had unconstitutional effect of "allow[ing] the jury find Gibson guilty of the charged offenses by relying on facts found only by a preponderance of the evidence").

- *Bartlett v. Alameida*, 366 F.3d 1020 (9th Cir. 2004) (per curiam) (trial court violated *Lambert v. California*, 355 U.S. (1957) by instructing jury in trial for failure to re-register as sex offender that "actual knowledge [of obligation to register] was not an element of the crime").

- Mollet v. Mullin, 348 F.3d 902 (10th Cir. 2003) (trial court violated *Simmons v. South Carolina*, 512 U.S. 154 (1994) by denying defense counsel's request for instructions "explaining] … the distinguishing feature under Oklahoma law between life imprisonment without parole" and instead "instructing] the jury that parole was not to be considered").

- *Ho v. Carey*, 332 F.3d 587 (9th Cir. 2003) (trial court violated "constitutional right to have a jury decide every element of the offense of second-degree murder based on implied malice … [by] erroneously instructing] jury that offense was a general-intent crime").

- *Patterson v. Haskins*, 316 F.3d 596 (6th Cir. 2003) (trial court's failure to instruct on "proximate causation" element of involuntary manslaughter violated due process, notwithstanding inclusion of instruction on same element with regard to two other charged offenses).

- *Bradley v. Duncan*, 315 F.3d 1091 (9th Cir. 2002), cert, denied, 540 U.S. 963 (2003) (trial court's refusal to instruct on state law defense of entrapment violated "due process right to present a full defense").

- *Cockerham v. Cain*, 283 F.3d 657 (5th Cir. 2002) (jury instructions, which could have been understood by jury to allow conviction without proof beyond reasonable doubt, violated *Cage v. Louisiana*, 498 U.S. 39 (1990) (per curiam)).

- *Davis v. Strack*, 270 F.3d 111 (2d Cir. 2001) (trial court violated due process by refusing to charge jury on defense of justification).

- *Johnson v. Gibson*, 254 F.3d 1155 (10th Cir.), cert, denied, 534 U.S. 1029 (2001) (judge's instruction to jury that "[i]t is inappropriate for you to consider" whether sentence of life imprisonment without parole absolutely bars possibility of parole violated rule of *Summons v. South Carolina*, 512 U.S. 154 (1994) and *Shafer v. South Carolina*, 532 U.S. 36 (2001)).

- *Barker v. Yukins*, 199 F.3d 867 (6th Cir. 1999), cert, denied, 530 U.S. 1229 (2000) (judge's refusal to give requested self-defense instruction violated due process right to present defense).

- *Conde v. Henry*, 198 F.3d 734 (9th Cir. 2000) (trial judge refused to instruct jury on theory of defense and defined crime in manner that reduced prosecution's burden of proof).

- *Caliendo v. Warden*, 365 F.3d 691 (9th Cir.), cert, denied, 543 U.S. 927 (2004) (state appellate court violated *Mattox v. United States*, 146 U.S. 140 (1892) by failing to apply "rebuttable presumption of prejudice" in assessing claim of juror misconduct based on 20-minute conversation between three jurors and key prosecution witness).

- *Weaver v. Thompson*, 197 F.3d 359 (9th Cir. 1999) (bailiff's statement to deliberating jurors that he had to reach verdict on all counts amounted to "an improper de facto Allen charge" in violation of due process).

- *Smalls v. Batista*, 191 F.3d 272 (2d Cir. 1999) ("Allen charge" unconstitutionally coerced deadlocked juror's by stating three times that "they had a duty and responsibility to convince other jurors that their views were correct" and by failing to "caution the jurors never to abandon their conscientiously held beliefs, even if holding firm will result in a deadlock").

- *Pham v. Kernan*, 1998 U.S. App. LEXIS 31015 (9th Cir. Dec. 7, 1998) (juror impermissibly provided other members of jury with extrinsic information about site where victim's body was buried, which bore on petitioner's ability to commit crime).

- *Lawson v. Borg*, 60 F.3d 608 (9th Cir. 1995) (juror's statement to other jurors that petitioner had "reputation for violence" constituted harmful due process violation because "extrinsic information directly related to a material issue in the case: intent to commit robbery").

CHAPTER FOURTEEN

CLAIMS CONCERNING EVIDENCE

"The right to the effective assistance of counsel is the right of the accused to require the prosecution's case to survive the crucible of meaningful adversarial testing. When a true adversarial criminal trial has been conducted, the kind of testing envisioned by the Sixth Amendment has occurred." *United States v. Cronic*, 466 U.S. 648.

The *Cronic* decision should bring to mind one of the greatest tricks the court and the government attempt to pull on the defense.

They will attempt to make you believe that it is the defendant who is on trial rather than the government's evidence. At many trials, you will discover that the government is presenting, and the defense counsel is questioning testimony rather than evidence.

This problem is most evident in drug-related conspiracy cases. Often, the government will round up witnesses who want to reduce their respective sentences and parade them through a circus-like trial rather than present actual evidence. In these cases, the defense lawyer takes a defensive posture and completely fails even to ask if the government has any evidence to offer.

As you might imagine, evidence is the due process backbone of any criminal trial. Without sufficient evidence to prove the elements of a crime, a conviction cannot stand under the Constitution of the United States. Any verdict of guilt without evidentiary support is invalid. So please pay special attention to the evidence in your case and understand the impact when it does not exist. See the cases that follow for a more comprehensive understanding.

- *Fiore v. White*, 531 U.S. 255 (2001) (per curiam) (granting federal *habeas corpus* relief because prosecution failed to present sufficient evidence to prove the element of crime and therefore petitioner's "conviction is not consistent with the demands of the Federal Due Process Clause").

- *Lee v. Superintendent*, 798 F.3d 159 (3d Cir. 2015) (given state's concessions that fire science evidence prosecution presented at trial has been shown by "scientific developments since Lee's trial" to be "invalid," and furthermore that "subsequent scientific developments and retesting of surviving materials from the crime scene have undermined the reliability" of chromatography evidence was not "sufficient to prove guilt beyond a reasonable doubt").

- *Owens v. Duncan*, 781 F.3d 360 (7th Cir. 2015), cert, dismissed, S. Ct. 651 (2016) (judge in bench trial violated due process and "right to have one's guilt or innocence adjudicated on the basis of evidence introduced at trial" by basing "verdict of guilty on ungrounded conjecture" with "no evidentiary support").

- *Langston v. Smith*, 630 F.3d 310 (2d Cir.), cert, denied, 132 S. Ct. 366 (2011) (evidence was constitutionally insufficient to support conviction of felony assault on theory that assault was "in furtherance of" only felony with which petitioner was charged, criminal possession of weapon).

- *Robertson v. Klem*, 580 F.3d 159 (3d Cir. 2009) (trial evidence, which was "sufficient to convict Robertson of a single conspiracy," was "insufficient to support Robertson's conviction on two counts of conspiracy to commit murder because the Commonwealth failed to prove that the murders at issue, which involved the same conspirators, the same murder weapon, and occurred at the same time and place, were the result of separate agreements or conspiratorial relationships").

- *O'Laughlin v. O'Brien*, 568 F.3d 287 (1st Cir. 2009), cert, denied, 558 U.S. 1158 (2010) ("the many strands of circumstantial evidence the prosecution has presented" were "far from sufficient to establish O'Laughlin's guilt under *Jackson* [*v. Virginia*]").

- *Kamienski v. Hendricks*, 332 Fed. Appx. 740, 2009 U.S. App. LEXIS 11456 (3d Cir. May 28, 2009), cert, denied, 558 U.S. 1147 (2010) (state appellate court unreasonably applied *Jackson v. Virginia* by reversing trial court's post-verdict entry of judgment ©f acquittal for accessory who had neither "the mental state required for a conviction of first degree murder or ... the knowledge required for a conviction of felony murder").

- *Newman v. Metrish*, 543 F.3d 793 (6th Cir. 2008), cert, denied, 558 U.S. 1158 (2010) (circumstantial evidence presented by prosecution at trial did not satisfy constitutional standard of sufficiency).

- *Perez v. Cain*, 529 F.3d 588 (5th Cir.), cert, denied, 555 U.S. 995 (2008) (accused "established at trial that he was insane at the time of the offense and that no rational juror could have found otherwise").

- *Smith v. Patrick*, 508 F.3d 1256 (9th Cir. 2007) (per curiam) ("opinion of the prosecution experts that [petitioner's] shaking of the infant had caused death was wholly unsupported by the physical evidence" and thus "evidence did not meet the standard of *Jackson v. Virginia*").

- *Torres v. Lytle*, 461 F.3d 1303 (10th Cir. 2006) (although "retaliating against a witness" charge required that retaliation was for victim's provision of information regarding "felony offense," evidence at trial indicated that threat of retaliation was for complainant's testimony against petitioner in misdemeanor trial).

- *Brown v. Palmer*, 441 F.3d 347 (6th Cir. 2006) (evidence was insufficient to support convictions of armed robbery and carjacking on theory of aiding and abetting).

- *Juan H. v. Allen*, 408 F.3d 1262 (9th Cir. 2005), cert, denied, 546 U.S. 1137 (2006) (evidence was insufficient to support delinquency adjudication for aiding and abetting murder and attempted murder).

- *McKenzie v. Smith*, 326 F.3d 721 (6th Cir. 2003), cert, denied U.S. 1158 (2004) (evidence in trial for assault with intent murder was insufficient to "establish, beyond a reasonable that McKenzie was the perpetrator of the assault").

CHAPTER FIFTEEN

CLAIMS AT SENTENCING

It goes without saying that we all know what sentencing is. Likewise, there is no need to pretend that anyone could list all of the possible errors or the countless number of winning cases. As I write this chapter, I continue to witness the fallout of *Sessions v. Dimaya*, 138 S. Ct. 1204 (2018).

The facts are simple: sentencing is the measure of funding. The longer the sentences are, the bigger the budgets are. In a proposed sentencing memorandum filed by Glennon F. Threatt, Jr., from the Federal Public Defender's Office in the Northern District of Alabama, the court-appointed defense counsel claimed that the judicial district would bill Congress, i.e., the taxpayers, over $28,000 per month to incarcerate Ray Allan. See *United States v. Allan*, Northern District of Alabama, Tuscaloosa (2013). In that case, "Little Ray" was encouraged to go to trial rather than take Glennon Threatt's advice to plead guilty. And he won at trial.

I only reference Mr. Allan's case because it is a clear reflection of the intentions of the lawyers involved. Even the defense lawyers.

One of the major devices which the federal judicial system uses to bolster and enhance federal criminal sentences are prior convictions for alleged "crimes of violence" or "controlled substance offenses." Because of recent changes in sentencing applications, at the time of writing this book, the number of winning cases were growing daily.

Any attempt I make here to encompass changes in sentencing enhancements would be outdated by the time this book is printed. Thus, in an attempt to point you in the right direction, I suggest that you review the cases that are causing all the changes in your own circuit. Also, keep in mind that correcting a sentence is the sole purpose of post-conviction relief.

A brief list of cases concerning enhancements:

- *Descamps v. United States*, 133 S. Ct. 2276 (2013)
- *Mathis v. United States*, 136 S. Ct. 2243 (2016)
- *Sessions v. Dimaya*, 138 S. Ct. 1204 (2018)
- *Bousley v. United States*, 523 U.S. 614 (1998)
- *Peugh v. United States*, 133 S. Ct. 2072 (2013)
- *Johnson v. United States*, 135 S. Ct. 2551 (2015)
- *Welch v. United States*, 136 S. Ct. 1257 (2016)

Again, let me remind you that at the time of this writing, the issue of sentencing enhancements was in an extreme state of flux.

Claims arising at sentencing

Solem v. Helm, 463 U.S. 277 (1983) (petitioner given life sentence for uttering a "no account" check for $100 following six minor prior convictions).

- *Bifulco v. United States*, 447 U.S. 381 (1980) (applicable federal criminal statute did not authorize trial court's imposition on section 2255 movant of special parole term to be served upon completion of imprisonment).

- *Dorszynski v. United States*, 418 U.S. 424 (1974) (district court lacked jurisdiction to impose sentence because judge failed to make specific finding that 19-year-old section 2255 movant would not derive benefit from treatment under Federal Youth Corrections Act).

- *United States v. Tucker*, 404 U.S. 443 (1972) (sentencing judge gave explicit consideration to two prior felony convictions stemming from cases in which section movant was denied right to counsel).

- *United States v. Behrens*, 375 U.S. 162 (1963) (district court modified original oral sentencing order and imposed section 2255 movant's final sentence in absence of movant and counsel).

- *Loher v. Thomas*, 2016 U.S. App. LEXIS 10971 (9th Cir. June 17, 2016) (enhancement of sentence "based on judge-found facts" violated *Apprendi v. New Jersey*, 530 U.S. 466 (2000)).

- *Harmon v. Lamar*, 2016 U.S. App. LEXIS 2275 (3d_ Cir. Feb. 10, 2016) ("consecutive sentences for aggravated assault and attempted murder arose out of a single incident and thus … violate[d] the Double Jeopardy Clause").

- *Austin v. Plumley*, 565 Fed. Appx. 175 (4th Cir. 2014) (per curiam), cert, denied, 135 S. Ct. 828 (2015) (judge's amendment of sentencing order to "extend … time in prison," which took place after prisoner petitioned appellate court to correct or rescind sentence on due process grounds, gave rise to "presumption of judicial vindictiveness" under *North Carolina v. Pearce*, 395 U.S. 711 (1969), and "State fail[ed] to rebut" presumption).

- *Balsavage v. Wetzel*, 545 Fed. Appx. 151 (3d Cir. 2013) (judge's resentencing of petitioner who prevailed in state post-conviction to "term of imprisonment seven times greater than his original probation violation sentence" must be presumed to be product of "judicial vindictiveness").

- *Moore v. Biter*, 725 F.3d 1184 (9th Cir. 2013) (petitioner's "term-of-years sentence of 254 years and four months for nonhomicide crimes he committed when he was sixteen years old" violated Supreme Court's holding in *Graham v. Florida*, 560 U.S. 48 (2010), that "Eighth Amendment prohibits the punishment of life without parole for juvenile nonhomicide offenders"; "Moore's sentence of 254 years is materially indistinguishable from a life sentence without parole because Moore will not be eligible for parole within his lifetime").

- *Brown v. Caraway*, 719 F.3d 583 (7th Cir. 2013) (granting section 2241 relief because Supreme Court decision issued after imposition of federal sentence established that state conviction of arson should not have been classified as "crime of violence" for purposes of career offender enhancement under federal sentencing guidelines).

- *Lovins v. Parker*, 712 F.3d 283 (6th Cir. 2013) ("three-year sentence enhancement was unconstitutional under the rule of *Blakely v. Washington* … because the sentence was enhanced based on facts that were not found by a jury").

- *Garrus v. Secretary*, 694 F.3d 394 (3d Cir. 2012) (en banc) ("state court unreasonably applied *Apprendi* [*v. New Jersey*] by allowing Garrus to be sentenced beyond the statutory maximum based on a judicial finding that Garrus burglarized an occupied building, despite his plea to the contrary").

- *Newton v. Avoyelles Women's Correctional Center*, 423 Fed. Appx. 419, 2011 U.S. App. LEXIS 8545 (5th Cir. April 26, 2011) (per curiam) (trial court violated *Apprendi v. New Jersey*, 530 U.S. 466 (2000), by assuming that jury's general verdict of guilty on indictment that charged two counts in conjunctive meant that jury had convicted on both and that judge accordingly could sentence on more serious offense).

- *Wilson v. Knowles*, 638 F.3d 1213 (9th Cir. 2011) (imposition of three-strikes sentence based upon judicial factfinding violated *Apprendi v. New Jersey*).

- *Villagarcia v. Warden*, 599 F.3d 529 (6th Cir. 2010) (trial judge enhanced sentence "beyond the statutory maximum by judicial fact-finding" in violation of *Blakely v. Washington*, 542 U.S. 296 (2004) and *Apprendi v. New Jersey*).

- *Gonzalez v. Duncan*, 551 F.3d 875 (9th Cir. 2008) (imposition of "three strikes" sentence of 28 years to life for "regulatory offense" of "failing to update … annual sex offender registration within five days of [one's] birthday" violated 8th Amendment).

- *Gautt v. Lewis*, 489 F.3d 993 (9th Cir. 2007), cert, denied, 552 U.S. 1245 (2008) (petitioner's "constitutional due process right to be informed of the charges against him was violated when he was charged with a sentencing enhancement: under one statute … of the California Penal Code … but had his sentence enhanced under a second, different statute").

- *Stokes v. Schriro*, 465 F.3d 397 (9th Cir. 2006) (five-year-sentencing enhancement, based upon aggravating circumstances involving "judicial fact-finding," violated *Apprendi v. New Jersey*, 530 U.S. 466 (2000)).

- *Williams v. Roe*, 421 F.3d 883 (9th Cir. 2005) (trial court violated Ex Post Facto Clause at resentencing by applying "amended statute [that] eliminated judicial discretion to impose a lower sentence afforded by the version in place at the time of Williams' offense").

- *Gill v. Ayers*, 342 F.3d 911 (9th Cir. 2003) (judge violated Due Process Clause by refusing to allow petitioner to testify at "three strikes" sentencing hearing to explain statements in earlier presentence report upon which prosecution relied to establish prior assaultive conduct).

- *Torres v. Berbary*, 340 F.3d 63 (2d Cir. 2003) (sentencing judge violated due process by determining, without hearing and based on hearsay report of petitioner's conduct in drug program, that petitioner failed to comply with conditions set at time of sentencing for replacing felony conviction and term of incarceration with misdemeanor conviction and sentence of time served).

- *Gunn v. Ignacio*, 263 F.3d 965 (9th Cir. 2001) (prosecutor breached plea agreement by seeking consecutive rather than concurrent sentences).

- *Henderson v. Norris*, 258 F.3d 706 (8th Cir. 2001) (sentence of life without eligibility for parole, imposed upon first offender for sale of .238 grams of cocaine base, was cruel and unusual punishment in violation of 8th Amendment).

- *Dunn v. Colleran*, 247 F.3d 450 (3d Cir. 2001) (prosecutor breached plea agreement by arguing for higher sentence than plea agreement had contemplated).

- *United States v. Mannino*, 212 F.3d 835 (3d Cir. 2000) (district court improperly calculated section 2255 movants' Sentencing Guideline sentences by attributing quantity of narcotics distributed throughout conspiracy to each movant).

- *Harris v. United States*, 149 F.3d 1304 (11th Cir. 1998) (district court lacked jurisdiction to enhance section 2255 movant's sentence on basis of prior conviction because government failed to file pre-plea information with respect to prior conviction).

Claims arising in death penalty sentencing

- *Estelle v. Smith*, 451 U.S. 454 (1981) (state-employed psychiatrist permitted to testify at death penalty phase based on petitioner's pretrial statements that were not freely and voluntarily given and that were made without counsel or waiver of counsel).

- *Gardner v. Johnson*, 247 F.3d 551 (5th Cir. 2001) (psychiatrists' pre-examination warnings were insufficient to apprise petitioner of possible, use of statements at capital sentencing proceeding).

- *Vanderbilt v. Collins*, 994 F,2d 189 (5th Cir. 1993) (at resentencing, state elicited statements petitioner made at time of first trial to psychiatrist appointed, at defense request, to asses petitioner's sanity and competency).

- *Buttrum v. Black*, 908 F.2d 695 (11th Cir. 1990) (state-hired psychiatrist's use of petitioner's uncounseled statements during competency evaluation to show future dangerousness violated *Estelle v. Smith*, supra).

- *Muniz v. Procunier*, 760 F.2d 588 (5th Cir.), cert, denied, 474 U.S. 934 (1985) (psychiatrist interviewed petitioner at direction of prosecutor without notice to defense counsel and without administering Miranda warnings, in violation of *Estelle v. Smith*, supra).

- *White v. Estelle*, 720 F.2d 415 (5th Cir. 1983) (judge granted state's motion for psychiatric examination of petitioner but neither petitioner nor counsel was advised that statements might be used as proof of future dangerousness at capital sentencing hearing).

- *Green v. Estelle*, 706 F.2d 148 (5th Cir. 1983) (per curiam) (finding violation of rule of *Estelle v. Smith* despite absence of contemporaneous objection because of state law exception to procedural rule).

- *Gholson v. Estelle*, 675 F.2d 734 (5th Cir. 1982) (uncounseled statements elicited in court-ordered psychiatric examination and also in additional interview conducted by another state psychiatrist without notice to defense counsel or judge violated rule of *Estelle v. Smith*, supra).

- *Battie v. Estelle*, 655 F.2d 692 (5th Cir. 1981) (petitioner did not waive claim under *Estelle v. Smith* by requesting psychiatric examination to determine competency to stand trial and sanity at time of offense).

- *Stringer v. Black*, 503 U.S. 222 (1992) (petitioner sentenced to death based on unconstitutionally vague "especially heinous, atrocious, or cruel" aggravating circumstance; state supreme court affirmed after invalidating aggravating circumstance without reweighing remaining aggravating and mitigating circumstances).

- *Maynard v. Cartwright*, 486 U.S. 356 (1988) (petitioner sentenced to death based on unconstitutionally vague "especially heinous, atrocious, or cruel" aggravating circumstance).

- *Rogers v. McDaniel*, 793 F.3d 1036 (9th Cir. 2015) (capital penalty-phase jury instruction on "depravity of mind aggravating factor" was unconstitutionally vague).

- *Pensinger v. Chappell*, 787 F.3d 1014 (9th Cir. 2015) ("trial court violated Pensinger's constitutional rights by failing to instruct the jury sua sponte in accordance with [state court decision holding that] … kidnap-murder special circumstance requires proof that the kidnapping was committed for an independent felonious purpose (i.e., not merely incidental to the murder)").

- *Robinson v. Schriro*, 595 F.3d 1086 (9th Cir.), cert, denied, 131 S. Ct. 566 (2010) ("Arizona state courts arbitrarily and capriciously applied the aggravating circumstance of especially cruel, heinous, or depraved conduct to Robinson").

- *Daniels v. Woodford*, 428 F.3d 1181 (9th Cir. 2005), cert, denied, 550 U.S. 968 (2007) (trial court failed to "instruct the jury that it could only consider the multiple-murder special circumstance as a single factor in aggravation").

- *Valerio v. Crawford*, 306 F.3d 742 (9th Cir. 2002) (en banc), cert. denied, 538 U.S. 994 (2003) (instruction at capital sentencing phase on "torture, depravity of mind, or mutilation of victim" was unconstitutionally vague and state supreme court failed to cure error on direct appeal by reweighing remaining aggravating and mitigating circumstances).

- *Hochstein v. Hopkins*, 113 F.3d 143 (8th Cir.), modified, 122 F.3d 1160 (8th Cir.), cert, denied, 522 U.S. 959 (1997) (petitioner sentenced to death based on unconstitutionally vague "exceptional depravity" aggravating circumstance).

- *McKenna v. McDaniel*, 65 F.3d 1483 (9th Cir. 1995), cert, denied, 517 U.S. 1150 (1996) (instruction on "depravity of mind" aggravating circumstance was unconstitutionally vague).

- *Houston v. Dutton*, 50 F.3d 381 (6th Cir.), cert, denied, 516 U.S. 905 (1995) (" 'heinous, atrocious or cruel' " jury instruction was "too vague and uninformative to properly guide the jury in reaching a death verdict").

- *Wade v. Calderon*, 29 F.3d 1312 (9th Cir. 1994) (sentence of death based on unconstitutionally vague special circumstance of torture-murder).

- *Beam v. Paskett*, 3 F.3d 1301 (9th Cir. 1993), cert, denied, 511 U.S. 1060 (1994) (death sentence premised in part on trial judge's distaste for petitioner's prior history of nonviolent "abnormal sexual relationships," including homosexuality and relationships with women substantially younger and older than petitioner).

- *King v. Puckett*, 1 F.3d 280 (5th Cir. 1993) (death sentence rested upon Mississippi's unconstitutionally overbroad "especially heinous, atrocious or cruel" aggravating factor).

- *Duest v. Singletary*, 997 F.2d 1336 (11th Cir. 1993), cert, denied, 510 U.S. 1133 (1994) (death sentence premised on prior conviction that was overturned on appeal).

- *Rust v. Hopkins*, 984 F.2d 1486 (8th Cir. 1993) (three-judge capital sentencing panel violated due process by failing to apply state law rule that aggravating circumstances must be proven beyond reasonable doubt; error was not cured by Nebraska Supreme Court's reweighing of circumstances on appeal because such reweighing exceeded permissible scope of principle of Stringer and deprived petitioner of state-created two-tiered process of sentencing followed by appellate review).

- *Smith v. Black*, 970 F.2d 1383 (5th Cir. 1992) (on remand from Supreme Court in light of *Stringer v. Black*, court concludes that use of Mississippi's vague "especially heinous, atrocious and cruel" aggravating circumstance rendered petitioner's death sentence unconstitutional).

- *Moore v. Clarke*, 951 F.2d 895 (8th Cir. 1991) (Nebraska's "heinous, atrocious, cruel or manifest[ing] exceptional depravity" aggravating circumstance was unconstitutionally vague on its face and as construed by state supreme court).

- *Davis v. Maynard*, 911 F.2d 415 (10th Cir. 1990) (per curiam) (applying rule of *Maynard v. Cartwright* to reverse death sentence because of vagueness of Oklahoma's "especially heinous, atrocious or cruel" aggravating circumstance).

- *Newlon v. Armontrout*, 885 F.2d 1328 (8th Cir. 1989), cert, denied, 497 U.S. 1038 (1990) (Missouri's "depravity of mind" aggravating circumstance was vague on its face and as construed by state supreme court).

- *Adamson v. Ricketts*, 865 F.2d 1011 (9th Cir. 1988) (en banc), cert. denied, 497 U.S. 1031 (1990) (Arizona's "especially heinous" aggravating circumstance was unconstitutionally vague).

- *Lewis v. Lane*, 832 F.2d 1446 (7th Cir. 1987), cert, denied, 488 U.S. 829 (1988) (defense counsel stipulated to, then prosecutor based successful argument in favor of death sentence on, "prior convictions" that did not exist).

Claims that trial court improperly restricted consideration of mitigating factors

- *Abdul-Kabir v. Quarterman*, 550 U.S. 233 (2007) ("trial judge's instructions to the Texas [capital sentencing] jury" violated 8th and 14th Amendments by creating "reasonable likelihood that … jurors [were prevented] from giving meaningful consideration to constitutionally relevant mitigating evidence").

- *Brewer v. Quarterman*, 550 U.S. 286 or (2007) (same as *Abdul-Kabir v. Quarterman*, supra).

- *Penry v. Johnson*, 532 U.S. 782 (2001) (same as *Penry v. Lynaugh*, infra: "to the extent the Texas Court of Criminal Appeals concluded that the substance of the jury instructions given at Penry's second sentencing hearing satisfied our mandate in Penry 1, that determination was objectively unreasonable" under AEDPA's section 2254(d) (1)).

- *Parker v. Dugger*, 498 U.S. 308 (1991) (trial court sentenced petitioner to death on basis of asserted absence of mitigating circumstances, though mitigating circumstances manifestly were present).

- *Hitchcock v. Dugger*, 481 U.S. 393 (1987) (petitioner sentenced to die by jury unconstitutionally instructed that, in passing on sentence, it could not consider fact that petitioner was brain damaged, had cooperated fully with police, and was capable of rehabilitation).

- *Penry v. Lynaugh*, 492 U.S. 302 (1989) (petitioner sentenced to die by jury unconstitutionally instructed in manner that prevented it from considering in mitigation, and only permitted it to consider in aggravation, fact that Penry was retarded).

- *Norris v. Davis*, 2016 U.S. App. LEXIS 11282 (5th Cir. June 21, 2016) ("jury instructions at the sentencing phase of Norris's trial violated his Eighth and Fourteenth Amendment rights under *Penry v. Lynaugh* … by not allowing the jury to give full effect to Norris's mitigating evidence").

- *McKinney v. Ryan*, 813 F.3d 798 (9th Cir. 2015) (en banc) ("For a period of a little over 15 years in capital cases, in clear violation of *Eddings* [*v. Oklahoma*], the Supreme Court of Arizona articulated and applied a 'casual nexus' test for non-statutory mitigation that forbade as a matter of law giving weight to mitigating evidence, such as family background or mental condition, unless the background or mental condition was casually connected to the crime." ; "Arizona Supreme Court applied its unconstitutional casual nexus test to McKinney's PTSD, refusing, as a matter of law, to treat it as a relevant non-statutory mitigating factor").

- *McGowen v. Thaler*, 675 F,3d 482 (5th Cir. 2011), cert, denied, 133 S. Ct. 648 (2012) ("punishment phase jury instructions" violated "*Penry v. Lynaugh* and its progeny" by "fail[ing] to provide an avenue to give effect to mitigating evidence").

- *Williams v. Ryan*, 623 F.3d 1258 (9th Cir. 2010) (trial court applied unconstitutional "nexus" requirement that evidence of drug use could only be considered in mitigation if prisoner showed impairment at time of crime).

- *Pierce v. Thaler*, 604 F.3d 197 (5th Cir. 2010-) (Texas "statutory special issues presented to the jury at Pierce's sentencing did not permit the jury to give meaningful consideration and effect" to "Pierce's mitigating evidence" of "troubled childhood" and "good character," and "prosecutor's closing comments may have exacerbated this problem by impressing upon the jury that its deliberations should be guided by the special issues alone").

- *Rivers v. Thaler*, 389 Fed. Appx. 360, 2010 U.S. App. LEXIS 16987 (5th Cir. Aug. 5, 2010) (same as *Abdul-Kabir v. Quarterman*, supra).

- *Coble v. Quarterman*, 496 F.3d 430 (5th Cir. 2007) (same as

- *Abdul-Kabir v. Quarterman*, supra).

- *Davis v. Coyle*, 475 F.3d 761 (6th Cir. 2007) (three-judge resentencing panel violated *Skipper v. South Carolina*, 476 U.S. 1 (1986), by refusing to consider petitioner's "evidence of his good behavior in prison during the five years he had spent on death row between the first and second sentencing hearings").

- *Nelson v. Quarterman*, 472 F.3d 287 (5th Cir. 2006) (en banc), cert. denied, 551 U.S. 1141 (2007) (same as *Abdul-Kabir v. Quarterman*, supra).

- *Bigby v. Cockrell*, 340 F.3d 259 (5th Cir. 2003) (instructions prevented jury from giving mitigating effect to evidence of petitioner's mental illness).

- *Blue v. Cockrell*, 298 F.3d 318 (5th Cir. 2002), overruled in part on other grounds by *Tennard v. Dretke*, 542 U.S. 274 (2004) (capital-sentencing instruction unconstitutionally limited jury's consideration of mitigating evidence of mental retardation and physical and sexual abuse).

- *Paxton v. Ward*, 199 F.3d 1197 (10th Cir. 1999) (trial court improperly applied per se rule barring polygraph evidence to prevent accused from showing—contrary to prosecutor's implication—that prior homicide charge was "dismissed because in the district attorney's view he had been cleared by a polygraph examination").

- *Murdaugh v. Ryan*, 724 F.3d 1104 (9th Cir. 2013), cert, denied, 134 S. Ct. 2840 (2014) (judicial sentencing in capital case violated *Ring, v. Arizona* "[because the existence or absence of mitigating circumstances directly affected whether Murdaugh was death eligible under Arizona law" and accordingly "he had a right to have a jury decide those facts").

- *Abu-Jamal v. Secretary*, 643 F.3d 370 (3d Cir.), cert, denied, 132 S. Ct. 400 (2011) (jury "verdict form together with the jury instructions" violated *Mills v. Maryland* by "creat[ing] a substantial probability that the jury believed it was precluded from finding a mitigating circumstance that has not been unanimously agreed upon").

- *Kindler v. Horn* 642 F.3d 398 (3d Cir. 2011), cert, denied, 132 S. Ct. 1089 (2012) (reaffirming, in pertinent part, *Kindler v. Horn*, 542 F.3d 70 (3d Cir. 2008), vac'd, 558 U.S. 53 (2009)) (granting writ because, inter alia, "jury instructions and verdict sheet used during the penalty phase of … trial denied … due process of law pursuant to the Supreme Court's holding in *Mills* [*v. Maryland*]").

- *Davis v. Mitchell*, 318 F.3d 682 (6th Cir. 2003) (combination of sentencing phase instructions and verdict form violated rule of *Mills v. Maryland*, 486 U.S. 367 (1988) and *McKoy v. North Carolina*, 494 U.S. 433 (1990) by creating "reasonable likelihood that the jury believed that it could not render a verdict in favor of life imprisonment rather than death unless the jury was unanimous with respect to its reasoning on the presence of mitigating factors and unless the jury was unanimous in rejecting the death penalty").

- *Wright v. Walls*, 288 F.3d 937 (7th Cir.), cert, denied, 537 U.S. 1015 (2002) ("sentencing court's statements [at capital sentencing hearing] reflect the wholesale exclusion of evidence offered by Wright in mitigation … [and establish] that Wright did not receive the individualized sentence as mandated by *Eddings* [*v. Oklahoma*, 455 U.S. 104 (1982)]").

- *Gall v. Parker*, 231 F.3d 265 (6th Cir. 2000), cert, denied, 533 U.S. 941 (2001) (combination of sentencing-phase instructions and verdict form violated *Mills v. Maryland*, 486 U.S. 367 (1988) and *McKoy v. North Carolina*, 494 U.S. 433 (1990), by creating reasonable likelihood that jury believed that findings of mitigating circumstances must be unanimous).

- *Frey v. Fulcomer*, 132 F.3d 916 (3d Cir. 1997), cert, denied, 524 U.S. 911 (1998) (sentencing-phase instruction violated *Mills v. Maryland* by creating reasonable likelihood that jury believed that unanimity was required for findings of mitigating circumstances).

- *Mak v. Blodgett*, 970 F.2d 614 (9th Cir. 1992) (per curiam) (unconstitutional exclusion of potentially mitigating evidence that petitioner was follower, rather than leader, in multiple murder).

- *Magwood v. Smith*, 791 F.2d 1438 (11th Cir. 1986) (sentencing judge's determination of inapplicability of two mitigating circumstances was not fairly supported by record and undermined reliability of capital sentencing process).

- *Pickens v. Lockhart*, 714 F.2d 1455 (8th Cir. 1983) (trial judge violated rule of *Lockett v. Ohio* by giving accessorial liability instruction that directed jury to punish petitioner "as if he were a principal," thereby negating mitigating circumstances of lesser participation in crime).

- *Cauthern v. Colson*, 736 F.3d 465 (6th Cir. 2013) (prosecutor committed misconduct in rebuttal argument at capital sentencing stage by comparing defendant to "two of the most widely despised criminals of the-then-recent past," making "biblical references" (citing "the Lord's Prayer" and calling defendant "the evil one"), and "encourag[ing] the jury to personally identify with the victims, and to feel as though failing to return sentences of death would endanger the families of the jury").

- *Weaver v. Bowersox*, 438 F.3d 832 (8th Cir. 2006), cert, dismissed, 550 U.S. 598 (2007) (prosecutor's penalty-phase closing argument contained improper and inflammatory statements analogizing jurors to soldiers with duty, expressing prosecutor's personal belief: in death penalty and invoking prosecutor's exercise of professional judgement in seeking death penalty, and urging jury to return death verdict to send message for future cases).

- *Bates v. Bell*, 402 F.3d 635 (6th Cir.), cert, denied, 546 U.S. 865 (2005) (prosecutor's closing argument, which was "laced … with personal opinion, attacks on opposing counsel, and undignified and unprofessional appeals to hatred and fear" unconstitutionally "operate[d] to preclude the jury's proper consideration of mitigation").

- *Cargle v. Mullin*, 317 F.3d 1196 (10th Cir. 2003) (prosecutor's sentencing stage argument that jury 11 1 can finish the job "begun by police and prosecutors" improperly suggest[ed] that jurors are part of "the team" of the prosecution and police, rather than impartial arbiters between the State and the defendant and thereby "profoundly mis[led] the jury" about its role in the criminal justice process).

- *Depew v. Anderson*, 311 F.3d 742 (6th Cir. 2002), cert, denied, 540 U.S. 888 & 938 (2003) (prosecutor's penalty stage argument violated 5th Amendment by referring to petitioner's failure to testify and violated 8th Amendment by using "inflammatory" and "misleading" statements to counter mitigating evidence of petitioner's lack of criminal history).

- *Sandoval v. Calderon*, 241 F.3d 765 (9th Cir.), cert, denied, 534 U.S. 847 (2001) (prosecutor's invocation of God in penalty stage closing argument violated 8th Amendment by implying that jury can rely on "higher law or extra-judicial authority" and by undercutting jurors' sense of responsibility).

- *Copeland v. Washington*, 232 F.3d 969 (8th Cir. 2000), cert, denied, 532 U.S. 1024 (2001) (prosecutor's penalty stage argument, which "referred to facts not in evidence (the other murders in all of Missouri's history); drew a comparison to violent drug gangs, evoking the jury's fear of crime; and made references to his son and the defense attorney's son[,] … was the sort of argument that would result in 'mob justice' rather than result in a reasoned deliberation").

- *Paxton v. Ward*, 199 F.3d 1197 (10th Cir. 1999) (prosecutor's closing argument in penalty stage deliberately misled jury about reasons for dismissal of prior homicide charge and improperly encouraged jury to draw incorrect and highly prejudicial inference from defense's failure to explain circumstances of charge's dismissal).

- *Shurn v. Delo*, 177 F.3d 662 (8th Cir.)> cert, denied, 528 U.S. 1010 (1999) (prosecutor's sentencing hearing summation violated due process by "emphasiz[ing] his position of authority," "express[ing] his personal opinion on the propriety of the 2 death sentence," "attempt[ing] to link [petitioner] to Charles Manson," and "appeal[ing] to jurors' fears and emotions").

- *Driscoll v. Delo*, 71 F.3d 701 (8th Cir. 1995), cert, denied, 519 U.S. 910 (1996) (prosecutor violated rule of *Caldwell v. Mississippi*, 472 U.S. 320 (1985), by minimizing significance of sentencing recommendation to judge that stage law required jury to make).

- *Miller v. Lockhart*, 65 F.3d 676 (8th Cir. 1995) (prosecutor's closing argument at penalty phase, which included expression of personal belief in propriety of death sentence, played on jurors' fears, and improperly commented on petitioner's decision not to testify, violated due process).

- *Christy v. Horn*, 28 F. Supp. 2d 307 (W.D. Pa. 1998) (prosecutor violated due process by disparaging petitioner's mental illness defense despite prosecutor's awareness of inadmissible evidence substantiating defense and by implicitly encouraging jury to believe, erroneously, that petitioner might be eligible for parole if sentenced to life imprisonment).

- *Sumner v. Shuman*, 483 U.S. 66 (1987) (statute mandating death penalty for murder committed by prisoner serving life sentence without possibility of parole violated 8th and 14th Amendments).

- *Brumfield v. Cain*, 808 F.3d 1041 (5th Cir. 2015), cert, denied, 136 S. Ct. 2411 (2016) ("Brumfield is intellectually disabled and, accordingly, ineligible for execution" under *Atkins v. Virginia*).

- *Williams v. Mitchell*, 792 F.3d 606 (6th Cir. 2015) (state postconviction court applied erroneous standard in assessing *Atkins v. Virginia* claim that petitioner's intellectual disability forecloses imposition of death penalty);

- *Pruitt v. Neal*, 788 F.3d 248 (7th Cir. 2015), cert, denied, 136 S. Ct. 1161 (2016) ("Pruitt has established that he is intellectually disabled and categorically ineligible for the death penalty").

- *Dodd v. Trannell*, 753 F.3d 971 (10th Cir. 2013), cert, denied, 134 S. Ct. 1548 (2014) ("testimony by the victims' relatives recommending the death penalty" violated *Payne v. Tennessee*, 501 U.S. 808 (1991)).

- *Magwood v. Warden*, 664 F.3d 1340 (11th Cir. 2011) (death sentence based on "unexpected and indefensible construction of" death penalty statute in Alabama Supreme Court decision issued two years after petitioner's crime, which created basis for capital sentence for offenders like petitioner that not previously exist—and which Alabama Supreme Court itself acknowledged twenty-five years later to have been wrongly decided—'.violated *Bouie v. City of Columbia*, 378 U.S. 347 (1964) and "fair-warning requirement of the Due Process Clause").

- *Hodges v. Epps*, 648 F.3d 283 (5th Cir. 2011) (capital sentencing instructions violated Due Process Clause by "incorrectly inform[ing] the jurors that Hodges would be eligible for parole" if jurors could not unanimously agree on punishment).

- *Wiley v. Epps*, 625 F.3d 199, 222 (5th Cir. 2010) ("Wiley is mentally retarded and therefore ineligible for a death sentence under *Atkins* [*v. Virginia*]").

- *Thomas v. Allen*, 607 F.3d 749 (11th Cir. 2010) (granting "penalty phase *habeas* relief" because "Thomas is mentally retarded and ineligible for execution pursuant to *Atkins v. Virginia*").

- *Ward v. Hall*, 592 F.3d 1144 (11th Cir.), cert, denied, 131 S. Ct. 647 (2010) ("constitutional right to a fair trial and a reliable sentence were violated when a bailiff improperly responded to a juror's question about parole during the penalty phase of trial").

- *Sechrest v. Ignacio*, 549 F.3d 789 (9th Cir. 2008), cert, denied, 558 U.S. 938 (2009) (prosecutor violated due process by repeatedly and falsely asserting to jury, in *voir dire* and sentencing stage closing argument, that LWOP sentence would likely result in release of petitioner by parole board).

- *Joseph v. Coyle*, 469 F.3d 441 (6th Cir. 2006), cert, denied, 549 U.S. 1280 (2007) (inaccurate capital murder specification in indictment and erroneous jury instructions violated Due Process Clause and 8th Amendment by depriving petitioner of adequate notice of charge and by producing death sentence that lacked finding of facts required for death-eligibility under state law).

- *Morris v. Woodford*, 273 F.3d 826 (9th Cir. 2001), cert, denied, 537 U.S. 941 (2002) (typographical error written jury instruction resulted in misstatement that non-unanimity would result in life sentence "with" rather than "without" parole).

- *Garter v. Bowersox*, 265 F.3d 705 (8th Cir. 2001), cert, denied, 535 U.S. 999 (2002) (trial court violated due process by omitting sentencing-phase instruction on effect of lack of unanimity on capital-sentencing verdict).

- *Mitchell v. Gibson*, 262 F.3d 1036 (10th Cir. 2001) (invalidation of rape and sodomy convictions should have resulted in invalidation of murder committed as part of same incident: "the rape and sodomy evidence impacted all three of the aggravating factors found by the jury").

- *Murtishaw v. Woodford*, 255 F.3d 926 (9th Cir. 2001), cert, denied, 535 U.S. 935 (2002) (trial court's use of capital-sentencing-phase jury instructions based on California's 1978 "Briggs death penalty initiative" violated Ex Post Facto Clause because Briggs initiative was not in effect at time of petitioner's crime, and instructions "infected the proceeding with the jury's potential confusion regarding its discretion to impose a life or death sentence" and prevented judicial "determin[ation] whether the jury sentenced [petitioner] to death under a confused and incorrect interpretation of the concededly wrong statute").

- *Rojem v. Gibson*, 245 F.3d 1130 (10th Cir. 2001) (trial court's failure to give "uniform jury instructions directing the jury to weigh the aggravating and mitigating circumstances when deciding whether to impose the death penalty" violated 8th and 14th Amendments by depriving jury of "clear, objective standards providing specific, detailed guidance [for] … deci[sion] whether to impose the death penalty" and by creating "reasonable likelihood that the jury applied the instructions in a way that prevented it from considering the mitigating evidence").

- *Coleman v. Calderon*, 210 F.3d 1047 (9th Cir. 2000) (jury instruction overstated Governor's power to "commute a sentence from life imprisonment without the possibility of parole to some lesser sentence that would include the possibility of parole").

- *Pickens v. Gibson*, 206 F.3d 988 (10th Cir. 2000) (sentencing jury viewed petitioner's videotaped confessing, which was unconstitutionally obtained, and which contained information about petitioner's commission of another murder under similar circumstances shortly before charged crime).

- *Paxton v. Ward*, 199 F.3d 1197 (10th Cir. 1999) (trial court violated Confrontation Clause by permitting prosecution to prove prior, unadjudicated homicide with hearsay statements by accused's then-three-year-old daughter who had no present recollection of events).

- *McLain v. Calderson*, 134 F.3d 1383 (9th Cir.), cert, denied, 525 U.S. 942 (1998) (instruction misled jury into believing that governor could commute death sentence on own when actually petitioner's record precluded commutation in absence of written recommendations from four state supreme court justices).

- *Grisby v. Blodgett*, 130 F.3d 365 (9th Cir. 1997) (Washington sentencing statute unconstitutionally penalized right to trial by permitting sentence of death or life without parole for defendants who opted for trial while prohibiting sentence greater than life with possibility of parole for those who pled guilty).

- *Gallego v. McDaniel*, 124 F.3d 1065 (9th Cir. 1997), cert, denied, 524 U.S. 917 (1998) (jury instruction concerning availability of executive clemency, although "not inaccurate as a general statement of the law, … could have prompted the jury into making erroneous speculations about the kind of sentence [petitioner] might actually serve")

•

CHAPTER SIXTEEN

POST SENTENCING CLAIMS

This can be a confusing chapter, so let's pay special attention to the context here. I am not talking about claims for your direct appeal, I am talking about claims that occur during your direct appeal and in other post-conviction proceedings. The procedures I am talking about include but are not limited to: post-trial, appellate, and/or post-conviction proceedings. Remember that each of these stages of the criminal justice process have their own specific and independent set of rules.

Reflecting back to previous books I have written, you will find that I have continuously directed you to read and follow court rules.

For instance, "Rules Governing 28 U.S.C. § 2255 Proceedings in the United States District Courts" is the standard set of rules for due process in 28 U.S.C. § 2255 proceedings. As you might imagine, I have seen nearly every district court in the United States violate a few of these rules and completely disregard 28 U.S.C. § 2255(b).

To be plain, the Fifth Amendment's due process clause pertains to each of these rules. When you arrive at this point in the process, you may also trigger the saving clause of 28 U.S.C. § 2255, so pay special attention. Most of these claims may also be eligible for review under 28 U.S.C. § 2241. As you read these cases for possible applications, keep an open mind, and watch out for "Post-Conviction Relief: Second Last Chance", distributed by Freebird Publishers, for additional reading.

Young v. Harper, 520 U.S. 143 (1997) (revocation of so-called "preparole" status, conducted without due process protections which *Morrissey v. Brewer*, 408 U.S. 471 (1972) assures individuals subject to parole revocation, violated Due Process Clause because "preparole" "program... differed from parole in name alone").

- *Lynce v. Mathis*, 519 U.S. 433 (1997) (1992 statute's retroactive revocation of five years' worth of good time credits that petitioner accumulated under regulations in effect in 1986 when offense and guilty plea occurred, and petitioner's re-arrest and reincarceration after being released based on accumulated credits, violated Ex Post Facto Clause).

- *Richmond v. Lewis*, 506 U.S. 40 (1992) (state supreme court's affirmance of death sentence unconstitutional and invalid because majority of state supreme court justices considered sentence to be constitutionally infirm).

- *Blackledge v. Perry*, 417 U.S. 21 (1974) (vindictive re-prosecution following successful appeal).

- *Price v. Warden*, 785 F.3d 1039 (5th Cir. 2015) (ex post facto clause bars retrospective application of state parole law – providing for forfeiture of all previously-earned good-time credits upon revocation of parole – to prisoner who was sentenced at time when state law provided for forfeiture of "no more than 180 days of good-time credit" upon parole revocation).

- *Grandberry v. Smith*, 754 F.3d 425 (7th Cir. 2014) (prison authorities' revocation of 30 days of good time credits was not supported by evidence).

- *Lujan v. Garcia*, 734 F.3d 917 (9th Cir. 2013), cert, denied, 135 S. Ct. 477 (2014) (state appellate court violated *Harrison v. United States*, 392 U.S. 219 (1968), by ruling that admission of inadequately Mirandized confession was rendered harmless by defendant's testimony at trial, in which defendant "explain[ed] the details of the offenses and the circumstances of his confession").

- *Mickens-Thomas v. Vaughn*, 407 Fed. Appx. 597, 2011 U.S. App. LEXIS 1318 (3d Cir. Jan. 20, 2011) ("Board has repeatedly failed to comply with our instructions to evaluate Thomas's request for parole under the parole laws and guidelines that existed at the time of Thomas's conviction, not under the laws and guidelines as amended in 1996 and thereafter").

- *Dorn v. Lafler*, 601 F.3d 439 (6th Cir. 2010) (prison officials' delay in processing and mailing prisoner's *pro se* direct appeal, which resulted in dismissal of appeal as untimely and relegated prisoner to less robust appellate and postconviction remedies, violated prisoner's right of access to courts; relief ordered is reinstatement of " 'the full appellate review [prisoner]… would have received but for the untimely submission of his papers' ").

- *Kamienski v. Hendricks*, 332 Fed. Appx. 740, 2009 U.S. App. LEXIS 11456 (3d Cir. May 28, 2009), cert, denied, 558 U.S. 1147 (2010) (state appellate court unreasonably applied *Jackson v. Virginia* by reversing trial court's post-verdict entry of judgment of acquittal for accessory who had neither "the mental state required for a conviction of first degree murder or… the knowledge required for a conviction of felony murder").

- *Styers v. Schriro*, 547 F.3d 1026 (9th Cir. 2008) (per curiam), cert, denied, 558 U.S. 932 (2009) (state appellate court, which had found aggravating factor to be invalid, "failed to properly re-weigh the aggravating and mitigating circumstances as required by *Clemons v. Mississippi*, 494 U.S. 738, 748-49 (1990)": state appellate court discounted mitigating evidence of post-traumatic stress disorder (PTSD) on impermissible ground that there was insufficient nexus between PTSD and crime).

- *Burbank v. Cain*, 535 F.3d 350 (5th Cir. 2008) (state appellate court improperly found curtailment of defense counsel's cross-examination to be harmless error).

- *Boyd v. Newland*, 455 F.3d 897 (9th Cir. 2006), amended, 467 F.3d 1139 (9th Cir. 2006), cert, denied, 550 U.S. 933 (2007) (given that petitioner raised "plausible *Batson* [*v. Kentucky*] claim," California appellate courts improperly denied petitioner's "request for a complete *voir dire* transcript and a full comparative analysis of the venire").

- *Clark v. Brown*, 450 F.3d 898 (9th Cir.), cert, denied, 549 U.S. 1027 (2006) ("California Supreme Court's retroactive application of a new interpretation of [prior state supreme court decision] and of the felony-murder special circumstances statute, on direct review violated Clark's due process right to fair warning that his conduct made him death-eligible").

- *Ruimveld v. Birkett*, 404 F.3d 1006 (6th Cir. 2005) (state supreme court, which found constitutional error in shackling of petitioner during trial, "unreasonably concluded that this harm did not substantially influence the jury's decision").

- *Brown v. Palmateer*, 379 F.3d 1089 (9th Cir. 2004) (parole board's postponement of petitioner's parole release date, based upon retroactive application of statutory amendment enacted after petitioner's commission of crimes, violated Ex Post Facto Clause).

- *Allen v. Lee*, 366 F.3d 319 (4th Cir.) (en banc) (per curiam), cert, denied, 543 U.S. 906 (2004) ("North Carolina Supreme Court's conclusion that the *McKoy* [*v. North Carolina*] error was harmless beyond a reasonable doubt" involved "unreasonable application of clearly established federal law as determined by the Supreme Court").

- *Caliendo v. Warden*, 365 F.3d 691 (9th Cir.), cert, denied, 543 U.S. 927 (2004) (state appellate court violated *Mattox v. United States*, 146 U.S. 140 (1892) by failing to apply "rebuttable presumption of prejudice" in assessing claim of juror misconduct based on 20-minute conversation between three jurors and key prosecution witness).

- *Cordova v. Baca*, 346 F.3d 924 (9th Cir. 2003) (state appellate court improperly treated defective waiver of counsel and consequent denial of right to counsel as subject to harmless error review rather than as prejudicial per se).

- *Himes v. Thompson*, 336 F.3d 848 (9th Cir. 2003) (determination of parole with standards that were "more onerous than those in place at the time Hines committed the offense for which he was incarcerated" violated Ex Post Facto Clause).

- *McQuillion v. Duncan*, 306 F.3d 895 (9th Cir. 2002) (rescission of parole without good cause violated Due Process Clause).

- *Valerio v. Crawford*, 306 F.3d 742 (9th Cir. 2002) (en banc), cert. denied, 538 U.S. 994 (2003) (state supreme court failed to cure instructional error at sentencing by reweighing aggravating and mitigating circumstances and instead engaged in impermissible procedure of de novo factfinding).

- *Alexander v. Cockrell*, 294 F.3d 626 (5th Cir. 2002) (per curiam) (parole must be reinstated because basis for revocation was conviction under criminal statute that was later declared unconstitutional and accordingly was "void ab initio").

- *Ghent v. Woodford*, 279 F.3d 1121 (9th Cir. 2002) (state appellate court erred in finding that admission, at "special circumstances" retrial, of testimony of psychiatrist who interviewed petitioner in violation of *Miranda v. Arizona* was harmless error).

- *Bulls v. Jones*, 274 F.3d 329 (6th Cir. 2001) (state appellate court erred in concluding that Confrontation Clause violation was harmless).

- *Carter v. Bowersox*, 265 F.3d 705 (8th Cir. 2001), cert. denied, 535 U.S. 999 (2002) (state supreme court refused to recall mandate despite plain error resulting from trial court's omission of sentencing-phase instruction on effect of lack of unanimity on capital-sentencing verdict).

- *Mitchell v. Gibson*, 262 F.3d 1036 (10th Cir. 2001) (invalidation of rape and sodomy convictions should have resulted in invalidation of murder committed as part of same incident: "the rape and sodomy evidence impacted all three of the apricating factors found by the jury").

- *Gall v. Parker*, 231 F.3d 265 (6th Cir. 2000), cert, denied, 533 U.S. 941 (2001) (state supreme court's review of sufficiency of evidence unconstitutionally relieved prosecution of burden of proving absence of "extreme emotional disturbance" beyond reasonable doubt).

•

SECTION THREE
CHAPTER SEVENTEEN

LONG ROAD HOME

I want to avoid giving you the wrong impression. Just because the cases I have shown you in this book are all winners doesn't mean they won easily. Please notice that out of all of these case citations, you do not find even one that was granted in a district court. The facts are simple: the district courts do not do justice – they do business. That business is a conviction for pay.

In my attempt to bring balance by exposing you to reality, I am going to share with you what I consider to be the worst-case scenario; yes, my own personal case. In my § 2255 case, a hostile court denied relief based on only three out of four grounds. The ground that the court decided to leave unanswered was where the court outright denied the appointment of counsel. Yes, I was required to act as my own counsel in a critical stage of the criminal proceeding.

Understand also that my criminal case is also very unique. Basically, Chief District Judge Karon Owen Bowdre allowed herself to get in too deep in three murders stemming from Birmingham, Alabama. Although she was drawn into the scheme to conceal murder innocently, she now has to conceal her own malfeasance. This is a very good example of a hostile court that's trying to conceal its own criminal conduct by denying justice to an innocent American citizen.

Take time to study the case record that follows. Doing so will open your eyes to unimaginable possibilities. It will also prepare you with tools you may need, even if only to a lesser degree. You will find many meaningful filings that can be amended and used in other proceedings. It not only serves as a "worst-case scenario," but it serves to illustrate every possible step in a post-conviction relief proceeding. Good luck – your success is on the other side of your very own fight for justice.

UNITED STATES DISTRICT COURT
NORTHERN DISTRICT OF ALABAMA
SOUTHERN DIVISION

KELLY PATRICK RIGGS V. UNITED STATES OF AMERICA	Case No.: 2:15-cv-8043-KOB 2:12-cr-297-KOB-JEO

MOTION FOR LEAVE TO AMEND

Kelly Riggs seeks leave to amend his § 2255 motion. Mr. Riggs's original *pro se* motion was over inclusive and needs to be more concise.

The amendment will not contain any new substantive claims but should clarify his two primary claims, i.e., constructive denial of counsel and actual innocence.

On November 10, 2015, Mr. Riggs filed his § 2255 motion. By March 30, 2016, all the primary pleadings were submitted. With the exception of a variety of pleadings Mr. Riggs filed in the equivalent of youthful (in the law) exuberance, the case has remained docile, presumably – at least in part – because of the extraneous pleadings and extraneous claims.

Mr. Riggs has matured in his legal studies, including accepting guidance from more experienced advocates. He now perceives his presentation as cluttered and confusing. He intends, by his amendment, to make his claims more precise and more amenable to efficient resolution. His claims reduce to:

1. Defense counsel's actual conflict of interest denied Mr. Riggs the effective assistance of counsel.

2. Mr. Riggs is actually innocent of the crimes of conviction, a claim supported by ten alibi witnesses; Mr. Riggs's guilty plea was coerced and unintelligent; thus, the conviction is invalid.

These two claims identify that a fundamental miscarriage of justice occurred. Succinctly, an actually innocent person was found guilty because conflicted counsel facilitated an involuntary guilty plea.

CONFLICT

In September, 2013, Mr. Riggs brought to the court's attention that his attorney, Glennon Threatt, Jr., and the Public Defender's Office had an actual conflict of interest. As a result of this notice – and because of the seriousness of the conflict – this court ordered Mr. Threatt to address Mr. Riggs's claim about the conflict.

Unsurprisingly, Mr. Threatt denied a conflict existed or that the dual representation conflict impaired his ability to represent Mr. Riggs. This representation was inaccurate. The conflict required counsel to avoid a trial because then the attorney's conflict would be apparent. Correspondingly, the attorneys, Mr. Threatt and Allison Case convinced Mr. Riggs to enter into a plea agreement, in essence advising Mr.

Riggs to forego his alibi defense, cooperate with authorities, and that both he and his family would receive assistance and protection. This representation likely was untrue rather than merely inaccurate.

In light of the seriousness of the conflict (Mr. Riggs's declaration succinctly describes the conflict), this court should have appointed unconflicted counsel to advise Mr. Riggs about the conflict. Because unconflicted counsel was not appointed, Mr. Riggs's trial was fundamentally unfair. A trial is uncontestably unfair when an accused has been actually or constructively denied the assistance of counsel. *United States v Cronic*, 466 U.S. 468 (1984). A conviction obtained in the absence of counsel must be reversed or vacated.

CONCLUSION

In sum, Mr. Riggs seeks leave to amend his motion to include only two grounds; (1) the guilty plea was involuntary, and (2) an actual conflict of interest denied him the assistance of counsel.

Respectfully submitted on the 13th day of June, 2017 by:

X_____

Kelly Patrick Riggs

CERTIFICATE OF SERVICE

I, the undersigned, do hereby Certify that I have served a copy of this instrument via U.S. Mail, First Class postage prepaid, properly addressed, to John B. Ward at:

U.S. Attorney's Office
1801 4th Ave. N.
Birmingham, AL 35203

Respectfully submitted on this 13th day of June, 2017 by:

X_____
Kelly Patrick Riggs

STATE OF FLORIDA
Sumter County

AFFIDAVIT

1. "My name is Kelly Patrick Riggs. I am over nineteen (19) years of age, under no legal disability, and make this affidavit based upon personal knowledge and belief of the facts contained herein."

2. "I am a federal inmate, currently incarcerated at Federal Correctional Complex- Low, Coleman, Florida, serving a federal sentence pursuant to a judgment in criminal case: UNITED STATES V. KELLY PATRICK RIGGS, 2:12-CR-297-KOB-JEO, in the Northern District of Alabama."

3. "During my pre-trial detention, I was exposed to an individual who confessed to the drug-related murder-for-hire of DeAndre Washington, a federal defendant. Within the confession of the "hit man," I was provided with the names of two residents of Birmingham, Alabama who hired him."

4. "As required by law, 18 U.S.C. § 4, I notified the U.S. District Court, the United States Marshal's Service, and the United States Federal Public Defender's Office."

5. "I was shocked to learn that the hit man was appointed the same Assistant Federal Public Defender that I was, Glennon F. Threatt, Jr."

6. "On or about August 31, 2013, I filed a *pro se* motion asking for a hearing to determine if it was a conflict of interest for the Federal Public Defender's office to represent me and someone whom I reported for murder at the same time, even more specifically, we were both represented by the very same lawyer. It was later discovered that Mr. Glennon F. Threatt, Jr. was aware of the unsolved murder."

7. "On September 3, 2013, my *pro se* motion was received and filed under seal by the United States District Court Clerk." Doc. #45.

8. "On September 4, 2013, the court issued an order setting a hearing to determine if a conflict of interest was indeed an issue."

9. "On or about September 5, 2013, I was taken from Cullman County Jail and transported to the United States Federal Court House (Hugo Black Bldg.) in Birmingham, Alabama. While in holding downstairs, I was counseled by Glennon F. Threatt, who advised me that I would soon be getting time served for my assistance."

10. "In the afternoon of September 5, 2013, I was taken into a hearing. The hearing was to determine if a conflict of interest existed between me and counsel Glennon F. Threatt, Jr. At that hearing, my position was that Mr. Threatt's representation was in conflict for serving two masters. Mr. Threatt was forced to decide which client he was going to be loyal to, the murderer or the one who is a witness to the murder."

11. "On September 5, 2013, Mr. Threatt's interests were in conflict with my own because he had to remain my representative so he could manipulate my testimony concerning his other client (Alvin Ray Johnson, Jr.). Silencing my testimony was the only way for Mr. Threatt to protect his other client from prosecution of an unsolved drug-related murder. That murder is still unsolved today."

12. "On September 5, 2013, Mr. Threatt was directed by the court to represent my position in the hearing where I challenged Mr. Threatt's loyalties. At that hearing, I was denied counsel at a critical stage. Mr. Threatt's interests were to represent his very own position that was in conflict with my own. This is a structural error."

13. "At the hearing on September 5, 2013, Magistrate Judge John E. Ott inquired of Mr. Threatt, who stated that he had advised me concerning the conflict. I also agreed, due to a misunderstanding, concerning the complexities of the conflict of interest that occurred where Mr. Threatt represented me in a controversy to which he was the adversarial party."

14. "Magistrate Judge John E. Ott determined that there was no conflict based upon Mr. Threatt's statement without further inquiry."

15. "Later that afternoon, Mr. Threatt and Allison Case advised me concerning the events and requirements of a downward departure pursuant to U.S.S.G. § 5K.1."

16. "I was then left alone with two United States Deputy Marshals. Deputy Keith Blankenship took my statement concerning Mr. Johnson without the advice of counsel."

17. "Upon my return to Cullman County Jail, I was confronted by the murderer because of my statement to the Marshals, and he then made threats against my family. He had ordered me to withdraw my statement."

18. "I immediately called Glennon Threatt about the confrontation. Having been advised earlier, I decided to take the offered plea, expecting the downward departure and, more importantly, protection for my family."

19. "At around 8:00 P.M., on September 5, 2013, Mr. Threatt arrived at Cullman County Jail, alone once again, and advised me about how a plea agreement would protect my family and get me moved for my protection. I was earlier advised that I would get time served for my assistance pursuant to a 5k.1 departure. I was, later that night, coerced to sign a plea agreement. Mr. Threatt led me to believe that the plea agreement would protect my family and myself, and then he would appeal for me."

20. "On September 6, 2013, I was rushed into a change of plea hearing only 18 hours later. The court was in such a hurry that it allowed the reading of the factual basis to be waived."

VERIFICATION

Under penalty of perjury pursuant to 28 U.S.C. § 1746, I declare that the factual statements contained in this Affidavit are true and correct to the best of my knowledge.

X_____
Kelly Patrick Riggs
June 13, 2017

KELLY PATRICK RIGGS

UNITED STATES COURT OF APPEALS
FOR THE ELEVENTH CIRCUIT

_____

CASE NO. _____

_____

In re: Kelly Patrick Riggs

[A.K.A. The Author]

_____

On Petition for a Writ of Mandamus
to the United States District Court,
Northern District of Alabama,
Case No: 2:15-cv-8043-KOB [§2255]

_____

PETITION FOR A WRIT OF MANDAMUS

_____

Prepared by/for

Kelly Patrick Riggs, *Pro se*

CERTIFICATE OF INTERESTED PERSONS

The parties that may be interested in the outcome of this action do not appear to have changed since the initial pleading.

PETITION FOR A WRIT OF MANDAMUS

Mr. Riggs moves this court to issue a writ of mandamus to Judge Karen Owen Bowdre in the Northern District of Alabama, ordering her to provide her honest service as a United States District Judge. Judge Bowdre has delayed protecting the public's interest in the finality of Mr. Riggs's criminal and post-conviction proceedings for the sole purpose of protecting her own personal reputation.

Mr. Riggs seeks resolution of his actual innocence and denial of counsel claims. Mr. Riggs filed for relief from a manifest miscarriage of justice in his *pro se* §2255 motion in good faith. He filed under §2255 because he erroneously believed that the section restated, clarified, and/or simplified the procedure in the nature of the ancient writ of error coram nobis. He had an unqualified belief that §2255 provided an expeditious remedy for correcting erroneous sentences and/or convictions without resorting to *habeas corpus*. Thus, if the courts provided their honest service as Congress intended, the resort to a writ of mandamus would be unnecessary.

ISSUE ONE

Mr. Riggs is confined in prison, where he has been for over five years, notwithstanding his actual innocence. His incarceration is a manifest miscarriage of justice in violation of the Thirteenth Amendment.

1.   Mr. Riggs is a former CI for a drug task force that was facilitated by the Vestavia Hills Police Department. Mr. Riggs has worked with several departments over the years, utilizing TFOs to include but not limited to: Mike Hale, Mr. Cole, Detective Goodwin, and countless others.

2.   By the summer of 2011, after over two years of diligence, Mr. Riggs discovered that a large-scale drug trafficking scheme was facilitated by the participation and a combined effort of Alabama public officials and Mexican Cartel members.

3.   Later, in 2011, Mr. Riggs learned that an agreement had been entered between the Mexican Cartel and Brad Taylor to murder Mr. Riggs. Mr. Riggs took his complaints to the F.B.I. in the Birmingham, Alabama field office. Mr. Taylor was later learned to be named as the electrician who performed maintenance services to Judge Bowdre's Birmingham, Alabama, rehabilitation center.

4.   After months of harassment by Hoover City Police personnel, the Hoover City Police Department staged a crime and kidnapped Mr. Riggs. Unknown to Hoover City Police personnel, those who staged the alleged offense chose a time period for which Mr. Riggs had an indisputable alibi. An alibi for every occurrence of the staged crime is sufficient to prove Mr. Riggs's actual innocence. Neither the court nor the government contest the alibi or actual innocence, only that the procedure requires that Mr. Riggs serve his sentence.

ISSUE TWO

Mr. Riggs has suffered a constructive denial of counsel at all stages of his trial proceedings and actual denial of counsel at three critical stages, which resulted in him entering a plea agreement under false pretenses.

1. Mr. Riggs was held hostage in Shelby County Jail for two days, after which he was alleged to be charged with an unidentified offense.

2. On or about May 29, 2012, Mr. Riggs was visited by attorney Jeffrey Bramer, who alleged that he was hired by Judge Bowdre personally.

3. After learning of the charged offense and the alleged time period, Mr. Riggs notified many alibi witnesses who began calling Mr. Bramer. Mr. Bramer stated that he was only hired to negotiate a plea agreement and that he wouldn't be taking statements or presenting an alibi defense.

4. Mr. David Luker was appointed after Mr. Bramer was dismissed. He also refused to take statements or raise an alibi defense because some of the witnesses were bar members.

5. The Federal Public Defender's Office was appointed after Mr. Luker was dismissed as counsel. After reviewing the case and talking with witnesses, Mr. Threatt gave notice of an alibi defense and subpoenaed ten witnesses. but later compelled Mr. Riggs to forego his alibi defense and trial, advising him to plead guilty in exchange for protection for his family. Mr. Threatt was forced to divide his loyalties between two different clients, a conflict of interest that required the replacement of counsel.

ISSUE THREE

1. Judge Bowdre lends the integrity of her office to her own personal interests in Mr. Riggs's case. Judge Bowdre has acted unprofessionally and with great prejudice to Mr. Riggs by knowingly incarcerating an innocent witness in DeAndre Washington's murder. Thus, Judge Bowdre has made herself an accessory after the fact.

2. Without mention of Mr. Riggs's previous efforts to assist law enforcement in the war on drugs, he also inadvertently became a witness in the drug-related murder-for-hire of DeAndre Washington. Mr. Riggs's counsel, Glennon F. Threatt, Jr., was later discovered to be acquainted with other conspirators in the murder. Thus, Mr. Threatt attempted to ruin MR. Riggs's credibility by compelling him to plead guilty.

3. Mr. Riggs moved the court to appoint new counsel to determine if a conflict of interest existed. The court guided Mr. Threatt, conflicted counsel, to address Mr. Riggs's claims.

4. On September 5, 2013, Mr. Riggs was present without the benefit of unconflicted counsel and was compelled to give information concerning murder and attempted murder to the United States Marshals Service, again without counsel.

5. Mr. Threatt was later successful in coercing Mr. Riggs's guilty plea under the duress of a scheme to murder Mr. Riggs's wife and children also.

6. After discovering that the Federal Public Defender's Office was responsible for the threat against his family, Mr. Riggs moved to withdraw his plea – before sentencing – presenting the affidavits of several of the alibi witnesses.

7. At the hearing, Mr. Riggs attempted, to the best of his ability, to express that Glennon Threatt and the Public Defender's Office deprived him of a fair trial by providing ineffective assistance of counsel. Mr. Riggs went on to show that the threat against his family caused him to enter the plea agreement and the appeal waivers unknowingly and unwillingly. At the 12/20/2013 hearing. Judge Bowdre found Mr. Threatt's testimony to be credible, meaning that Mr. Riggs had an alibi defense. On April 22, 2014, however. Judge Bowdre sentenced Mr. Riggs to 120 months so he could "Learn to tell the truth."

8. On March 17, 2016, Judge Bowdre, in her order (DE-33) determined that Glennon Threatt's testimony was credible and Mr. Riggs's §2255 "Ripe for Summary Disposition." Mr. Riggs agrees because he is due relief, but yet has languished in prison for an additional 21 months.

FACTS OF THE CASE

Mr. Riggs's conviction is a product of a structural error where he was outright denied counsel at a critical, pre-plea stage of his criminal proceeding. Mr. Riggs shows the court the following:

1. During his pre-trial detention, Mr. Riggs was exposed to an individual who confessed to the drug-related murder-for-hire of DeAndre Washington, a federal defendant. Within the confession of the "hit man," Mr. Riggs was provided with the names of two residents of Birmingham, Alabama who hired him.

2. Mr. Riggs notified the U.S. District Court, the U.S. Marshals Service, and the U.S. Federal Defender's Office. Mr. Riggs was shocked to learn that the hit man was appointed the same Assistant Federal Public Defender as Mr. Riggs: Glennon F. Threatt, Jr.

3. On or about August 31, 2013, Mr. Riggs filed a *pro se* motion asking for a hearing to determine if it was a conflict of   interest for the Federal Public Defender's Office to represent Mr. Riggs and someone who he reported for murder at the same time, even more specifically, they were both represented by the very same lawyer. It was later discovered that Mr. Glennon F. Threatt, Jr. was aware of the unsolved murder.

4. On September 4, 2013, Mr. Riggs's *pro se* motion was received and filed under seal by the United States District Court Clerk. (DE-51)

5. On September 4, 2013, the court issued an order setting a hearing to determine if a conflict of interest was indeed an issue.

6. On or about September 5, 2013, Mr. Riggs was taken from Cullman County Jail and transported to the United States Courthouse (Hugo L. Black Bldg.) in Birmingham, Alabama. While in holding downstairs, Mr. Riggs was counseled by Glennon F. Threatt, Jr., who advised Mr. Riggs that he would soon be getting time served for his assistance.

7. In the afternoon of September 5, 2013, Mr. Riggs was taken into a hearing. The hearing was to determine if a conflict of interest existed between Mr. Riggs and counsel Glennon F. Threatt, Jr. At that hearing, Mr. Riggs's position was that Mr. Threatt's representation was in conflict for serving two masters. Mr. Threatt was forced to decide which client he was going to be loyal to: the murderer, or Mr. Riggs, who is a witness to the murder.

8. On September 5, 2013, Mr. Threatt's interests were in conflict with Mr. Riggs's own, because Mr. Threatt had to remain Mr. Riggs's representative, so he could manipulate Mr. Riggs's testimony concerning his other client, Alvin Ray Johnson, Jr. Silencing Mr. Riggs's testimony

was the only way for Mr. Threatt to protect his other client from a prosecution of an unsolved, drug-related murder.

9. On September 5, 2013, Mr. Threatt was directed by the court to represent Mr. Riggs's position in the hearing where Mr. Riggs challenged Mr. Threatt's loyalties. At that hearing, Mr. Riggs was denied counsel at a critical stage. Mr. Threatt's interests were to represent his very own position that was in conflict with Mr. Riggs's own. This is a structural error.

10. At the hearing on September 5, 2013, Magistrate Judge John E. Ott inquired of Mr. Threatt, who stated that he had advised Mr. Riggs concerning the conflict. Mr. Riggs also agreed, due to a misunderstanding, concerning the complexities of the conflict of interest that occurred where Mr. Threatt represented Mr. Riggs in a controversy to which Mr. Threatt was the adversarial party.

11. Magistrate Judge John E. Ott determined that there was no conflict based upon Mr. Threatt's statement, without further inquiry. Later that afternoon, Mr. Threatt and Allison Case advised Mr. Riggs concerning the events and requirements of a downward departure pursuant to U.S.S.G. §5kl.l. Mr. Riggs was then left alone with two United States Deputy Marshals. Deputy Keith Blankenship took Mr. Riggs's statement concerning Mr. Johnson without the advice of counsel.

12. Upon Mr. Riggs's return to Cullman County Jail, Mr. Riggs was confronted by the murderer because of Mr. Riggs's statement to the Marshal, and Mr. Johnson then made threats against Mr. Riggs's family. Mr. Johnson ordered Mr. Riggs to withdraw his statement.

13. Mr. Riggs immediately called Glennon Threatt about the confrontation. Having been advised earlier, Mr. Riggs decided to take the offered plea, expecting the downward departure, and more importantly, protection for his family.

14. At around 8:00 P.M. on September 5, 2013, Mr. Threatt arrived at Cullman County Jail, alone once again, and advised Mr. Riggs about how a plea agreement would protect Mr. Riggs's family and get Mr. Riggs moved for his protection. Mr. Riggs was earlier advised that he would get time served for his assistance pursuant to a 5k. 1 departure. Mr. Riggs was, later that night, coerced to sign a plea agreement. Mr. Threatt led Mr. Riggs to believe that the plea agreement would protect his family and himself, and then Mr. Threatt would appeal for Mr. Riggs.

15. On September 6, 2013, Mr. Riggs was rushed to a change of plea hearing only 18 hours later. The court was in such a hurry that it allowed the reading of the factual basis to be waived.

16. Mr. Riggs continued to provide information to Mr. Threatt by mail as Mr. Threatt directed, which Mr. Threatt shared with a colleague in the Federal Defender's Office named Sabra Barnett. On or about October 5, 2013, Mr. Riggs learned through a fellow inmate, incarcerated for illegal re-entry and distribution of methamphetamine, that Ms. Barnett advised Cartel associates that Mr. Riggs was providing information that was dangerous to their case. On or about October 5, 2013,

17. Mr. Riggs filed a motion to withdraw his plea agreement, which was entered into on false pretenses. (DE-57)

18. On or about October 18, 2013, Mr. Riggs was once again denied counsel at another conflict of interest hearing. (DE-58)

19. On or about December 20, 2013, Mr. Riggs was denied leave to withdraw his plea of guilty, notwithstanding two structural errors. (Cronic)

20. On appeal, counsel promptly filed an Anders brief, identifying there were no possible issues for appeal. Once notified by this court of his right to object, Mr. Riggs filed his own brief – particularizing to the best of his ability raising the claim of actual innocence and the outright denial of counsel at a critical stage. On January 8, 2015, this court issued an order granting counsel's motion to withdraw and affirming the sentence and conviction.

21. Mr. Riggs promptly filed for rehearing en banc, once again to the best of his ability, being, at the time, completely ignorant to Federal Criminal and Appellate Procedure. On March 2, 2015, the panel of this court denied Mr. Riggs a rehearing.

REASONS TO GRANT THE WRIT

Mr. Riggs has attempted everything that he has learned in an effort to compel review of his undisputed actual innocence. This case has been pending since March 17, 2016, 21 months after the court determined it ripe for summary disposition.

The court's standard of review is:

> "Mandamus is an extraordinary remedy, and it is appropriate only when 'No other adequate means are available to remedy a clear usurpation of power or abuse of discretion by the district court.'" *Carpenter v. Mohawk Indus., Inc.*, 541 F.3d 1048, 1055 (11th Cir. 2008) (quoting in re Loudermich, 158 F.3d 1143, 1144 (11th Cir. 1998).

This court has previously held that, "Mandamus may be used to direct a district court to decide a pending case when there has been unreasonable delay in rendering a decision. See *Johnson v. Rogers*, 917 F.2d 1283, 1284 (10th Cir. 1990).

This is Mr. Riggs's second request for this court's active protection in the form of a writ of mandamus. Over one year ago, Mr. Riggs received this court's denial and followed the court's direction to wait longer. Mr. Riggs has shown that no other adequate remedy remains available, that he is indisputably innocent, and is currently the longest waiting innocent prisoner in the Eleventh Circuit.

Mr. Riggs has shown that the district judge delays with deliberate indifference for the sole purpose of concealing her own malfeasance. A government official who uses his or her public position for self-enrichment breaches the duty of honest service owed to the public and the government. So, for instance [and much like], a public official who accepts a bribe or corrupt payment [even protection of one's own reputation] breaches the duty of honest, faithful, and disinterested service. While outwardly appearing to be exercising independent judgment in his or her work, the public official instead has been paid privately for his or her public conduct. Thus, the public is not receiving the public official's honest and faithful service to which it is entitled.

Moreover, the Supreme Court has previously stated that,

> "The purpose of a criminal court is not to provide a forum for the ascertainment of private rights. Rather it is to vindicate the public interest in the enforcement of the criminal law while at the same time safeguarding the rights of the individual defendant." *Standefer v. United States*, 447 U.S. 10, 25, 100 S. Ct. 1999, 64 L. Ed. 2d 689 (1980).

CONCLUSION

Mr. Riggs moves this court to issue a writ of mandamus, considering also the obvious history of this case, and the court's effort to maintain the conviction of even the innocent, Mr. Riggs moves, alternatively, for this court to determine what Congress meant by, "an expeditious remedy for correcting erroneous sentences…" in a single line definition of "expeditions."

Respectfully submitted on this 2nd day of January, 2018, by:

_____

Kelly Patrick Riggs, *Pro se*

KELLY PATRICK RIGGS

CERTIFICATE OF SERVICE

I certify that I served a copy of this foregoing instrument on the Clerk of this Court, via U.S. Mail, first class postage prepaid, and properly addressed to:

Judge Karen Owen Bowdre
1729 5th Ave. North
Birmingham, AL 35203

Clerk of the Court
United States District Court
1729 5th Ave. North
Birmingham, AL 35203

U.S. Attorney's Office
John Ward
1801 4th Ave. North
Birmingham, AL 35203

On this 2nd day of January, 2018.

Submitted by:

Kelly Patrick Riggs, *Pro se*

IN THE UNITED STATES DISTRICT COURT
FOR THE NORTHERN DISTRICT OF ALABAMA
SOUTHERN DIVISION

KELLY PATRICK RIGGS,	]	
	]	
Plaintiff,	]	
	]	
v.	]	2:15-cv-08043-KOB
	]	
UNITED STATES OF AMERICA	]	
	]	
Defendant.	]	

ORDER

This matter is before the court on movant Kelly Patrick Riggs' motion to amend his 28 U.S.C. § 2255 motion to vacate sentence. (Doc. 59). Mr. Riggs states that his "original pro se motion was overinclusive and needs to be more concise," and that the amended § 2255 motion will clarify his primary claims. (*Id.* at 1). The court GRANTS Mr. Riggs' motion. **Mr. Riggs may file his amended § 2255 motion on or by February 17, 2018.**

The court notes that Mr. Riggs has filed four other motions that remain pending in this case: a "Motion for Summary Judgment" (doc. 29); a "Motion to Call into Question the Government's Authority to Prosecute Attempted Second Degree Rape without Subject-Matter Jurisdiction" (doc. 31); a "Motion for Expansion of the Record" (doc. 35); and a "Motion for an Evidentiary Hearing" (doc. 46). In light of the coming amendment to Mr. Riggs' § 2255 motion, the court DENIES AS MOOT those four motions.

DONE and **ORDERED** this 12th day of January, 2018.

KARON OWEN BOWDRE
CHIEF UNITED STATES DISTRICT JUDGE

AMENDED

MOTION UNDER 28 U.S.C. § 2255 TO VACATE, SET ASIDE, OR CORRECT

SENTENCE BY A PERSON IN FEDERAL CUSTODY.

United States District Court	District Northern District of Alabama	
Name *(under which you were convicted)*: Kelly Patrick Riggs		Docket or Case No.: 2:15-CV-8043-KOB
Place of Confinement: FCC Coleman- Low	Prisoner No.: 29821-001	
UNITED STATES OF AMERICA	Movant *(include name under which convicted)*	
V.	Kelly Patrick Riggs	

MOTION

1. (a) Name and location of court which entered the judgment of conviction you are challenging:

   U.S.D.C. Northern District of Alabama
   Southern Division
   Birmingham, AL

   (b) Criminal docket or case number (if you know): 2:12-CR-297-KOB-JEO

2. (a) Date of the judgment of conviction (if you know): September 6, 2013

   (b) Date of sentencing: April 22, 2014

3. Length of sentence: 120 Months

4. Nature of crime (all counts):

   Count One: Enticing a Minor 18 U.S.C. §2422(b)

   Count Two: Transferring Obscene Material to a Minor 18 U.S.C. §1470

5. (a) What was your plea? (Check one)

   (1) Not guilty ☐   (2) Guilty [X]   (3) Nolo contendere (no contest) ☐

   (b) If you entered a guilty plea to one count or indictment, and a not guilty plea to another count or what did you plead guilty to and what did you plead not guilty to?   N/A

6. If you went to trial, what kind of trial did you have? (Check one) N/A   Jury ☐   Judge only ☐

7. Did you testify at a pretrial hearing, trial, or post-trial hearing?   Yes ☐   No [X]

8. Did you appeal from the judgment of conviction?   Yes X   No ☐

9. If you did appeal, answer the following:

   (a) Name of court: Eleventh Circuit

   (b) Docket or case number (if you know): 14-11917-CC

   (c) Result: Affirmed

   (d) Date of result (if you know): March 2, 2015

   (e) Citation to the case (if you know): Unknown

   (f) Grounds raised:

   Ineffective assistance of counsel, deprived of counsel, conflict of interest, lack of jurisdiction, and rush to judgment.

   (g) Did you file a petition for certiorari in the United States Supreme Court?   Yes [X]   No [ ]

   If "Yes," answer the following:

   (1) Docket or case number (if you know): 14-9985

   (2) Result: Certiorari denied

   (3) Date of result (if you know): June 29, 2015

   (4) Citation to the case (if you know): WL 245 7924(U.S.), 83 USLW 3929

   (5) Grounds raised:

   Fraud on the court, ineffective assistance of counsel, plain error, manufactured jurisdiction, falsified indictment, prosecution without jurisdiction, rush to judgment, entered plea under threat and duress.

0. Other than the direct appeals listed above, have you previously filed any other motions, petitions, or applications, concerning this judgment of conviction in any court?

   Yes [X]   No [ ]

1. If your answer to Question 10 was "Yes," give the following information:

   (a) (1) Name of court: U.S.D.C Northern District of Alabama

   (2) Docket or case number (if you know): 2:15-CV-8005-KOB

   (3) Date of filing (if you know): March 9, 2015

   (4) Nature of the proceeding: Recharacterized as motion under §2255

   (5) Grounds raised: Fraud on the court, outrageous government conduct, ineffective assistance of counsel, deprived of civil rights, prosecution

without jurisdiction, and manufactured jurisdiction,.

(6) Did you receive a hearing where evidence was given on your motion, petition, or application?
Yes ☐   No ☒

(7) Result: Dismissed without prejudice

(8) Date of result (if you know): March 19, 2015

(b) If you filed any second motion, petition, or application, give the same information:

(1) Name of court: U.S.D.C. Northern District of Alabama

(2) Docket of case number (if you know): 2:12-CR-297-KOB-JEO

(3) Date of filing (if you know): April 11, 2015

(4) Nature of the proceeding: Writ of error coram nobis

(5) Grounds raised:

Fraud on the court, outrageous government conduct, depravation of civil rights, prosecution without jurisdiction, and prosecutorial misconduct.

(6) Did you receive a hearing where evidence was given on your motion, petition, or application?
Yes ☐   No ☒

(7) Result: Denied

(8) Date of result (if you know): May 6, 2015

(c) Did you appeal to a federal appellate court having jurisdiction over the action taken on your motion, petition, or application?

(1) First petition: Yes ☒   No ☐
(2) Second petition: Yes ☒   No ☐

(d) If you did not appeal from the action on any motion, petition, or application, explain briefly why you did not:

N/A

12. For this motion, state every ground on which you claim that you are being held in violation of the Constitution, laws, or treaties of the United States. Attach additional pages if you have more than four grounds. State the facts supporting each ground.

GROUND ONE:

Mr. Riggs' Criminal Judgement violates due process because it was not intelligent, knowing, or voluntary.

Mr. Riggs is actually innocent, and his conviction was cultivated by conflicted counsel who provided false information. Thus, Mr. Riggs' trial process was fundamentally unfair. These two claims identify that a fundamental miscarriage of justice occurred. Succinctly, an actually innocent person was found guilty because conflicted counsel facilitated an involuntary plea agreement.

(a) Supporting facts (Do not argue or cite law. Just state the specific facts that support your claim.):

Mr. Riggs believed that if he did not sign the plea agreement then his wife and children would be at risk of being killed by Mr. Alvin Ray Johnson, Jr., whom Mr. Riggs gave a statement against hours earlier. At the time of the plea agreement, Mr. Riggs informed counsel about a threat against Mr. Riggs' wife and children. Counsel stated that the Marshals Service would provide protection for Mr. Riggs' family and move Mr. Riggs away from Mr. Johnson, but only if Mr. Riggs would plead guilty. Counsel did not apprise Mr. Riggs of his right to protection from other inmates or his right to proceed to trial. Mr. Riggs did not understand the options available to him at the time of the guilty plea, nor did he know the consequences of the choices he was presented. Therefore, Mr. Riggs' guilty plea was invalid, which in turn invalidates his conviction. This court should set aside the Judgement and return Mr. Riggs to the pre-plea agreement stage of the proceedings.

Mr. Riggs' prosecution stems from his efforts as a C.I. who provided information to law enforcement entities in the State of Alabama. As the records obtained from the Freedom of Information Act show, Mr. Riggs has provided critical information to task force officers in Cherokee, Blount, Shelby, and Jefferson counties. Over a ten-year period he has discovered public officials who were involved in the drug trade. By 2010, Mr. Riggs had inadvertently identified the involvement of a state prosecutor, in Shelby County, and his relation to Mexican Cartel members. By 2011, Mr. Riggs suffered two attempts on his life and then notified of a contract, to kill him, with the Cartel. Mr. Riggs made reports to Cornelius Harris in the FBI's Birmingham field office and, shortly after, police officers and confidential informants, from Shelby County, Alabama, i.e. Hoover City Police Department, staged a crime and then kidnapped Mr. Riggs three days later. He was held without official charge until May 28, 2012. when he was charged by Homeland Security.

1. In or around December of 2011, and while still recovering from surgery after donating a kidney, Mr. Riggs committed to rent space in his home in an effort to supplement his income.

2. In or around February of 2012, Mr. Riggs, with the assistance of an acquaintance, listed said space for rent in an ad on craigslist.com.

3. Mr. Riggs' ad was answered by a Hoover City Police Detective in or around March, 2012. After much consideration, Mr. Riggs rented the space to police informant Joy Brown, who was operating under the alias Laney Jones. Police informant Joy Brown moved into the home of Mr. Riggs on May 14, 2012.

4. On or about May 16, 2012, Ms. Brown purchased an internet-ready cellular phone at Wal-Mart in Trussville, Alabama. Upon purchasing the phone, Ms. Brown asked for Mr. Riggs' permission to use one of the SIM cards from his broken cellular phone for the new phone she had purchased.

5. On or about May 23, 2012, Ms. Brown engaged in a detailed conversation with a Hoover City Police detective on her new cellular phone while Mr. Riggs was elsewhere with many alibi witnesses. The text messages were a very explicitly detailed sexual dialogue between Ms. Brown, pretending to be Mr. Riggs, and the police detective, pretending to be a 14-year-old girl.

6. On or about May 26, 2012, Mr. Riggs arrived at an insurance company, riding a newly obtained motorcycle, to purchase insurance. While waiting for the insurance agent he was brutally attacked by 6-8 heavily armed men. He was then transported to Hoover City Police Department where he met and was interviewed by Special Agent Daniel McKenzie. Agent McKenzie discovered that Mr. Riggs was confused about why the police personnel would kidnap him while he was shopping for insurance.

7. On or about May 30, 2012, Mr. Riggs was appointed counsel, Jeffrey Bramer, and appeared in court for a preliminary hearing. During trial preparations, many; alibi witnesses called and attempted to visit Jeffrey Bramer to offer their testimony. Jeffrey Bramer refused to take any of the many witness statements and/or memorialize their testimony.

8. From on or about May 30, 2012, through on or about October 9, 2012, Jeffrey Bramer refused to assert Mr. Riggs' alibi defense, take witness statements, and/or prepare for trial.

9. On or about June 1, 2012, Joy Brown, while attempting to extract evidence against Mr. Riggs, inadvertently confessed to staging the crime for which he is incarcerated for, to include but not limited to, sending obscene pictures to detectives and having dialogue with detectives on May 23, 2012, on her phone. This confession was memorialized on jail telephone recordings at Shelby County Jail.

10. On or about October 10, 2012, David Luker was appointed by the court to defend Mr. Rigg' interests. David Luker refused to assert Mr. Riggs' alibi defense, interview a single witness, and/or do any other meaningful thing to benefit Mr. Riggs.

11. On or about May 29, 2012, Mr. Riggs, being refused assistance of counsel, filed a *Pro se* motion to appeal to the District Judge. Mr. Riggs was attempting, by his filing, to inform the Judge that he had an air-tight alibi defense that a second lawyer refused to assert or otherwise defend his interests.

12. On or about June 4, 2013, the court appointed the Federal Public Defender's Office to represent Mr. Riggs' interests.

13. During his pre-trial detention Mr. Riggs was exposed to an individual who confessed to the drug-related murder-for-hire of DeAndre Washington, a federal defendant. Within the confession of the "hit-man," Mr. Riggs was provided with the names of two residents of Birmingham, Alabama who hired him.

14. Mr. Riggs notified the U.S. District Court, the U.S. Marshal's Service, and the U.S. Federal Defender's Office. Mr. Riggs was shocked to learn that the "hit-man" was appointed the same Assistant Federal Public Defender as Mr. Riggs, Glennon F. Threatt, Jr.

15. In or around August, 2013, Mr. Johnson had contact with his court-appointed counsel, Glennon Threatt, who informed Mr. Johnson that there would be no downward departure because Mr. Johnson informed others that he had murdered Mr. Washington. Mr. Johnson began making arrangements to kill his counsel, Glennon Threatt.

16. Mr. Riggs, and fellow detainee Greg Robinson, reported this threat to the U.S. District Court in an effort to prevent harm to Glennon Threat. Additionally, Mr. Riggs personally alerted Glennon Threatt by phone.

17. On or about August 31, 2013, Mr. Riggs filed a *Pro se* motion asking for a hearing to determine if it was a conflict of interest for the Federal Public Defender's Office to represent both Mr. Riggs and someone who he reported for murder at the same time, while even more specifically, they were both being represented by the very same lawyer. It was later discovered that Mr. Glennon F. Threatt, Jr. was aware of the unsolved murder.

18. On September 4, 2013, Mr. Riggs' *Pro se* motion was received and filed under seal by the United States District Court Clerk. The court issued an order setting a hearing to determine if a conflict of interest was indeed an issue.

19. On or about September 5, 2013, Mr. Riggs was taken from Cullman County Jail and transported to the United States Courthouse (Hugo L. Black Bldg.) in Birmingham, Alabama. While in holding downstairs, Mr. Riggs was counseled by Glennon F. Threatt, Jr., who advised Mr. Riggs that he would soon be getting time served for his assistance. That afternoon Mr. Riggs was taken into a hearing. The hearing was to determine if a conflict of interest existed between Mr. Riggs and counsel Glennon F. Threatt, Jr. At that hearing, Mr. Riggs' position was that Mr. Threatt's representation was in conflict for serving two masters. Mr. Threatt was forced to decide which client he was going to be loyal to: Mr. Riggs, who is a witness to the murder confession, or the murderer.

20. At the hearing, Mr. Threatt's interests were in conflict with Mr. Riggs' own because Mr. Threatt had to remain Mr. Riggs' representative so he could manipulate Mr. Riggs' testimony concerning his other client, Alvin Ray Johnson, Jr. Silencing Mr. Riggs' testimony was the only way for Mr. Threatt to protect his other client from a prosecution of an unsolved, drug-related murder, which is subject of an FBI investigation.

21. On September 5, 2013, Mr. Threatt was directed by the court to represent Mr. Riggs' position in the hearing where Mr. Riggs challenged Mr. Threatt's loyalties. At that hearing, Mr. Riggs was denied counsel at a critical stage. Mr. Threatt's interests were to represent his very own position that was in conflict with Mr. Riggs' interests. Magistrate Judge John E. Ott inquired of Mr. Threatt, who stated he had advised Mr. Riggs that no conflict existed. Mr. Riggs also agreed due to a misunderstanding concerning the complexities of the conflict of interest that occurred where Mr. Threatt represented Mr. Riggs in a controversy to which Mr. Threatt was the adversarial party.

22. Magistrate Judge John E. Ott determined that there was no conflict based upon Mr. Threatt's statement without further inquiry. Later that afternoon Mr. Threatt and Allison Case advised Mr. Riggs concerning the events and requirements of a downward departure pursuant to U.S.S.G. §5k.1.

23. On or about September 5, 2013, shortly after following a hearing, court-appointed counsel, Glennon Threatt, compelled Mr. Riggs to provide statements to Deputy Marshal Keith Blakenship concerning Alvin Ray Johnson, Jr.'s confession to murdering DeAndre Washington and Mr. Johnson's threat to murder Glennon Threatt and his family.

24. Upon Mr. Riggs' return to Cullman County Jail, Mr. Riggs was confronted by Mr. Johnson because of Mr. Riggs' statement to the Marshals. Mr. Johnson then made threats against Mr. Riggs' family and, additionally, Mr. Johnson ordered Mr. Riggs to withdraw his statement.

25. Mr. Riggs immediately called Glennon Threatt about the confrontation. Having been advised earlier, Mr. Riggs decided to take the offered plea, expecting the downward departure, and more importantly, protection for his family.

26. At around 8:00 P.M. on September 5, 2013, Mr. Threatt arrived at the Cullman County Jail, once again alone, and advised Mr. Riggs about how a plea agreement would protect Mr. Riggs' family and get Mr. Riggs moved for his protection. Mr. Riggs was earlier advised that he would get time served for his assistance pursuant to a §5k.1 departure. Mr. Riggs was, later that night, coerced into signing a plea agreement. Mr. Threatt led Mr. Riggs to believe that the plea agreement would protect his family and himself, and then Mr. Threatt would appeal for Mr. Riggs.

27. On September 6, 2013, Mr. Riggs was rushed into a change of plea hearing only 18 hours later. The court was in such a hurry that it allowed the reading of the factual basis to be waived.

28. Mr. Riggs continued to provide information to Mr. Threatt by mail which Mr. Threatt shared with a colleague in the Federal Defender's Office by name of Sabra Barnett.

29. On or about October 5, 2013, Mr. Riggs learned through a fellow inmate, who was incarcerated for illegal re-entry and distribution of methamphetamine, that Ms. Barnett advised Cartel associates that Mr. Riggs was providing information that was dangerous to their case. On or about October 5, 2013, Mr. Riggs filed a motion to withdraw his plea agreement.

30. On or about October 18, 2013, Mr. Riggs was once again denied counsel at another conflict of interest hearing.

31. On or about October 21, 2013, the court granted Mr. Riggs' motion for appointment of new counsel.

32. On or about December 20, 2013, the court heard Mr. Riggs' motion to withdraw his guilty plea. Mr. Riggs and court-appointed counsel Brett Bloomston were present in court before United States Chief District Judge Karen Owen Bowdre. During the course of the hearing the court attempted to determine the claims in Mr. Riggs' *Pro se* motion. Mr. Riggs' motion was not refined or clarified by court-appointed counsel Brett Bloomston. The court received testimony from former counsel Glennon Threatt. Mr. Threatt testified in particular part, and relevant to this action, that he, Mr. Threatt, did give the court and the government Notice of Alibi in Mr. Riggs' case. Furthermore, Mr. Threatt testified that he had issued subpoenas to ten (10) witnesses in Mr. Rigg's case Court-appointed counsel Brett Bloomston was present in the court when Mr. Threatt testified in support of Mr. Riggs' alibi defense to support his actual innocence. Mr. Bloomston was also present when the court took judicial notice of the accuracy of Glennon Threatt's testimony. Mr. Riggs was denied leave to withdraw his plea of guilty, notwithstanding two structural errors.

33. On or about April 22, 2014, at a sentencing hearing before Judge Karen 0. Bowdre, Mr. Riggs was sentenced notwithstanding his protest and unequivocal assertation of innocence. While in court, and subsequent to the court's rendering an unlawful sentence, Mr. Riggs stood and made his Declaration of Verbal Notice of Appeal based on his alibi defense, alibi witnesses, and his actual innocence, all in the presence of counsel Brett Bloomston.

34. On appeal, counsel promptly filed an Anders brief, identifying there were no possible issues for appeal. Once notified by the Court of Appeals of his right to object, Mr. Riggs filed his own brief – particularizing to the best of his ability – raising the claim of actual innocence and the outright denial of counsel at a critical stage. On January 8, 2015, the Court of Appeals issued an order granting counsel's motion to withdraw and affirming the sentence and convict ion. (App-1)

35. On or about November 10, 2015, Mr. Riggs blindly filed for post-conviction relief pursuant to 28 U.S.C. §2255 without his case file or any other discovery materials.

(b) **Direct Appeal of Ground One:**

(1) If you appealed from the judgment of conviction, did you raise this issue?

Yes ☒   No ☐

(2) If you did not raise this issue in your direct appeal, explain why:

N/A

(c) **Post-Conviction Proceedings:**

(1) Did you raise this issue in any post-conviction motion, petition, or application?

Yes ☒   No ☐

(2) If you answer to Question (c)(1) is "Yes," state:

Type of motion or petition: §2255

Name and location of the court where the motion or petition was filed:

U.S.D.C. Northern District of Alabama

Docket or case number (if you know): 2:15-CV-8043-KOB

Date of the court's decision: January 12, 2018

Result (attach a copy of the court's opinion or order, if available):

Mr. Riggs granted leave to amend his §2255

(3) Did you receive a hearing on your motion, petition, or application?

Yes ☐   No ☒

(4) Did you appeal from the denial of your motion, petition, or application? N/A

Yes ☐   No ☐

(5) If your answer to Question (c)(4) is "Yes," did you raise the issue in the appeal? N/A

Yes ☐   No ☐

(6) If your answer to Question (c)(4) is "Yes," state:

Name and location of the court where the appeal was filed:

N/A

Docket or case number (if you know):

Date of the court's decision:

Result (attach a copy of the court's opinion or order, if available):

(7) If your answer to Question (c)(4) or Question (c)(5) is "No," explain why you did not appeal or raise this issue:

This is a step in an ongoing litigation that is not yet final.

GROUND TWO:

Mr. Riggs was deprived of the effective assistance of counsel at all stages of his criminal proceedings. Thus, he was denied a speedy and public trial.

(a) Supporting facts (Do not argue or cite law. Just state the specific facts that support your claim.):

Mr. Riggs Mr. Riggs adopts by reference the facts contained in ground One. Mr. Riggs is further explicating that the trial counsel either misapprehended the settled law concerning guilty pleas or misrepresented the law to Mr. Riggs. Under either scenario, counsel breached his duty to ensure Mr. Riggs' decision to plead guilty was informed. Counsel's breach of duty not only caused Mr. Riggs to plead guilty unintelligently but also deprived Mr. Riggs of the effective assistance of counsel at a fair trial.

Mr. Riggs is actually innocent of the crimes of conviction, a claim supported by ten alibi witnesses, Mr. Glennon F. Threatt, Jr 's testimony, and this court's judicial notice issued on March 17, 2016. Mr. Riggs has raised issue concerning defense counsel's actual conflict of interest that denied Mr. Riggs the effective assistance of counsel.

These two claims identify that a fundamental miscarriage of justice occurred. Succinctly, an actually innocent person was found guilty because conflicted counsel facilitated an involuntary guilty plea.

In September of 2013, Mr. Riggs alerted the court concerning an actual conflict of interest that affected Mr. Riggs, his attorney Glennon Threatt, the Federal Public Defender's Office, and Alvin Ray Johnson, Jr. As a result of this notice, and because of the seriousness of the claim, the court ordered Mr. Threatt to address

Mr. Riggs' claim about the conflict, without the benefit of unconflicted counsel to protect Mr. Riggs' interests.

Unsurprisingly, Mr. Threatt denied a conflict existed or that the dual representation conflict impaired his ability to represent Mr. Riggs. Mr. Threatt's representation was inaccurate. The conflict required counsel to avoid a trial because the evidence and facts of Mr. Riggs trial had he had the opportunity to proceed to trial – would have made Mr. Threatt's conflict apparent. Correspondingly, the attorneys, Mr. Threatt and Allison Case, convinced Mr. Riggs to enter into a plea agreement, in essence advising Mr. Riggs to forgo his alibi defense, cooperate with authorities, and that both he and his family would receive assistance and protection. This representation likely was untrue rather than merely inaccurate.

Due to the seriousness of the conflict, the court should have appointed unconflicted counsel to advise Mr. Riggs about the conflict. Because unconflicted counsel was not appointed, Mr. Riggs' trial was fundamentally unfair. This court should set aside the judgement and return Mr. Riggs to the pre-plea agreement stage of the proceedings.

1. During Mr. Riggs' pre-trial detention, he was exposed to Alvin Ray Johnson, Jr., who confessed to the drug-related murder-for-hire of DeAndre Washington. Within the confession, Mr. Johnson provided the names of others involved in the scheme. Mr. Riggs reported Mr. Johnson's confession to the district court, the U.S. Marshals Service, and Glennon Threatt. Mr. Threatt in turn advised Mr. Johnson that he would not be receiving the expected downward departure because he had told other inmates about the murder. Mr. Johnson then made additional threats against the lives of both Mr. Threatt and his family.

2. These events were again reported by inmate Gregory Robinson and Mr. Riggs. Following the second event, Mr. Riggs' trial preparations were reduced to discussing Mr. Johnson's case and Mr. Riggs' reports. After two weeks of failed trial preparation – and discovering that Mr. Threatt's representation of Mr. Johnson was a distraction – Mr. Riggs filed a motion raising a conflict of interest in *pro se*.

3. Mr. Riggs' motion, filed on September 3, 2012, requested a hearing to determine if it was a conflict of interest for the Federal Public Defender's Office to represent Mr. Riggs, a witness to a confession of murder. More specifically, Mr. Riggs and Mr. Johnson were both represented by the same lawyer, Mr. Threatt.

4. On or about September 5, 2013, Mr. Riggs was transported to the federal court house in Birmingham, Alabama. While being held in the court's basement Mr. Riggs was counseled by Mr. Threatt, who advised that Mr. Riggs would soon be getting time served for his assistance if he would plea guilty.

5. Later that afternoon, Mr. Riggs was taken into a hearing to determine if a conflict of interest existed. The court failing to appoint unconflicted counsel, conducted the hearing with Mr. Threatt as Mr. Riggs' counsel. On the day of the hearing Mr. Riggs' interests were to prove a conflict of interest existed. Mr. i Threatt's interest was to prove that a conflict did not exist. The interests of Mr. Riggs and Mr. Threatt were in conflict on September 5, 2013. On that day Mr. Riggs was either represented by conflicted counsel or he had no counsel at all.

6. Based upon Mr. Threatt's representation. Magistrate Judge John E. Ott determined that no conflict existed. Upon returning to the basement, Mr. Threatt and Ms. Case visited with Mr. Riggs, giving counsel concerning the events and requirements of a downward departure under U.S.S.G. §5k.1. Mr. Riggs gave protest because he was going to trial and a downward departure would be meaningless. Just the same, Mr. Riggs provided his statement to U.S. Deputy Marshal Keith Blakenship without the benefit of counsel.

7. Upon returning to his place of detention Mr. Riggs was confronted by Mr. Johnson, who declared that Mr. Riggs gave a statement against him. Mr. Johnson made threats against the lives of Mr. Riggs' wife and children. Mr. Riggs, distraught about the events and possibility of yet more killings by Mr. Johnson, this time of Mr. Riggs' own family, called Mr. Threatt after hours. Mr. Riggs, having been earlier advised, decided to take the offered plea, expecting the downward departure and, more importantly, protection for his family.

8. At or around 8:00 P.M on September 5, 2013, Mr. Threatt arrived at Cullman County Jail and advised Mr. Riggs about how the plea agreement would protect his family. Mr. Riggs was earlier advised that he would get time served for his assistance under a §5k.1 departure. Mr. Threatt represented that the plea agreement would provide protection for his family. It was unknown to Mr. Riggs that he was being directed by conflicted counsel to plea guilty under false pretenses. Mr. Riggs was deprived of a speedy and public trial by conflicted counsel.

(b) Direct Appeal of Ground Two:

    (1) If you appealed from the judgment of conviction, did you raise this issue?

        Yes [X]   No [ ]

    (2) If you did not raise this issue in your direct appeal, explain why:

        N/A

(c) Post-Conviction Proceedings:

    (1) Did you raise this issue in any post-conviction motion, petition, or application?

        Yes [X]   No [ ]

    (2) If you answer to Question (c)(1) is "Yes," state:

Type of motion or petition: §2255

Name and location of the court where the motion or petition was filed:

U.S.D.C. Northern District of Alabama

Docket or case number (if you know):   2:15-CV-8043-KOB

Date of the court's decision: January 12, 2018

Result (attach a copy of the court's opinion or order, if available):
Mr. Riggs granted leave to amend his §2255

    (3) Did you receive a hearing on your motion, petition, or application?

        Yes [ ]   No [X]

    (4) Did you appeal from the denial of your motion, petition, or application? N/A

        Yes [ ]   No [ ]

    (5) If your answer to Question (c)(4) is "Yes," did you raise the issue in the appeal? N/A

        Yes [ ]   No [ ]

    (6) If your answer to Question (c)(4) is "Yes," state:

Name and location of the court where the appeal was filed: N/A

N/A

Docket or case number (if you know):

Date of the court's decision:

Result (attach a copy of the court's opinion or order, if available):

    (7) If your answer to Question (c)(4) or Question (c)(5) is "No," explain why you did not appeal or raise this issue:

This a step in an ongoing litigation that is not yet final.

GROUND THREE:

Mr. Riggs was deprived of counsel of multiple critical stages in his criminal case. Thus, he was deprived of a speedy public trial with a compulsory process* for compelling his ten alibi witness.

(a) Supporting facts (Do not argue or cite law. Just state the specific facts that support your claim.):

Mr. Riggs adopts by reference the facts contained in grounds One and Two, here in ground Three. Mr. Riggs is further explicating that he was deprived of counsel at three critical stages in his criminal case. Because of these errors Mr. Riggs was deprived of the trial he so desperately desired.

The record reflects two constants throughout Mr. Riggs' criminal case: One) He demanded a fair trial; and Two) He repeatedly requested the appointment of the effective assistance of counsel. One such record entry was memorialized on or about December 13, 2012. In that hearing Mr. Riggs made verbal requests of the court for the effective assistance of counsel, that would present his alibi defense, in a fair trial. The court concluded that Mr. Riggs needed "a more extensive mental evaluation." Mr. Riggs shows:

1. On or about September 5, 2013, Mr. Riggs was brought to court to determine if a conflict of interest existed between Mr. Riggs, the Federal Public Defender's Office, and Mr. Alvin Ray Johnson, Jr.

2. At the hearing Mr. Riggs and Glennon Threatt, assistant public defender, were present repressing opposite sides of the controversy. The Court did not appoint unconflicted counsel for the hearing. Mr. Riggs was forced to decide between proceeding without counsel or proceeding with conflicted counsel. Mr. Riggs did not waive his right to counsel and/or unconflicted counsel. The court did not advise Mr. Riggs concerning the dangers of proceeding through the hearing with conflicted counsel. Thus, Mr. Riggs fell prey to the effects of counsel who represented interests that were in conflict to Mr. Riggs'.

3. A conflict of interest hearing is a critical stage in the trial process because it holds significant consequences for the accused. A conflict of interest hearing is a qualitatively distinct, discrete, and separate phase or step of a criminal proceeding where the defendant has a right to counsel.

4. In Mr. Riggs' case counsel desperately endeavored to avoid a trial because, in the event of trial, counsel's conflict would have become known. If Mr. Riggs had been allowed to proceed to trial, the proceeding would have implicated others known to Mr. Riggs and Mr. Threatt in criminal conduct that was, or is still not yet, indicted in state proceedings. People such as Brad Taylor, Lakendrick Dunn, Eric Mariano, Brandon Moody, and others.

5. Had the court appointed unconflicted counsel, Mr. Threatt and the Federal Public Defender's Office would have been dismissed from Mr. Riggs' case. He would have proceeded to trial, where proof of official misconduct at the state level, Mr. Riggs' alibi defense, and his efforts as a CI would have been proven. Mr. Riggs would have proven his innocence rather than just legal insufficiency; his life and social status would have been restored years ago. Mr. Riggs would have also proven that Mr. Threatt and Allison Case employed the services of Alvin Ray Johnson, Jr. – who was known to intimidate

witnesses – to coerce guilty pleas from other witnesses. Such as Ray Allen, Gregory Robinson, and others.

6. On or about September 27, 2013, Mr. Threatt engaged in a conversation with another assistant federal public defender, Sabra M. Barnett, concerning Mr. Riggs' activities as a C.I. against a Mexican cartel operating in the Northern District of Alabama. Ms. Barnett advised her client, Lois Rodriguez, that Mr. Riggs was a danger to the criminal cases of cartel members Mr. Riggs was incarcerated with. Ms. Barnett represented to the Alabama State Bar that Mr. Rodriguez was "naive about prison life," notwithstanding his extensive criminal history that extended from Birmingham, Alabama to Barstow, California. MR. Rodriguez was formerly a subject of information Mr. Riggs supplied to a multi-agency task force.

7. On or about October 5, 2013, Mr. Rodriguez advised Mr. Riggs about Ms. Barnett's notification and advised Mr. Riggs that he could not remain in the same cell block with the Cartel. Upon making this discovery Mr. Riggs moved to withdraw his plea agreement, realizing he was only endangered by the Federal Public Defender's Office.

8. On or about October 18, 2013, Mr. Riggs was present in another hearing to determine if a conflict existed. Mr. Riggs had filed for the appointment of unconflicted counsel once again and again present in the court room without the benefit of counsel. The motion for counsel was granted.

9. On or about October 30, 2013, Mr. Brett Bloomston filed his notice of appearance. (DE-60) Mr. Bloomston filed no substantive motion from the time of his appointment. Although Mr. Riggs' filing of motions in prose and the governments motions in response constituted a lengthy dialog, Mr. Bloomston failed to even amend or clarify Mr. Riggs' motion to withdraw his guilty plea. Mr. Riggs was constructively denied counsel at a critical, post plea but pre-sentence, stage in his criminal proceeding.

10. On or about April 30, 2014, Mr. Riggs filed his notice of appeal and Mr. Bloomston was appointed as appellate counsel. Notwithstanding the obvious errors, Mr. Bloomston withdrew as appellate counsel. Mr. Riggs was once again abandoned by counsel at a critical stage of his criminal proceeding. Mr. Riggs was forced to proceed in appeal without the benefit of counsel.

(b) **Direct Appeal of Ground Three:**

   (1) If you appealed from the judgment of conviction, did you raise this issue?

       Yes ☒   No ☐

   (2) If you did not raise this issue in your direct appeal, explain why:

     N/A

(c) **Post-Conviction Proceedings:**

   (1) Did you raise this issue in any post-conviction motion, petition, or application?

       Yes ☒   No ☐

   (2) If you answer to Question (c)(1) is "Yes," state:

Type of motion or petition: §2255

Name and location of the court where the motion or petition was filed:

  U.S.D.C. Northern District of Alabama

Docket or case number (if you know): 2:15-CV-8043-KOB

Date of the court's decision: January 12, 2018

Result (attach a copy of the court's opinion or order, if available):

  Mr. Riggs granted leave to amend his §2255

   (3) Did you receive a hearing on your motion, petition, or application?

       Yes ☐   No ☒

   (4) Did you appeal from the denial of your motion, petition, or application? N/A

       Yes ☐   No ☐

   (5) If your answer to Question (c)(4) is "Yes," did you raise the issue in the appeal? N/A

       Yes ☐   No ☐

   (6) If your answer to Question (c)(4) is "Yes," state: N/A

Name and location of the court where the appeal was filed:

     N/A

Docket or case number (if you know):

Date of the court's decision:

Result (attach a copy of the court's opinion or order, if available):

   (7) If your answer to Question (c)(4) or Question (c)(5) is "No," explain why you did not appeal or raise this issue:

  This is a step in an ongoing litigation that is not yet filed.

GROUND FOUR

Mr. Riggs incarceration is unconstitutional because his conviction is a manifest miscarriage of justice:

Mr. Riggs is actually innocent and has been incarcerated without the benefit of a fair trial.

(a) Supporting facts (Do not argue or cite law. Just state the specific facts that support your claim.):

Mr. Riggs adopts by reference the facts contained in grounds One, Two, and Three here in ground Four. Mr. Riggs is further explicating that his actual innocence serves to overcome all procedural bars. Thus, his claims require resolution on their merits. The claims and facts herein must be presumed as true unless definitively rebutted by the record.

Had Mr. Riggs been appointed adequate representation he would have been able to present the evidence in his criminal case, above and beyond his alibi defense that would have proven his innocence at a fair trial. At trial Mr. Riggs would have proven:

1. In or about October of 2008, Mr. Riggs and his family moved to St. Clair County Alabama. By the next spring Mr. Riggs began work in Jefferson County Alabama, the Northern district of Alabama. A short time into employment Mr. Riggs found himself, once again, assisting law enforcement. He was helping to identify opioid and amphetamine dealers who catered to those employed in the construction fields.

2. Within 18 months of service, to random task force officers, Mr. Riggs' efforts began to take its toll on Mr. Riggs' marriage. After giving birth to her fourth child Mrs. Riggs had little toleration for the long nights and sporadic absences of Mr. Riggs. By the fall of 2011 a separation was imminent.

3. In November of 2011, Mr. Riggs donated a kidney to a fellow veteran at the University of Alabama at Birmingham Hospital. Upon his discharge Mr. Riggs was required to find another home. The voluntary surgery was an additional stress Mrs. Riggs could not bear. Mr. Riggs then rented an additional home at 801 Argo Margarette Road; Trussville, Alabama.

4. Within a couple of months Mr. and Mrs. Riggs began to see each other romantically on a regular basis. Mrs. Riggs would often stay overnight with Mr. Riggs at his home. During their courtship Mr. and Mrs. Riggs had taken amateur nude pictures of one another which they maintained in their cellular phones.

5. In March or possibly in early April of 2012, Mrs. Riggs fell ill. Mr. Riggs, unable to reach Mrs. Riggs, went to Mrs. Riggs' hone and found her unresponsive on her living room floor. Once hospitalized, Mr. Riggs stayed by Mrs. Riggs' side for approximately three days.

6. Upon Mrs. Riggs being discharged from the hospital, Mr. Riggs took her to her home. Upon arrival Mr. Riggs found her home had been broken into. Mr. and Mrs. Riggs left and went to Mr. Riggs' home and found it had been broken into as well. After evaluating the damages to both properties Mr.

and Mrs. Riggs discovered that their only losses were two door locks, a SIM card belonging to Mrs. Riggs, and a phone from Mr. Riggs' home.

7. In or around March, 2012, Mr. Riggs' roommate ad was answered. Unknown to Mr. Riggs, however, it was answered by police informant Joy Brown, who was operating under the alias "Laney Jones." Ms. Brown and Mr. Riggs had become acquainted over the next couple of months. Mr. Riggs also introduced her to others acquainted to Mr. Riggs. Ms. Brown took a specific interest in Tim Simons and his cousin Breanna.

8. On or about May 14, 2012, Ms. Brown rented the space in Mr. Riggs' home—the next day. On May 15, 2012, Ms. Brown asked that Mr. Riggs allow an internet connection in his home. Mr. Riggs refused.

9. On or about May 16, 2012, Ms. Brown purchased an internet-ready cellular phone at Wal-Mart in Trussville, Alabama. After purchasing her new phone Ms. Brown asked to use the SIM card of one of Mr. Riggs' broken cellular phones.

10. After Mr. Riggs' arrest, and within the first week, Ms. Brown, speaking with Mr. Riggs over jail house phone, admitted to sending nude pictures of Mr. Riggs from her cellular phone.

11. In a meeting with his first appointed lawyer, Jeffrey Bramer, Mr. Riggs expressed what he had talked to Ms. Brown about during their phone conversation. Mr. Riggs also gave Mr. Bramer a list of many alibi witnesses and discussed everything he knew about "Breanna." Mr. Riggs informed Mr. Bramer that he had only known Breanna for a couple of months. Mr. Riggs explained that he had worked on her car, that she was a waitress at Olive Garden in Gardendale, Alabama, and that he had only talked to her a couple of times over the phone.

12. Mr. Bramer had shown Mr. Riggs pictures of Mr. Riggs and Mrs. Riggs – the nude pictures they had made of each other and kept in their respective phones – and Mr. Riggs immediately identified the pictures as the ones contained only in the phones that had been stolen during the break-ins. Mr. Bramer had also disclosed that the alleged girl in the charged offense used the name "Breanna."

13. Mr. Bramer was adamant that Mr. Riggs was set up for some unknown reason and that he would have the case in a trial very quickly. After only a few days Mr. Bramer had confirmed all that Mr. Riggs had told him. Mr. Bramer informed Mr. Riggs that Joy Brown was working-off charges.

14. A couple of weeks later Mr. Bramer visited Mr. Riggs at Shelby County Jail and asked only one additional question. Mr. Bramer asked Mr. Riggs if he had been assisting law enforcement officers in drug related investigations. After Mr. Riggs answered in the affirmative, Mr. Bramer advised that Mr. Riggs should plea guilty if he knew what was good for him.

Had Mr. Riggs been granted the opportunity to present the facts of his criminal case in a fair trial with the effective assistance of counsel Mr. Riggs could have proven that he is innocent. Additionally, and as a matter of fact, Mr. Riggs could have proven he wasn't even present when the alleged conduct occurred.

(b) **Direct Appeal of Ground Four:**

    (1) If you appealed from the judgment of conviction, did you raise this issue?

        Yes [X]   No [ ]

    (2) If you did not raise this issue in your direct appeal, explain why:

    N/A

(c) **Post-Conviction Proceedings:**

    (1) Did you raise this issue in any post-conviction motion, petition, or application?

        Yes [X]   No [ ]

    (2) If you answer to Question (c)(1) is "Yes," state:

    Type of motion or petition: §2255

    Name and location of the court where the motion or petition was filed:

    U.S.D.C. Northern District of Alabama

    Docket or case number (if you know):   2:15-CV-8043-KOB

    Date of the court's decision: January 12, 2018

    Result (attach a copy of the court's opinion or order, if available):

    Mr. Riggs granted leave to amend his §2255

    (3) Did you receive a hearing on your motion, petition, or application?

        Yes [ ]   No [X]

    (4) Did you appeal from the denial of your motion, petition, or application?   N/A

        Yes [ ]   No [ ]

    (5) If your answer to Question (c)(4) is "Yes," did you raise the issue in the appeal? N/A

        Yes [ ]   No [ ]

    (6) If your answer to Question (c)(4) is "Yes," state:

    Name and location of the court where the appeal was filed:

    N/A

Docket or case number (if you know): _____

Date of the court's decision: _____

Result (attach a copy of the court's opinion or order, if available):

    (7) If your answer to Question (c)(4) or Question (c)(5) is "No," explain why you did not appeal or raise this issue:

    This is a step in an ongoing litigation that is not yet final.

13. Is there any ground in this motion that you have <u>not</u> previously presented in some federal court? If so, which ground or grounds have not been presented, and state your reasons for not presenting them:

No

14. Do you have any motion, petition, or appeal <u>now pending</u> (filed and not decided yet) in any court for the ground you are challenging?　　　Yes ⎡X⎤　　　No ⎡　⎤

If "Yes," state the name and location of the court, the docket or case number, the type of proceeding, and the issues raised.

This amended motion is in continuation to the original §2255 proceeding initiated on November 10, 2015, in Case No.: 2:15-CV-8043-KOB

15. Give the name and address, if known, of each attorney who represented you in the following stages of the proceedings you are challenging:

(a) At the preliminary hearing:

Jeffrey Bramer and David Luker

(b) At the arraignment and plea:

Glennon Threatt and Allison Case

(c) At the trial:

N/A

(d) At sentencing:

Brett Bloomston

(e) On appeal:

Brett Bloomston

(f) In any post-conviction proceeding:

Pro Se

(g) On appeal from any ruling against you in a post-conviction proceeding:

N/A

16. Were you sentenced on more than one court of an indictment, or on more than one indictment, in the same court and at the same time? Yes [X] No [ ]

17. Do you have any future sentence to serve after you complete the sentence for the judgment that you are challenging? Yes [ ] No [X]

    (a) If so, give name and location of court that imposed the other sentence you will serve in the future:

    N/A

    (b) Give the date the other sentence was imposed: N/A

    (c) Give the length of the other sentence: N/A

    (d) Have you filed, or do you plan to file, any motion, petition, or application that challenges the judgment or sentence to be served in the future? N/A Yes [ ] No [ ]

18. TIMELINESS OF MOTION: If your judgment of conviction became final over one year ago, you must explain why the one-year statute of limitations as contained in 28 U.S.C. § 2255 does not bar your motion.*

    This amended motion is timely because all claims relate back to claims in Mr. Riggs' original §2255, and amendment was authorized by an order of the district court.

---

* The Antiterrorism and Effective Death Penalty Act of 1996 ("AEDPA") as contained in 28 U.S.C. § 2255, paragraph 6, provides in part that:

  A one-year period of limitation shall apply to a motion under this section. The limitation period shall run from the latest of –

  (1) the date on which the judgment of conviction became final;

  (2) the date on which the impediment to making a motion created by governmental action in violation of the Constitution or laws of the United States is removed, if the movant was prevented from making such a motion by such governmental action;

  (3) the date on which the right asserted was initially recognized by the Supreme Court, if that right has been newly recognized by the Supreme Court and made retroactively applicable to cases on collateral review; or

  (4) the date on which the facts supporting the claim or claims presented could have been discovered through the exercise of due diligence.

Therefore, movant asks that the Court grant the following relief: Mr. Riggs asks this court to vacate his sentence and conviction. Thus, returning him to the pre plea stage of his trial process.

or any other relief to which movant may be entitled.

_____

Signature of Attorney (if any)

I declare (or certify, verify, or state) under penalty of perjury that the foregoing is true and correct and that this Motion under 28 U.S.C. § 2255 was placed in the prison mailing system on _____ .

(month, date, year)

Executed (signed) on _____ (date)

_____

Signature of Movant

If the person signing is not movant, state relationship to movant and explain why movant is not signing this motion.

IN THE UNITED STATES DISTRICT COURT FOR THE
NORTHERN DISTRICT OF ALABAMA
SOUTHERN DIVISION

KELLY PATRICK RIGGS,   )
)
       Petitioner,   )
)
v.   )   Case No. 2:15-CV-08043-KOB
)
UNITED STATES OF AMERICA,)
       Respondent.   )

ORDER TO SHOW CAUSE

This matter is before the court on Kelly Patrick Riggs's Amended Motion to Vacate, Set Aside, or Correct Sentence filed pursuant to 28 U.S.C. § 2255. (Doc. 63).

The court ORDERS that the Government appear and show cause in writing within **twenty-one days** from the date of this Order why the court should not grant the relief requested by the movant. The answer or return furnished by the Government should provide a thorough discussion of all matters of fact and law relating to the movant's claims.

The court ORDERS the Government to furnish copies of any court records, briefs, transcripts, or other documents that may be pertinent to the matters discussed in its answer.

The court DIRECTS the Clerk to serve a copy of this Order upon the movant and to serve a copy of this Order and a copy of the movant's amended motion (doc. 63) upon the United States Attorney for the Northern District of Alabama.

DONE and ORDERED this 2nd day of March, 2018.

_____
KARON OWEN BOWDRE
CHIEF UNITED STATES DISTRICT JUDGE

UNITED STATES DISTRICT COURT
NORTHERN DISTRICT OF ALABAMA
SOUTHERN DIVISION

KELLY PATRICK RIGGS

v.

UNITED STATES OF AMERICA

_____ /

Case No.:

2:15-CV-8043-KOB

MOTION FOR THE APPOINTMENT OF COUNSEL

Mr. Riggs moves the court to appoint counsel as authorized under 18 U.S.C. §3006A. He believes good cause exists because this §2255 action has become complex. He shows the following in support:

1. That his criminal prosecution and subsequent conviction, appeal, and post-conviction proceedings are by-products of previous interactions with State of Alabama law enforcement entities.

2. It is quite likely that many who are involved, in the federal level of this case, are unaware of all the aspects involved. With the possible exception of Glennon Threatt, who is acquainted with LaKendrick Dunn, and Sabra Barnett, who discussed Mr. Riggs' efforts as a C.I. with Glennon Threatt on 9-27-13 and with Cartel associates on 10-5-13.

3. Mr. Riggs has identified 64 possible witnesses that include unnoticed bar members both state and federal; federal agents from three different field offices; local task force officers; and the seven remaining alibi witnesses.

4. That this case also has an unaddressed correlation with the murder of Sambo Hazelrig and that the Obstruction of Justice by Hoover City Police Department may have been a factor in facilitating that murder.

Wherefore, Mr. Riggs seeks counsel to prepare for further proceedings. In his §2255 motion, its Amendment, and the court's docket, three claims are presented that are untenable by the government. Thus, he moves this court to appoint counsel to assist him.

Kelly P. Riggs
_____
Kelly Patrick Riggs

CERTIFICATE OF SERVICE

Mr. Riggs has served all parties as required by law and rule.

(signature)

Kelly Patrick Riggs

UNITED STATES DISTRICT COURT
NORTHERN DISTRICT OF ALABAMA
SOUTHERN DIVISION

KELLY PATRICK RIGGS,   Case No.:

Petitioner

V.   2:15-CV-8043-K0B

UNITED STATES,

      Respondent

_____/

MOTION FOR AN ORDER TO PROVIDE SERVICE
OF GOVERNMENTS RESPONSE

Mr. Riggs moves this court to provide its active protection in securing his constitutional right to due process. The record reflects that Mr. Riggs filed an amendment to his §2255 in good faith. This court issued an order for the government to show cause. On or about April 2, 2018, Mr. Riggs was notified, by an independent advocacy organization, that the government filed its response on March 20, 2018, but failed to serve Mr. Riggs. It is well established that due process requires the government to provide service to a party or the party's attorney.

Mr. Riggs is convinced the governments conduct in this matter is simply an oversight rather than nefarious behavior. Thus, requiring only a reminder from this court.

Wherefore, Mr. Riggs moves this court to issue an order requiring the government to provide service, to Mr. Riggs, through authorized legal mail channels and a specified adequate time for Mr. Riggs to file any appropriate reply. Mr. Riggs needs only 15 days from the date he signs for delivery of the government's response, thus moves this court to specifically particularize this request in its order.

Kelly P. Riggs
_____
Kelly Patrick Riggs

CERTIFICATE OF SERVICE

I hereby certify that a true and correct copy of this motion has been served on all parties as required by rule and law.

Respectfully submitted this 4 day of April, 2018

Kelly Patrick Riggs

IN THE UNITED STATES DISTRICT COURT
FOR THE NORTHERN DISTRICT OF ALABAMA
SOUTHERN DIVISION

KELLY PATRICK RIGGS	)	
	)	
v.	)	CaseNo.
	)	2:15-CV-8043-KOB
UNITED STATES OF AMERICA	)	

UNITED STATES' RESPONSE TO PETITIONER KELLY PATRICK RIGGS' AMENDED 28 U.S.C. S 2255 MOTION TO VACATE

The United States respectfully responds to Petitioner Kelly Patrick Riggs' amended 28 U.S.C. § 2255 motion to vacate his sentence (Doc. 63). In his amended motion, Riggs asserts a freestanding claim of actual innocence. He also renews his claim that each of his Court-appointed counsel was ineffective. For the following reasons, the Court should deny Riggs' motion without a hearing.

BACKGROUND

Following an undercover operation, Riggs was charged with one count of enticement of a minor, in violation of 18 U.S.C. § 2242(b), and one count of transfer of obscene material to a minor, in violation of 18 U.S.C. § 1470. Riggs subsequently pled guilty to both counts, in a binding plea agreement. See Cr. Doc. 55, 89.[1] One month later, Riggs moved to withdraw his plea. Cr. Doc. 57, 58. After holding a hearing and finding "no legitimate reason to set aside the guilty plea," the Court denied the motion. Cr. Minute Entry (Dec. 20, 2013); Cr. Doc. 114 at 92:4. In accordance with the binding plea agreement, the Court sentenced Riggs to concurrent sentences of 120 months, followed by 60 months of supervised release. Cr. Doc. 89.

During the course of the case, Riggs was represented by four Court-appointed attorneys. Riggs was initially represented by Jeffrey Bramer, until Mr. Bramer moved to withdraw citing ethical concerns. See Cr. Doc. 3, 18. Next, Riggs was represented by David Luker, until Riggs asked to represent himself and Mr. Luker informed the Court that his relationship with Riggs "had devolved to the point that it was not reconcilable." Cr. Doc. 34 at 3; see Cr. Doc. 100. Assistant Federal Public Defenders Glennon Threatt and Allison Case then represented Riggs, until Riggs moved to withdraw his guilty plea and again asked to represent himself. Cr. Doc. 57, 58. Brett Bloomston represented Riggs for the remainder of the proceedings.

Riggs appealed the judgment against him. Mr. Bloomston filed an Anders brief asserting there were no issues of arguable merit and sought to withdraw from representation. Riggs then filed a *pro se* response claiming, among other things, that he was innocent, that he had not knowingly and voluntarily pled guilty,

---

[1] Documents from Riggs' underlying criminal case are cited in this brief as "Cr. Doc." Pursuant to the Court's order (Doc. 4 at 2), the United States provided documents pertinent to Riggs' petitions in an appendix filed with its original response.

that each of his Court-appointed counsel had provided ineffective assistance, and that his speedy trial rights had been violated. *Pro se* Br. of Appellant, Riggs v. United States, No. 14-11917 (11th Cir. filed Sept. 26, 2014). The Eleventh Circuit affirmed Riggs' convictions and sentences, finding there were "no arguable issues of merit." United States v. Riggs, 589 Fed. Appx. 523, 524 (11th Cir. 2015).

On November 16, 2015, Riggs filed his original Section 2255 motion. Doc.1 Riggs claimed, among other things, that his Court-appointed counsel were ineffective and that he did not knowingly and voluntarily plea guilty. On December 2015, the United States filed a response asking the Court to deny Riggs' motion without a hearing. Doc. 13.

ARGUMENT

The Court should deny Riggs' motion without a hearing. Riggs is barred from litigating his Section 2255 claims because the Eleventh Circuit has already adjudicated those claims against him. In addition, Riggs' arguments are patently frivolous, conclusory, or affirmatively contradicted by the record—and completely without merit. See *Diveroli v. United States*, 803 F.3d 1258, 1263 (11th Cir. 2015) ("a district court need not hold a hearing if the allegations are patently frivolous, based upon unsupported generalizations, or affirmatively contradicted by the record") (internal quotations omitted).[2]

I.   The Court Should Reject Riggs' Claim of Actual Innocence

Riggs claims he is entitled to *habeas* relief because he is actually innocent of the crimes of conviction (Doc. 63 at 4). Riggs' claim is not valid, it is procedurally barred, and it is without merit.

Riggs does not present a valid claim. In non-capital cases, a substantive claim of actual innocence is not a ground for *habeas* relief. See *Herrera v. Collins*, 506 U.S. 390, 400 (1993) (holding that in non-capital cases, federal *habeas* relief is not available for freestanding claims of actual innocence); Jordan v. Sec'y, Dep't of Corr., 485 F.3d 1351, 1356 (11th Cir.2007) (same). Actual innocence is merely a "gateway" for petitioners to request courts to consider Section 2255 claims that are otherwise procedurally defaulted, or time barred. Rozzelle v. Sec 'y, Fla. Dep't of Corr., 672 F.3d 1000, 1011 (11th Cir. 2012); United States v. Montano, 398 F.3d 1276, 1284 (11th Cir. 2005) (Actual innocence "serves only to lift the procedural bar" to a Section 2255 motion). At most, Riggs' claim of actual innocence could excuse a procedural default in his Section 2255 claims.

Even if Riggs' claim were cognizable, Riggs cannot litigate it here because the Eleventh Circuit has already adjudicated that claim against him. Defendants may not collaterally attack matters "decided adversely to [them] on direct appeal."

United States v. Nyhuis, 211 F.3d 1340, 1343 (11th Cir. 2000).[3] On appeal, Riggs asked the Eleventh Circuit to "revers[e]" his conviction because he was "actually innocent" of the crimes of conviction. See *Pro se* Br. of Appellant at 19. The Eleventh Circuit rejected that argument and affirmed Riggs'

---

2 The Court is required to hold a hearing, however, if, "accepting] all of the petitioner's alleged facts as true," the petitioner has alleged facts that "would entitle him to relief." *Diaz v. United States*, 930 F.2d 832, 834 (11th Cir. 1991).

3 Similarly, Riggs is barred from re-litigating matters decided by this Court under the law-of-the-case doctrine. See Toole v. Baxter Healthcare Corp., 235 F.3d 1307, 1313 (11th Cir. 2000); see also *Rozier v. United States*, 701 F.3d 681, 684 (11th Cir. 2012) (applying the doctrine in the context of a § 2255 proceeding).

convictions. Riggs, 589 Fed. Appx. at 524.[4] Therefore, Riggs is barred from challenging the sufficiency of the evidence in this petition.[5]

In any event, Riggs' claim is meritless. Riggs clearly enticed and transferred obscene material to a minor, as proscribed by federal law.[6] Law enforcement arrested Riggs after he arranged to have sex with a minor. See Cr. Doc. 55 at 4-5. Riggs admitted to the offenses in a Mirandized, videotaped confession. See, e.g, Cr. Doc. 114 at 45:4-23 (Mr. Threatt testifying about the confession); id. at 88:14- lb. At the change of plea hearing, Riggs admitted—under oath—that he knowingly used the internet and a cell phone to "entice" a person he believed to be fourteen years old "to engage in sexual activity," and that he transferred "obscene matter" to that person. Cr. Doc. 62 at 27:6-17. He also admitted that the facts contained in the plea agreement were "accurate." Id. at 26:21-24. As the Court stated in denying Riggs' motion to withdraw his guilty plea, the evidence against Riggs is "very strong." Cr. Doc. 114 at 88. Riggs presents no reason to reconsider that determination.[7]

In sum, Riggs' actual innocence claim is not valid, it is procedurally barred, and it is entirely without merit.

II. The Court Should Reject Riggs' Claims of Ineffective Assistance of Counsel

Riggs renews his claims that his various Court-appointed counsel – Mr. Bramer, Mr. Luker, Mr. Threatt, Ms. Case, and Mr. Bloomston – provided ineffective assistance. Riggs' claim is procedurally barred and without merit.[8]

---

4 This Court also rejected Riggs' claim, stating it did not have a "glimmer" Riggs was innocent of the charges against him. Cr. Doc. 114 at 88:9-22.

5 Riggs also waived his right to challenge the sufficiency of the evidence in his guilty plea. See Cr. Doc. 55 at 10-11 (waiving all appellate and post-conviction rights except for claims relating to illegal sentences, sentences imposed above the advisory guideline range, and ineffective assistance of counsel); Cr. Doc. 62 at 9:13, 13:8-15:2 (in-court colloquy regarding the rights Riggs would waive by pleading guilty).

6 Notably, actual innocence means factual innocence, not "mere legal insufficiency." *Bousey v. United States*, 523 U.S. 614, 623 (1998); *McKay v. United States*, 657 F.3d 1190, 1197 (11th Cir. 2011).

7 Riggs' claims otherwise are flatly contradicted by the record. Riggs alleges he talked to an adult woman, and not the minor, when he committed the crimes in question. Doc. 63 at 23. At Riggs' hearing to withdraw his guilty plea, however, Mr. Threatt testified that he had interviewed this woman, who "denied ever having spoken to [Riggs]." Cr. Doc. 114 at 77. Likewise, the Court can summarily dismiss Riggs' claim that he was framed by a police informant. As the Court noted, Riggs has a long history of deceitfulness and manipulation. See, e.g., Cr. Doc. 114 at 15:3- 16:9; 18:13-16; 89:14-24; 91:2-10; see also Cr. Doc. 116 at 22:7-18 (describing Riggs' "contradictory" statements throughout the course of the case, and stating that Riggs was either "the most brazen liar who has ever been in my court" or someone with absolutely...no idea what the truth is"). Finally, both the Eleventh Circuit and this Court have rejected Riggs' claim that his plea was coerced. Riggs, 589 Fed. Appx. at 524; Cr. Doc. 114 at 88:14-90:3.

8 In its original response, the United States argued that Riggs waived any ineffective-assistance claims relating to pre-plea conduct when he knowingly and voluntarily pled guilty. See Doc. 13 at 7. Although this is generally true, see, e.g., *Wilson v. United States*, 962 F.2d 996, 997 (11th Cir. 1992), the plea agreement states that Riggs reserved his right to raise ineffective assistance of counsel claims in any appeal or post-conviction proceeding. Cr. Doc. 55 at 10-11. Accordingly, the United States will not argue that Riggs waived his ineffective-assistance claims.

Riggs cannot re-litigate his ineffective-assistance claims because the Eleventh Circuit already adjudicated that matter against him. On appeal, Riggs claimed that each of his trial counsel was ineffective: Mr. Bloomston, see *Pro se* Br. of Appellant at 5-7, 10; Mr. Threatt and Ms. Case, see id. at 11-12; Mr. Luker, see id. at 13; and Mr. Bramer, see id. at 14-15.[9] The Eleventh Circuit rejected those claims. Riggs, 589 Fed. Appx. at 524. Therefore, Riggs is barred from re-litigating the matter in this petition. See Nyhuis, 211 F.3d at 1343.

In any event, Riggs' ineffective-assistance claims are meritless. To prevail on a claim of ineffective assistance of counsel, one must show that (1) "counsel's performance was deficient," i.e., it "fell below an objective standard of reasonableness," and (2) "the deficient performance prejudiced the defense." Strickland v. Washington, 466 U.S. 668, 687-88 (1984). As discussed in greater detail in the United States' original response (Doc. 13 at 6-17), Riggs has not established—and cannot establish—either Strickland prong.

Riggs has not demonstrated any deficiency in Mr. Bramer or Mr. Luker's performance as counsel. Conclusory allegations of an inadequate pre-trial investigation—that these attorneys failed to investigate defenses or meet witnesses[10]—do not "warrant an evidentiary hearing," let alone relief. United States v. Chandler, 950 F. Supp. 1545,1558 (N.D. Ala. 1996). Additionally, Riggs has not shown that correcting any of these supposed deficiencies would have made a difference in the outcome, i.e., would have resulted in an acquittal or, at the very least, would have led Riggs to elect a trial over a guilty plea. See Hill v. Lockhart, 474 U.S. 52, 59 (1985).

Similarly, Riggs has not demonstrated any deficiency in the representation provided by Mr. Threatt and Ms. Case. This Court has already rejected Riggs' claims (Doc. 63 at 7-9) that Mr. Threatt and Ms. Case provided information about his case to prison gang members, and coerced Riggs to plea guilty in exchange for protection from a fellow inmate. See Cr. Doc. 114 at 88. Likewise, Magistrate Judge John E. Ott rejected Riggs' claim (Doc. 63 at 12-14) that Mr. Threatt's representation of that inmate disqualified him from representing Riggs. See Cr. Doc. 109 at 7; see also Cr. Doc. 114 at 5:17-6:11. Further, Riggs' claims (Doc. 63 at 9) that these attorneys failed to investigate the case, or interview or subpoena witnesses, lies in square conflict with Mr. Threatt's testimony concerning the assistance the Federal Public Defender's Office provided Riggs. See, e.g., Cr. Doc. 114 at 55:18-22 (Mr. Threatt explaining that subpoenas were issued for "at least ten people," and that he had spoken to "at least eight of them" about matters Riggs had asked Mr. Threatt to investigate); 74:14-75:10 (Mr. Threatt explaining his advice not to assert an alibi defense inconsistent with Riggs' videotaped confession); 85:3-14 (Mr. Threatt testifying that he "conscientiously represented" Riggs "to the best of [his] ability").

Riggs also has not shown that Mr. Bloomston performed deficiently. Riggs' allegation that Mr. Bloomston failed to clarify or amend Riggs' motion to withdraw his guilty plea (Doc. 63 at 19) can be dismissed summarily. Mr. Bloomston strongly advocated on Riggs' behalf, arguing that the Court should allow Riggs to withdraw his plea because Riggs had been denied the close assistance of counsel, and because granting Riggs' request would conserve judicial resources and would not prejudice the United States. See Cr. Doc. 114 at 31-32. Moreover, there is no prejudice. The Court correctly determined that

---

9 Mr. Bloomston stated in his Anders brief that Riggs had "no viable claim of ineffective assistance of counsel." Br. of Appellant at 8.

10 The Court should reject any ineffective-assistance claims relating to Riggs' assertions that he believed he was communicating to an adult woman, or that he was framed by a police informant. These allegations are flatly contradicted by the record. See note 5, supra

Riggs had knowingly and voluntarily pled guilty, with the close assistance of "three outstanding defense attorneys." Cr. Doc. 114 at 88-89. Riggs cannot demonstrate any defect in the Court's ruling, or any non-frivolous basis to challenge it.

Riggs' claim that Mr. Bloomston was ineffective because he did not file any substantive motions (Doc. 63 at 19) likewise fails. By the time Mr. Bloomston represented Riggs, Riggs had already pled guilty to the mandatory minimum sentence. Any deficiency, therefore, could not have affected the convictions or sentences Riggs received. Finally, Mr. Bloomston was not ineffective for filing an Anders brief. As the Eleventh Circuit stated, there were "no arguable issues of merit" for appeal. Riggs, 589 Fed. Appx. at 524.[11]

In sum, Riggs' ineffective-assistance claims are procedurally barred and entirely without merit.

CONCLUSION

The Court should deny Riggs' motion without a hearing. The Court also should not issue Riggs a certificate of appealability because Riggs has not made "a substantial showing" that he was denied a constitutional right. 28 U.S.C. § 2253(c) (2).

Respectfully submitted on March 20, 2018.

JAY E. TOWN
United States Attorney

/s/Manu K. Balachandran
MANU K. BALACHANDRAN
Assistant United States Attorney

---

[11] Riggs also claims that the ineffective assistance of his attorneys violated his right to a speedy trial. Doc. 63. at 12. As noted (Doc. 13 at 14), Riggs waived his right to a speedy trial. That waiver, moreover, operated to Riggs' advantage because it provided his new counsel—Mr. Luker, who had been appointed less than two weeks before—time to prepare for trial. Any further delays are attributable to Riggs who, as the Court stated, repeatedly "manufactured" problems with each of his attorneys "every time [h]e got close to trial." Cr. Doc. 114 at 16:5

KELLY PATRICK RIGGS

CERTIFICATE OF SERVICE

I hereby certify that on March 20, 2018,1 filed a copy of the foregoing notice with the Clerk of the Court using the CM/ECF system, which will provide defense counsel with a copy of the same.

/s/*Manu K. Balachandran*
MANU K. BALACHANDRAN
Assistant United States Attorney

ADDRESS OF COUNSEL:

United States Attorney's Office
1801 Fourth Avenue North
Birmingham, AL 35203
Telephone: (205)244-2108
Fax: (205)244-2182
Email: Manu.Balachandran@usdoj.gov

UNITED STATES DISTRICT COURT
NORTHERN DISTRICT OF ALABAMA
SOUTHERN DIVISION

KELLY PATRICK RIGGS

v.

UNITED STATES OF AMERICA

_____/

Case No.:

2:15-CV-8043-KOB

MR. RIGGS' REPLY TO "UNITED STATES' RESPONSE"

Mr. Riggs has recently filed his amended 28 U.S.C. §2255 motion. The government opposes the motion, notwithstanding the fact that the A.U.S.A conceded several critical issues. Moreover, the government's response merely places some of Mr. Riggs' allegations into contest. Consequently, governing authorities requires this court to conduct an evidentiary hearing to determine the facts. 28 U.S.C. §2255(b). Alternatively, this court should predicate its decision on Mr. Riggs' facts and events as they are presented in his amended §2255.

Mr. Riggs addresses the government's response in three parts:

1. Mr. Riggs demonstrates that on the existing record he was deprives of counsel at critical stages of the criminal proceedings. This claim is conceded by the government.

2. Mr. Riggs demonstrates that on the existing record he has a judicially noticed alibi defense establishing his actual innocence. This claim is conceded by the government.

3. Mr. Riggs demonstrates that on the existing record he was deprived of the effective assistance of counsel where Glennon F. Threatt, Jr. provided false information to his client, Mr. Riggs, and the district court. This claim is conceded by the government.

Mr. Riggs provides a clarifying explanation for each claim in turn.

1. Mr. Riggs demonstrates that on the existing record he was deprived of counsel at critical stages of the criminal proceeding. This claim is conceded by the government.

First, Mr. Riggs points out that ground Two of his amended §2255 raises a *Cronic* error that the government conceded by failing to address the issue. Mr. Riggs stands firmly on all points raised in his original and amended §2255 motions. This reply will address only the points raised in the government's response that require a reply and reiterate claims the government conceded.

The crux of the government's response is hinged on an erroneous belief that the Eleventh Circuit Court of Appeals' decision serves as a bar, and that "Riggs cannot relitigate his ineffective-assistance claims because the Eleventh Circuit already adjudicated that matter against him." The government's contention that "The court should deny Riggs' motion without a hearing. Riggs is barred from litigating his section §2255 claims because the Eleventh Circuit has already adjudicated those claims against him" is clearly wrong.

In Mr. Riggs' Ground Two he claimed that he "… was deprived of the effective assistance of counsel …" Due to Mr. Riggs being abandoned by counsel at direct appeal, coupled with his ignorance of law, this claim—that he was without counsel—was never raised on direct appeal. Thus, the court of appeals was unable to adjudicate the claim.

Moreover, the court could easily find what the higher courts have previously held, that it is a constitutional right to have the assistance of counsel at trial, but yet a violation that is ordinarily unreviewable on direct appeal. The Eleventh Circuit Court of Appeals holds that "A claim of ineffective assistance of counsel may not be raised on direct appeal where the claim has not been heard by the district court nor a factual record developed."

United States v. Khoury, 901 F.2d 948, 969 (11th Cir. 1990); "The preferred method of raising the issue of ineffective assistance of counsel is not on direct appeal, but instead in a 28 U.S.C. §2255 motion to vacate." *Massaro v. United States*, 538 U.S. 500 (2003); "only when the record is sufficiently developed will we consider an ineffective assistance claim on direct appeal." *United States v. Bender*, 290 F.3d 1279, 1284 (11th Cir. 2002).

In Mr. Riggs' claim Two he showed in pertinent part that,

> "...Mr. Riggs was taken into a hearing to determine if a conflict of interest existed. The court failing to appoint unconflicted counsel, conducted the hearing with Mr. Threatt as Mr. Riggs' counsel. On the day of the hearing Mr. Riggs' interests were to prove a conflict of interest existed. Mr. Threatt's interest was to prove that a conflict did not exist. The interests of Mr. Riggs and Mr. Threatt were in conflict on September 5, 2013. On that day Mr. Riggs was either represented by conflicted counsel or he had no counsel at all."

In either scenario, Mr. Riggs suffered a Sixth Amendment violation because the primary concern of a conflict of interest could not have been determined at a hearing where Mr. Riggs had no counsel. See *Strickland* and *Cronic* both supra.

The conflict of interest hearing in Mr. Riggs' case was a critical stage in his trial proceeding that was rendered unconstitutional because the court failed to appoint unconflicted counsel. In *United States v. Roy*, 855 F.3d 1133 (11th Cir. 2017) (en banc), the court of appeals asked, "What, then is a 'critical stage' of a trial?" In the case of *Roy*, counsel's seven-minute absence did not rise to a *Cronic* error because counsel only missed a small portion of the trial itself and not "an entire 'stage of the trial'." See *Cronic*, 466 U.S. at 659. As noted by the Eleventh Circuit Court of Appeals sitting en banc, "The Supreme Court has instructed us that it has used the term 'critical stage "to denote a step of a criminal proceeding, such as arraignment, that held significant consequences for the accused.' Bell v. Cone 535, U.S. at 695-96, 122 S. Ct at 1851." And decision after decision shows that what the court means when it does use the term 'stage' for *Cronic* purposes is a qualitatively distinct, discrete, and separate phase or step of a criminal proceeding where the defendant has a right to counsel, such as an arraignment, a post-indictment line-up, a preliminary hearing, a plea hearing, closing arguments as a whole, or a sentence proceeding as a whole. See *Monte.jo v. Louisiana*, 556 U.S. 778 (2009) (describing post indictment interrogation as a critical stage); *Iowa v. Tovar*, 541 U.S. 77 (2004) ('A plea hearing qualifies as a "critical stage'."); *Gardner v. Florida* 430 U.S. 349, (1977) ("Sentencing is a critical stage of the criminal proceeding at which the defendant is entitled to the effective assistance of counsel."); *Gilbert v. California*, 388 U.S. 263, (1967) ("A post-indictment pretrial lineup...is a critical stage of the criminal prosecution..."); *White*, 373 U.S. at 59-60,83 S. Ct. at 1051 ("Whatever may be the normal function of the 'preliminary hearing' under Maryland law, it was in this case as 'Critical' a stage as arraignment..."); *Hamilton*, 368 U.S. at 53, (describing arraignment as "a critical stage in a criminal proceeding"); See also *Harrington v. Gillis*, 456 F.3d 118, 132 (3rd Cir. 2006) (noting that "an appeal is a critical stage of a criminal proceeding"); *United States v. Sanchez-Barreto*, 93 F.3d 17, 20 (1st Cir. 1996) (Noting that a "plea withdrawal hearing" is a critical stage).

Mr. Riggs' primary contention is that his counsel's conflict caused damage to his defense. When the district court failed to appoint unconflicted counsel at a conflict of interest hearing, Mr. Riggs was outright denied counsel at a critical stage of his criminal proceeding. Thus, Mr. Riggs, acting alone against his own counsel, failed to present his claim adequately. Ultimately, Mr. Riggs was deprived of a public speedy trial by conflicted counsel who encouraged him to forgo trial, his alibi defense, and enter into a defunct plea agreement with the expectation of protection for him and his family.

Mr. Riggs contends that he has met both prongs of the Strickland test. See *Jae Lee v. United States*, 582 U.S., 137 S. Ct., holding that "when a defendant alleges his counsel's deficient performance led him to accept a guilty plea rather than go to trial, courts consider whether the defendant was prejudiced by the denial of the entire judicial proceeding to which he had a right. When a defendant claims that his counsel's deficient performance deprived him of a trial by causing him to accept a plea, the defendant can show prejudice by demonstrating a reasonable probability that, but for counsel's errors, he would not have pleaded guilty and would have insisted on going to trial."

Notwithstanding the government conceding to the foregoing claim, Mr. Riggs reminds that the Eleventh Circuit said in *Roy* that "The Cronic decision limited the presumption of prejudice to cases where defense counsel 'entirely fails to subject the prosecution's case to meaningful adversarial testing in the trial or where there is the complete denial of counsel' at a 'critical stage of [the] trial.' *Cronic* 466 U.S. at 659, 104 S. Ct. at 2047 (emphasis added)"

This claim alone presents a claim of constitutional magnitude that is not only untenable, but also the government concedes in its response. This court should return Mr. Riggs to the pre-plea stage of the criminal proceeding. In the alternative, this court could require Mr. Riggs' presence at an evidentiary hearing.

2. Mr. Riggs demonstrates that on the existing record he has a judicially noticed alibi defense establishing his actual innocence. This claim is conceded by the government.

In all of the claims in Mr. Riggs amended §2255 he showed that an alibi existed. The government in its reply conceded the fact and went on to say that "Riggs' claims that these attorneys failed to investigate the case, or interview or subpoena witnesses, lies in square conflict with Mr. Threatts testimony concerning the assistance the federal public defender's office provided Riggs." The government goes on to make note of." ..Mr. Threatt explaining his advice not to assert an alibi defense inconsistent with Riggs' videotaped confession," makes known that an alibi did in fact exist where the government raised no contest to the claim.

What is most interesting is that Mr. Threatt, on December 20, 2013, testified that he gave notice of alibi and that ten subpoenas were issued. Mr. Threatt's testimony is in clear conflict with the record because the docket reflects neither a notice of alibi nor a witness list for the defense.

Moreover, on December 20, 2013, in a conversation Mr. Riggs was having with Judge Bowdre, she testified that she did not issue a subpoena. Thus, even Mr. Threatt's own testimony is contradicted by the record, where he made false statements to the court.

Alibi is defined as, "a defense based on the physical impossibility of a defendant's guilt by placing the defendant in a location other than the scene of the crime at the relevant time. Fed. R. Crim. P. 12.1. Black's Law Dictionary, third pocket edition.

Mr. Riggs has shown that he was elsewhere and with many alibi witnesses when the alleged offense occurred and electronically recorded. Glennon F. Threatt, Jr. claimed in court record that he filed a notice of alibi and subpoenaed ten witnesses. The district court took judicial notice that Mr. Threatts testimony was accurate.

In Mr. Riggs case, either Mr. Threatt was ineffective for making false claims to the court concerning Mr. Riggs and the court was in error for taking judicial notice, or Mr. Riggs is actually innocent supported by a judicially noticed alibi defense. In either scenario Mr. Riggs is due an evidentiary hearing. Thus, the government's argument that "the court should deny Riggs' motion without a hearing" is misplaced. See. *McQuiggin v. Perkins*, 569 U.S. (2013), where even ." ..a prisoner otherwise subject to defense of abuse or successive use of the writ [of *habeas corpus*] may have his federal constitutional claim considered on the merits if he makes a proper showing of actual innocence."

In Mr. Riggs' case he has made a proper showing of actual innocence. Thus, this court should at a minimum hold an evidentiary hearing.

3.   Mr. Riggs demonstrates that on the existing record he was deprived of the effective assistance of counsel where Glennon F. Threatt, Jr. provided false information to his client, Mr. Riggs, and the district court. This claim is conceded by the government.

In Mr. Riggs' amended §2255 motion he raised issue with Glennon F. Threatt, who provided false testimony to the court, which is established by the record; who presented an edited version of the videotaped interview that the government now relies on; and who provided information to a collogue who represented cartel members Mr. Riggs provided information against. These claims were unaddressed in the government's response, thus conceded.

Under such circumstances the prosecutor, even when new to a case, has an obligation to seek justice. The A.B.A. Model Rules of Professional Conduct, Rule 3.8: Special Responsibilities of a Prosecutor, 3.8(g) and (h). Mr. Riggs has shown and goes unaddressed that he has been, since 2001, an informant for several law enforcement agencies. He presented facts and claims that if true would constitute grounds for relief. The government, however, in violation of A.B.A. standards has shirked its duty to seek justice and asks this court to preserve a miscarriage of justice.

Mr. Riggs has shown in his amended §2255 that Glennon F. Threatt, Jr. has obstructed justice in several investigations by presenting false information to Mr. Riggs and the court. The actions of Glennon Threatt constitute a criminal act where he actually aided and abetted Alvin Ray Johnson, Jr., Lakendrick Dunn, and Ronny Davis in the concealment of Mr. Deandrea Washington's murder. Mr. Threatt and Sabra Barnett took an active role in aiding and abetting uncharged persons in facilitating the murder of Sambo Hazelrig and his girlfriend. A minimum level of investigation would reveal that Mr. Riggs is in fact a witness in multiple cases; that Mr. Riggs' testimony proved harmful to Alabama State officials; that state officials including, but not limited to, Hoover Police Dept, have effectively weaponized a United States government effort; and that Glennon F. Threatt, Jr. concealed evidence, made false statements, and manipulated Mr. Riggs' case in an effort to obstruct justice.

This claim has gone unanswered by the government and is therefore conceded. The court should at a minimum require Mr. Riggs' presence in court and hold an evidentiary hearing where he may present his case.

Wherefore, Mr. Riggs shows that his claims are not procedurally barred, and this court is established for the purpose of addressing the merits of constitutional claims, just like these, among other things. Mr. Riggs moves this court to vacate his sentence and/or set the courts judgment aside in an effort to seek justice in this case.

Respectfully submitted this 23rd day of April, 2018.

Kelly Patrick Riggs

KELLY PATRICK RIGGS

CERTIFICATE OF SERVICE

Mr. Riggs certifies that he has served all parties as required by rule and law to include and not limited to the clerk of this court and the United States at 1801 4th Ave. N; Birmingham, AL 35203.

Respectfully submitted this 23rd day of April, 2018.

_____

Kelly Patrick Riggs

USPS TRACKING #
& CUSTOMER
RECEIPT

9114 9012 3080 1329 5933 72
For Tracking or inquiries go to USPS.com
or call 1-800-222-1811.

OFFICE OF THE FEDERAL PUBLIC DEFENDER
NORTHERN DISTRICT OF ALABAMA

BIRMINGHAM OFFICE
505 20th Street North, Suite 1425
Birmingham, Alabama 35203
T: (205) 208-7170
F: (205) 307-2567
Toll Free: 888-703-4316

HUNTSVILLE OFFICE
200 Clinton Avenue West, Suite 503
Huntsville, Alabama 35801
T: (256) 684-8700
F: (256) 519-5948

KEVIN L. BUTLER
Federal Public Defender

November 14, 2013

Alabama State Bar
The Disciplinary Commission
P.O. Box 671
Montgomery, Alabama 36101
Attn: Ms. Carol Wright

Subject: Bar Complaint - CSP 2013-1977
              Mr. Kelly Riggs

Dear Ms. Wright:

Thank you for the opportunity to respond to the Complaint filed by Mr. Kelly Riggs. In his complaint, Mr. Riggs alleges that I did "enter into an agreement and or conspire" with his appointed attorney, Glennon Threatt, to forward information regarding his cooperation against the Mexican Cartel to the "Mexican Community" at the jail in which he was being held at the time. Specifically, he states that I conspired with Mr. Threatt to inform the Mexican Cartel that Mr. Riggs was supplying information to the U.S. Marshals "concerning a shipment of 'ICE'". These allegations are completely false.

Although I did not provide counsel to Mr. Riggs, my office did represent him for a period of time. Throughout our office's representation, I was not aware and am not aware of Mr. Riggs supplying information about a shipment of "ICE" by the Mexican Cartel. I did warn Mr. Rodriguez to stop relying on legal advice that I believed Mr. Riggs was giving Mr. Rodriguez, but this was the extent of the conversation that I had with Mr. Rodriguez regarding Mr. Riggs.

For background, while Mr. Riggs was an inmate in Cullman, I had one client tell me that he had provided legal advice to him regarding his case. That same week, possibly even the same day, I had another client tell me that he had received some advice about his case but would not name the source. I assumed that it was Kelly Riggs because the advice was similar to the advice he had provided my other client and because all of the advice was counterproductive to the counsel that I

(Document #3)

159

was providing to them.[1] On September 27, 2013, I received a letter from Mr. Rodriguez, which I thought was peculiarly formatted. I also thought that the tone of the letter was unusual for Mr. Rodriguez. That same day, I went into Mr. Threatt's office and saw a letter on his desk that was formatted the same as Mr. Rodriguez' letter. I inquired about the author of the letter. Mr. Threatt stated that it was from Mr. Riggs. I did not read Mr. Riggs letter and am still unaware of the content. However, I assumed, based on my previous knowledge regarding Mr. Riggs' advice to other clients, that Mr. Riggs had either drafted or assisted Mr. Rodriguez in drafting the letter that was sent to me by Mr. Rodriguez.

When I next met with Mr. Rodriguez regarding his case, I shared my concern regarding the letter. I told him that Mr. Riggs had provided him with bad advice and incorrect information regarding the United States Sentencing Guidelines and that he should not rely on Mr. Riggs for legal advice. I also told him that the tone of the letter was offensive. Finally, I told Mr. Rodriguez that if he wanted to send a letter to Judge Coogler regarding his sentencing, he needed to write it because I was concerned that any letter written by Mr. Riggs would be considered disrespectful by the Court. I believe that during that meeting I also gave Mr. Rodriguez general advice about watching his back in prison, something I typically tell clients that appear to be somewhat naive about prison life.[2] However, that advice was not connected with Mr. Riggs.

In closing, I did not do what Mr. Riggs has alleged. Since I was unaware of Mr. Riggs' informing about a shipment of ICE, it would have been impossible for me to provide this information to Mr. Rodriguez.

Thank you for your time and consideration. Please let me know if I can provide additional information.

Sincerely,

Sabra M. Barnett
Assistant Federal Public Defender

---

[1] I do not recall the names of the clients that provided me with this information. If the Bar wishes to pursue, I could try to make a best guess by reviewing my time records and comparing them to the time that Mr. Riggs was housed in Cullman.

[2] If the Bar requests, I can provide information regarding Mr. Rodriguez that led me to give him the "watch your back" advice. I also can provide you with information that Mr. Rodriguez provided to me regarding the drafting of the letter. However, because Mr. Rodriguez is not a party to this Complaint, I do not feel comfortable providing that information unless so ordered.

(Document #3)

[DO NOT PUBLISH]

IN THE UNITED STATES COURT OF APPEALS

FOR THE ELEVENTH CIRCUIT

_____

No. 14-11917
Non-Argument Calendar

_____

D.C. Docket No. 2:12-cr-00297-KOB-JEO-1

UNITED STATES OF AMERICA,

Plaintiff-Appellee,

versus

KELLY PATRICK RIGGS,

Defendant-Appellant.

_____

Appeal from the United States District Court
for the Northern District of Alabama

_____

(January 8, 2015)

Before TJOFLAT, WILSON and JULIE CARNES, Circuit Judges.

PER CURIAM:

Brett N. Bloomston, appointed counsel for Kelly Patrick Riggs, has filed a

motion to withdraw on appeal, supported by a brief prepared pursuant to *Anders v.*

California, 386 U.S. 738, 87 S.Ct. 1396, 18 L.Ed.2d 493 (1967). Our independent review of the entire record reveals that counsel's assessment of the relative merit of the appeal is correct. Because independent examination of the entire record reveals no arguable issues of merit, counsel's motion to withdraw is **GRANTED**, and the defendant's convictions and sentences are **AFFIRMED**.

APP-2

UNITED STATES COURT OF APPEALS
For the Eleventh Circuit

No. 14-11917

District Court Docket No.
2:12-cr-00297-KOB-JEO-1

UNITED STATES OF AMERICA,

Plaintiff - Appellee,

versus

KELLY PATRICK RIGGS,

Defendant - Appellant.

Appeal from the United States District Court for the
Northern District of Alabama

JUDGMENT

It is hereby ordered, adjudged, and decreed that the opinion issued on this date in this appeal is entered as the judgment of this Court.

Entered: January 08, 2015
For the Court: John Ley, Clerk of Court
By: Djuanna Clark

ISSUED AS MANDATE 03/23/2015

APP-4

IN THE UNITED STATES COURT OF APPEALS

FOR THE ELEVENTH CIRCUIT

No. 14-11917-CC

UNITED STATES OF AMERICA,

Plaintiff - Appellee,

versus

KELLY PATRICK RIGGS,

Defendant - Appellant.

Appeal from the United States District Court
for the Northern District of Alabama

ON PETITION(S) FOR REHEARING AND PETITION(S) FOR REHEARING EN BANC

BEFORE: TJOFLAT, WILSON and JULIE CARNES, Circuit Judges

PER CURIAM:

The Petition(s) for Rehearing are DENIED and no Judge in regular active service on the Court having requested that the Court be polled on rehearing en banc (Rule 35, Federal Rules of Appellate Procedure), the Petition(s) for Rehearing En Banc are DENIED.

ENTERED FOR THE COURT:

UNITED STATES CIRCUIT JUDGE

ORD-42

APP-3

164

1 presented, unless you took the stand, that you believed

2 that person was over the age of eighteen?

3   DEFENDANT RIGGS: Yes, ma'am, I understand

4 that.

5   THE COURT: So you had that conversation with

6 Mr. Threatt?

7   DEFENDANT RIGGS: We had a conversation. Like

8 I said, he's mixing some of the quotes of the video as

9 to what I actually said.

10   But I'm moving on to the next point of the same

11 thing.

12 Q.   Was that not after you told me you would not assert

13 an alibi defense?

14 A.   No, it was not. The conversation about the alibi

15 defense was a completely different conversation. And we

16 actually had that conversation about the alibi defense

17 on two or three occasions.

18 Q.   Did you assert the alibi defense?

19 A.   We actually filed a notice of alibi.

20 Q.   Did you file it or did I?

21 A.   You filed it. And let me tell you why. Let me tell

22 you why.

23   Because we had several conversations about the

24 alibi. With respect to the alibi, alibi means that an

25 individual is asserting that they were at a place other

APP-6

1   indicated that he didn't wish to do that.

2   Q.   I understand.

3   MR. BLOOMSTON: Mr. Riggs, do you have any

4   questions of Mr. Threatt?

5   If the Court will entertain, there may be some

6   questions.

7   BY MR. RIGGS:

8   Q.   As far as the level of assistance, do you remember

9   how many motions I requested you to file?

10 A.   I don't remember how many. But I have

11 correspondence from you.

12 Q.   Do you remember the substance?

13 A.   There were numerous. You asked me to file motions

14 to challenge the findings of competency. You asked me

15 to file motions to challenge statements made by Alton

16 Margotto. You asked me to file motions to actually have

17 you determined to be incompetent.

18   You asked me to file motions to force -- to

19 issue subpoenas, which we did, we subpoenaed at least

20 ten people in the case. Also spoke to at least eight of

21 them on the phone about the matters that you had asked

22 me about.

23   You asked me to try to find surveillance

24 videotapes that you alleged that Mr. Bramer had promised

25 you that he was going to get that he never got.

**IN THE UNITED STATES DISTRICT COURT
FOR THE NORTHERN DISTRICT OF ALABAMA
SOUTHERN DIVISION**

KELLY PATRICK RIGGS,   ]
                                             ]
    Plaintiff,   ]
                                             ]
v.   ]   **2:15-cv-08043-KOB**
                                             ]
UNITED STATES OF AMERICA   ]
                                             ]
    Defendant.   ]

<u>ORDER</u>

This matter comes before the court on Kelly Patrick Riggs' "Motion for an Order to

Provide Service of Government's Response." (Doc. 69). The court ORDERS the Government

to SHOW CAUSE, in writing, **on or before April 25, 2018,** how service of its response to

Mr. Riggs' amended 28 U.S.C. § 2255 motion to vacate sentence was proper.

DONE and **ORDERED** this 23rd day of April, 2018.

Karon O. Bowdre
KARON OWEN BOWDRE
CHIEF UNITED STATES DISTRICT JUDGE

FILED
2018 Apr-23 PM 01:3.
U.S. DISTRICT COUR
N.D. OF ALABAM,

IN THE UNITED STATES DISTRICT COURT
FOR THE NORTHERN DISTRICT OF ALABAMA
SOUTHERN DIVISION

KELLY PATRICK RIGGS   )
)

v.   )   **Case No.**
)   **2:15-CV-8043-KOB**

UNITED STATES OF AMERICA   )

UNITED STATES' RESPONSE TO THE COURT'S ORDER
TO SHOW CAUSE

The United States respectfully submits the following response to the Court's

April 23, 2018, Order to Show Cause (Doc. 71).

On March 20, 2018, the United States responded to Petitioner Kelly Patrick

Riggs' Amended Section 2255 motion. Doc. 68. The United States submitted its

response via the CM/ECF system, not realizing Riggs would not receive a copy of

the filing.

On April 9, 2018, Riggs alerted the United States to its oversight. Doc. 69.

That same day, the United States mailed Riggs a copy of the filing, via first-class

mail, to the address he provided in Doc. 69. On April 10, 2018, the United States

notified chambers that it had mailed the filing to Riggs.

Respectfully submitted on April 23, 2018.

JAY E. TOWN
United States Attorney

/s/ Manu K. Balachandran
MANU K. BALACHANDRAN
Assistant United States Attorney

FILED
2018 Apr-24 AM 11:08
U.S. DISTRICT COURT
N.D. OF ALABAMA

IN THE UNITED STATES DISTRICT COURT
FOR THE NORTHERN DISTRICT OF ALABAMA
SOUTHERN DIVISION

KELLY PATRICK RIGGS,   ]
                            ]
      Plaintiff,   ]
                            ]
v.   ]   2:15-cv-08043-KOB
                            ]
UNITED STATES OF AMERICA   ]
                            ]
      Defendant.   ]

ORDER

This matter comes before the court on Kelly Patrick Riggs' "Motion for an Order to Provide Service of Government's Response." (Doc. 69). The Government responded that, after Mr. Riggs alerted it to the oversight in service, on April 9, 2018, it sent him a copy of the response by first-class mail. (Doc. 72). In light of the Government's response, the court DENIES AS MOOT Mr. Riggs' motion.

DONE and ORDERED this 24th day of April, 2018.

KARON OWEN BOWDRE
CHIEF UNITED STATES DISTRICT JUDGE

FILED
2018 Apr-24 AM 11:11
U.S. DISTRICT COURT
N.D. OF ALABAMA

IN THE UNITED STATES DISTRICT COURT
FOR THE NORTHERN DISTRICT OF ALABAMA
SOUTHERN DIVISION

KELLY PATRICK RIGGS,　　　　　　　　　]

　　　　Plaintiff,　　　　　　　　　　　]
　　　　　　　　　　　　　　　　　　　]
v.　　　　　　　　　　　　　　　　　　]　　　　2:15-cv-08043-KOB
　　　　　　　　　　　　　　　　　　　]
UNITED STATES OF AMERICA　　　　　　　]
　　　　　　　　　　　　　　　　　　　]
　　　　Defendant.　　　　　　　　　　　]

ORDER REGARDING SUMMARY DISPOSITION

On March 2, 2018, Kelly Patrick Riggs filed an amended 28 § 2255 motion to vacate, set aside, or correct sentence. (Doc. 63). In response to this court's Show Cause Order (doc. 65), the Government filed its response on March 20, 2018 (doc. 68).

The court deems the case ripe for summary disposition. *See McBride v. Sharpe*, 25 F.3d 962 (11th Cir. 1994). The purpose of this Order is to notify Mr. Riggs that the court will treat the motion as ripe for summary disposition and to further inform him of his right to file affidavits or other materials to show why the court should not summarily deny the motion on the basis of the Government's response.

The court gives Mr. Riggs until **May 15, 2018,** twenty days after the date of this Order, to supply any additional evidentiary materials or legal arguments he may wish to offer regarding whether the motion is subject to summary disposition. Thereafter, the court will take the motion under advisement for consideration in light of the Government's response, court record, and any additional materials supplied by the movant.

The court DIRECTS the Clerk to send a copy of this Order to Mr. Riggs and to counsel for the Government.

KELLY PATRICK RIGGS

DONE and **ORDERED** this 24th day of April, 2018.

Karon O. Bowdre

KARON OWEN BOWDRE
CHIEF UNITED STATES DISTRICT JUDGE

**UNITED STATES DISTRICT COURT
NORTHERN DISTRICT OF ALABAMA
SOUTHERN DIVISION**

USPS TRACKING # **9114 9012 3080 1329 6154 32**
& CUSTOMER   For Tracking or inquiries go to USPS.com
RECEIPT   or call 1-800-222-1811.

KELLY PATRICK RI〈

v.   2:15-CV-8043-KOB

UNITED STATES OF AMERICA

_____ /

**MR. RIGGS' OBJECTION AND OPPOSITION TO THE COURT'S
ORDER REGARDING SUMMARY DISPOSITION**

Mr. Riggs objects to the court's intention to "Summarily deny the motion" based only "on the basis of the government's response." He has repeatedly shown the court that he was deprived of counsel during his criminal proceeding in which the court knowingly enslaved an innocent American citizen. Neither the government or the court deny that Mr. Riggs was deprived of counsel at critical stages of his criminal proceeding and therefore concede the issue. Mr. Riggs provided the court with a full discussion concerning the outright denial of counsel at critical stages in his "Reply to 'United States' Response'," which was received by the clerk of this court on April 27, 2018, at 10:25am. See U.S. postal tracking #9114-9012-3080-1329-5933-72.

Mr. Riggs' constitutional challenges are premised upon violations of the Fifth and Sixth amendments to the United States Constitution. The Fifth amendment provides that no criminal defendant may be "deprived of life, liberty, or property, without due process of law." The Sixth amendment provides that "in all criminal prosecutions, the accused shall enjoy the right…to have the assistance of counsel for his defense."

Mr. Riggs is seeking to vacate his convictions and sentences pursuant to 28 U.S.C. §2255(a), which allows a federal inmate whose sentence was imposed in violation of the constitution or law of the United States to "move the court which imposed the sentence to vacate, set aside, or correct the sentence." Herenow, the court notifies Mr. Riggs that it intends to deny his §2255 motion without the benefit of a hearing pursuant to 28 U.S.C §2255(b), which is mandatory "unless the motion and the files and records of the case conclusively show that the prisoner is entitled to no relief." Thus, the court's intended denial, without a hearing, is both a violation of due process and a rush to judgment.

The Supreme Court of the United States has stressed, "Judges must be vigilant and independent in reviewing petitions for the writ, a commitment that entails substantial judicial resources." *Harrington v. Richter*, 562 U.S. 86, 91 (2011). Reviewing capital cases, which are a matter of life and death, the Supreme Court has repeatedly demonstrated what a vigilant and independent review entails, particularly when the defendant alleges counsel failed to provide effective assistance. See, e.g., *Buck v. Davis*, 137 S. Ct. 759 (2017); *Rompilla v. Beard*, 545 U.S. 374 (2005); *Wiggins v. Smith*, 539 U.S. 510 (2003); *Williams v. Taylor*, 529 U.S. 362 (2003).

Though Mr. Riggs has been convicted of sexual offences rather than murder, he still suffers a life altering change, he will be subject to a lifelong banishment from his life as he knew it. Thus, his case also can result in a matter of life and death.

Additionally, Mr. Riggs has effectively shown that he was outright deprived of counsel at critical stages of his criminal proceeding. The court has failed to address the issue, that is plain in the record, and gives notice it intends to deny without the benefit of the hearing required by 28 U.S.C. §2255(b). In the courts April 24, 2018, order, DE-74, the court notifies "Mr. Riggs that the court will treat the motion as ripe for summary disposition … on the basis of the government's response." It is clear that the court fails to provide a "vigilant and independent" review of the "…motion and the files and record of the case …" to determine if the "…records of the case conclusively show that the prisoner is entitled to no relief."

Wherefore, Mr. Riggs objects to the court's intention to summarily deny his §2255 claims without a "vigilant and independent" review of the "motion and the files and record of the case." Mr. Riggs moves this court to issue an order of *Habeas corpus* to the end that he be present at a hearing to determine the facts of this case pursuant to 28 U.S.C. §2255(b).

Respectfully submitted this day of May, 2018.

Kelly Patrick Riggs

CERTIFICATE OF SERVICE

Mr. Riggs certifies that he has served all parties as required by rule and law, to include, but not limited to, the clerk of this court and the U.S. Attorney at 1801 4th Ave. N.; Birmingham, AL 38203.

Respectfully submitted this 3 day of May, 2018

_____

**UNITED STATES DISTRICT COURT
NORTHERN DISTRICT OF ALABAMA
SOUTHERN DIVISION**

KELLY PATRICK RIGGS

v.

UNITED STATES OF AMERICA

_____ /

Case No.

2:15-CV-8043-K0B

REQUEST FOR JUDICIAL NOTICE

Mr. Riggs seeks a judicial notice of undisputable facts that exist in the record. The purpose of his request serves to preserve precious judicial resources by leaving only contested factual issues before the court for resolution. Mr. Riggs moves the court to notice the following:

1. That the criminal record, in Case 2:12-CR-297-KOB-JEO, reflects that on September 4, 2013, a sealed document was recorded as document 51.

2. That on September 5, 2013, an order of the court was recorded that states in pertinent part that "The court, at a hearing this morning, addressed the recent *Pro se* ex-parte pleading filed in this matter 51. The court is convinced there is no conflict in the representation of the defendant by present counsel."

3. That between the filing of the *Pro se* ex-parte motion, on September 4, 2013, and the conflict of interest hearing held on September 5, 2013, the court DID NOT appoint independent unconflicted counsel to represent Mr. Riggs' interests at the conflict of interest hearing.

4. That Mr. Riggs raised the issue of conflicted counsel in a 28 U.S.C. §2255 emotion on November 16, 2015. DE-157, 2:12-CR-297-K0B-JE0

5. That on or about March 17, 2016, the court issued an order giving a notice of summary judgment.

6. That on or about May 17, 2017, and over a year later, Mr. Riggs filed a motion "Requesting leave to withdraw pending motions."

7. That on or about June 13, 2017, Mr. Riggs filed a "Motion for leave to amend."

8. That on or about January 2, 2018, nearly two years after Mr. Riggs received the notice of summary judgment, he filed a "Petition for a Writ of Mandamus" in the United States Court of Appeals for the Eleventh Circuit and providing service to Karen Owen Bowdre.

9. That on January 11, 2018, Judge Bowdre issued an order granting Mr. Riggs leave to withdraw a number of motions. DE-61-1, 2:15-CV-8043-KOB.

10. That on or about January 12, 2018, Judge Bowdre issued an order that "grants Mr. Riggs' motion." [he filed six months earlier] "Mr. Riggs may filed his amended §2255 motion on or by February 17, 2018."

11. That on or about February 14, 2018, Mr. Riggs filed a detailed amended §2255 that included, inter alia, a claim that he was deprived of counsel at a critical stage of the criminal proceeding. See Ground Two, DE-63.

12. That on or about March £, 2018, Judge Bowdre issued an "Order to Show Cause," giving the government twenty-one days.

13. That on or about March 9, 2018, Mr. Riggs filed a "Motion for the Appointment of Counsel."

14. That on or about April 4, 2018, Mr. Riggs filed a "Motion for an Order to Provide Service of Government's Response" after he learned from an independent non-profit organization that the government filed its response on March 20, 2018, without serving Mr. Riggs. DE-69

15. That within Mr. Riggs' motion for service, DE-69, he specifically moved the court to order a "specified adequate time for Mr. Riggs to file any appropriate reply. Mr. Riggs needs only 15 days from the date he signs for delivery of the government's response…"

16. That on or about April 12, 2018, Mr. Riggs received a copy of the government's response. DE-68.

17. That Mr. Riggs filed a reply and I he has attached a certificate of service that indicates that his reply was served on April 23, 2018. Only eleven days after Mr. Riggs received the government's response.

18. That on April 23, 2018, Judge Bowdre issued an order demanding that the government is "To show cause…how service of its response to Mr. Riggs' amended 28 U.S.C. §2255 motion to vacate sentence was proper."

19. That on April 23, 2018, the government filed, "United States' Response to the Courts' Order to Show Cause," in which the government shows service was not proper, stating that, "The United States submitted its response via the CM/ECF system, not realizing Riggs would not receive a copy of the filing." DE-72

20. That on April 24, 2018, Judge Bowdre issued an order that "Denies as Moot Mr. Riggs' motion," seeking 15 days to reply.

21. That on April 24, 2018, Judge Bowdre issues an "Order Regarding Summary Disposition" in which she attempts to manipulate the court record by making false statements. In the very first line of her order she claims that Mr. Riggs' amended §2255 was filed on March 2, 2018, two weeks after the ordered deadline of February 17, 2018. Mr. Riggs shows, for the purpose of publication and/or impending appeal, that his amended §2255 arrived in the court house for filing on or about February 14, 2018. See U.S. Postal tracking #9114-9012-3080-1329-5910-88.

22. That Mr. Riggs began to seek and expeditious resolve to his claim on or about February 10, 2014, DE-73, over four years ago. Mr. Riggs has continually shown that he was outright deprived of counsel in his criminal proceeding. The government, although given ample opportunity still to this day, fails to address the issue.

23. Mr. Riggs shows that the denial of counsel at a critical stage of a criminal proceeding violates both the Fifth and Sixth amendments to the constitution. He shows that "unless the motion and the files and records of the case conclusively show that the prisoner is entitled to no relief, the court SHALL cause notice thereof to be served upon the United States attorney, grant a prompt hearing thereon, determine the issues, and make findings of fact and conclusions of law with respect thereto" 28 U.S.C. §2255(b).

Wherefore, Mr. Riggs moves this court to take judicial notice based upon his motion and federal court rules. He further contends that this notice will preserve the judicial resources of the reviewing court after this court deprives Mr. Riggs of the due process guaranteed by 28 U.S.C. §2255(b).

Respectfully submitted this 3 day of May, 2018

_____

Kelly Patrick Riggs

CERTIFICATE OF SERVICE

Mr. Riggs certifies that he has served all parties as required by rule and law to include, but not limited to, the clerk of this court and the United States at 1801 4th Ave. N.; Birmingham, AL 35203.

Respectfully submitted this 3 day of May, 2018

_____

Kelly Patrick Riggs

**IN THE UNITED STATES DISTRICT COURT
FOR THE NORTHERN DISTRICT OF ALABAMA
SOUTHERN DIVISION**

KELLY PATRICK RIGGS,	]	
	]	
Plaintiff,	]	
	]	
v.	]	**2:15-cv-08043-KOB**
	]	
UNITED STATES OF AMERICA	]	
	]	
Defendant.	]	

MEMORANDUM OPINION

The movant Kelly Patrick Riggs pled guilty to one count of attempted enticement of a

minor to engage in sexual activity, in violation of 18 U.S.C. § 2422(b), and one count of transfer

of obscene material to a minor, in violation of 18 U.S.C. § 1470. (Cr. Doc. 89).[1] The court

sentenced him to 120 months imprisonment on each count, to run concurrently. (*Id.*). Mr. Riggs

moved, under 28 U.S.C. § 2255, to vacate his sentence. (Doc. 1). After the government

responded (doc. 13), Mr. Riggs moved to amend his § 2255 motion. (Doc. 59). The court

granted the motion to amend, and Mr. Riggs filed an amended § 2255 motion and a motion for

appointment of counsel. (Docs. 63, 67). The Government responded to the amended § 2255

motion and Mr. Riggs replied. (Docs. 72, 75).

In his amended § 2255 motion, Mr. Riggs contends that (1) his guilty plea was not

intelligent, knowing, and voluntary; (2) counsel was ineffective because he had a conflict of

interest; and (3) he is actually innocent. (Doc. 63). The court WILL DENY Mr. Riggs' § 2255

motion because the record confirms that Mr. Riggs' challenge to his guilty plea is procedurally

barred and procedurally defaulted; Mr. Riggs waived the alleged conflict of interest; and

---

[1] The court cites documents from Mr. Riggs' underlying criminal case, *United States v. Riggs*, 2:12-cr-00297-KOB-JEO, as "Cr. Doc. __."

Mr. Riggs' freestanding claim of actual innocence is not cognizable in a § 2255 motion. The court WILL DENY AS MOOT Mr. Riggs' request for appointment of counsel.

I.   BACKGROUND

In 2012, a grand jury charged Mr. Riggs with one count of enticing a minor to engage in criminal activity in violation of 18 U.S.C. § 2422(b) and one count of transfer of obscene material to a minor in violation of 18 U.S.C. § 1470. (Cr. Doc. 6). The court appointed Jeffrey Bramer as his defense attorney. (Cr. Doc. 3). Mr. Bramer, however, quickly withdrew as counsel based on an undisclosed "ethical issue." (Cr. Doc. 18 at 2; Cr. Doc. Minute Entry, Oct. 9, 2012).

Next, the court appointed David Luker as Mr. Riggs' defense attorney. (Cr. Doc. 20). While represented by Mr. Luker, Mr. Riggs filed a *pro se* motion seeking to represent himself. (Cr. Doc. 28). A magistrate judge held a hearing, at which he allowed Mr. Luker to withdraw and appointed the Federal Public Defender to represent Mr. Riggs. (Cr. Doc. 100 at 16–17).

Allison Case and Glennon Threatt entered appearances as Mr. Riggs' public defenders. (Cr. Docs. 35, 36). While they were representing him, Mr. Riggs filed a *pro se* motion seeking subpoenas for various witnesses, including seven alleged alibi witnesses and three character witnesses. (Cr. Docs. 45, 105). After holding a hearing on the motion, the magistrate judge issued all of the requested subpoenas. (Cr. Docs. 46, 105).

Mr. Riggs next filed a *pro se* motion requesting that the court hold a hearing on whether Mr. Threatt had a conflict of interest. (Cr. Doc. 51). Mr. Riggs alleged that members of a prison gang had threatened to harm or kill Mr. Threatt and his family, and stated that he had also told Mr. Threatt about "a confession to killing a co-conspirator and the intent to kill witnesses of that event." (*Id.* at 2). Although that *pro se* motion itself did not state who the alleged co-conspirator was, who made the alleged confession, or what its relation to Mr. Riggs' criminal case was,

Mr. Riggs' current § 2255 motion makes it apparent that Mr. Riggs was referring to another of

Mr. Threatt's clients, a man named Alvin Johnson, who Mr. Riggs says confessed to killing

another man named DeAndre Washington. (*See* Doc. 63 at 6–8).

On September 5, 2013, the magistrate judge held a hearing on Mr. Riggs' allegation

about Mr. Threatt's alleged conflict of interest. (Cr. Doc. 109). The magistrate judge indicated

that Mr. Threatt "was aware of [the threat against Mr. Threatt] and [he] has already discussed it

with the Federal Defender, Mr. Butler, and they reached the conclusion that no further action

would be taken on their part at the present time . . . . And they also did make their own

independent inquiry as to whether or not there's a conflict issue. And . . . Mr. Threatt . . . and

Mr. Butler did not believe there was a conflict." (*Id.* at 7). Mr. Riggs then told the magistrate

judge that he had discussed the issue with Mr. Threatt several days earlier and they had

"determined that it was not going to be an issue," but by then, he had already mailed the motion.

(*Id.*). After the hearing, the magistrate judge entered an order stating that he was "convinced

there is no conflict in the representation of the defendant by present counsel." (Cr. Doc. Minute

Entry, Sept. 5, 2013).

At the same hearing, Mr. Riggs stated that when he mailed the motion requesting a

hearing on Mr. Threatt's alleged conflict, he also mailed two other pleadings, one of which was a

notice of alibi. (Doc. 109 at 3–5). The magistrate judge noted that the court had not yet received

those filings. (*Id.* at 3–4). Mr. Riggs stated that, since mailing the notice of alibi, he had spoken

with Mr. Threatt and they had "come to a point." (*Id.* at 5). Neither Mr. Riggs nor Mr. Threatt

disclosed the content of their discussion, but Mr. Riggs indicated that he was "satisfied with the results of [that] conversation," and Mr. Threatt indicated that he was not planning to file a notice of alibi. (*Id.* at 5–6).

Mr. Riggs requested to withdraw the two pleadings that he had mailed. (*Id.* at 13–14). The magistrate judge stated that he would review them before allowing Mr. Riggs to withdraw them. (*Id.*). The record does not include an order permitting withdrawal, nor does it contain the two pleadings.

The day after the conflict hearing, Mr. Riggs entered a plea agreement with the Government, in which he agreed to plead guilty to both counts against him. (Cr. Doc. 55). The plea agreement described the factual basis of the crime. (*Id.* at 3–5). It stated that, on May 23, 2012, Mr. Riggs responded to an internet advertisement and emailed an undercover law enforcement officer whom he believed to be a 14 year old girl. (*Id.* at 2–3). Over the next few days, he emailed and texted with the undercover officer, sending her nude pictures of an adult man's body and asking for nude pictures in return. (*Id.* at 3–4). He eventually arranged to meet the purported 14 year old girl at a bowling alley around 10:00 am on May 26, 2012, but when he arrived there at 10:20 am, law enforcement officers arrested him. (*Id.* at 4–5).

At Mr. Riggs' change of plea hearing, Mr. Riggs stipulated that the factual basis set forth in the plea agreement was accurate. (Cr. Doc. 62 at 25–26). The court asked Mr. Riggs: "Has anyone promised you anything or threatened you in any way to encourage you to enter this plea of guilty?" (*Id.* at 16). Mr. Riggs responded, "No." (*Id.*). The court also asked Mr. Riggs if he was "satisfied with Mr. Threatt and the work that he has done," to which Mr. Riggs responded, "Yes." (*Id.* at 24).

The next month, Mr. Riggs filed a *pro se* motion to withdraw his guilty plea and to replace his attorney. (Cr. Doc. 57). In the motion, he stated that he had entered the plea

183

agreement under duress because (1) a gang had threatened his family, and (2) Mr. Threatt had

told him the only way to get a reduction in his sentence was to plead guilty. (*Id.* at 1–2). He

explained that, on the day of the prior conflict hearing, he had given a statement against

Mr. Threatt's other client, Alvin Johnson, because Mr. Johnson had made a jailhouse confession

to the murder of DeAndre Washington and had threatened Mr. Threatt and Mr. Threatt's family.

(*Id.* at 2, 6, 8). According to Mr. Riggs, after he notified Mr. Threatt of those matters,

Mr. Threatt told Mr. Johnson that Mr. Riggs "was a problem to [Mr. Johnson's] case." (*Id.* at 6).

Mr. Riggs also alleged that Mr. Threatt had told a United States marshal that "this was a

conflict." (*Id.*).

The magistrate judge held a hearing on the portion of the motion seeking to discharge

counsel. (Cr. Doc. 111). Expressing concern about potentially breaching attorney-client

privilege and revealing defense strategy, the magistrate judge told Mr. Riggs not to reveal any

confidential communications between his attorney and himself. (*Id.* at 7–8). But when the

magistrate judge asked Mr. Threatt if he opposed Mr. Riggs' motion for a new attorney,

Mr. Threatt said he did not. (*Id.* at 6).

After that hearing, the magistrate judge entered an order stating that "the interests of

justice warrant the release of the Federal Defender and the appointment of new counsel. The

court notes that the decision in no way reflects on the performance of counsel, but is indicative of

the defendant's narcissistic personality." (Cr. Doc. 59 at 4). The magistrate judge appointed

Brett Bloomston as Mr. Riggs' fifth appointed attorney. (Cr. Doc. 60).

The court then held a hearing on the motion to withdraw Mr. Riggs' guilty plea.

(Cr. Doc. 114). Mr. Riggs told the court that after the first conflict hearing on September 5,

2013, at which the court had ruled that Mr. Threatt had no conflict, Mr. Riggs met with a United

States deputy marshal about Mr. Johnson's statements. (*Id.* at 4–5). At that time, Mr. Threatt

told the marshal that because Mr. Johnson was another of his clients, he could not represent

Mr. Riggs during the marshal's interview of Mr. Riggs. (*Id.* at 5). The court asked if Mr. Riggs

understood that "the conflict that Mr. Threatt was referring to had to do with your conversation

with the marshal about Mr. Johnson . . . [h]ad nothing to do about his continued representation

with you at trial or at your plea." (*Id.* at 6). Mr. Riggs stated that he understood the difference.

(*Id.*).

The court pointed out that Mr. Riggs' change of plea hearing took place after the meeting

with the United States marshal about Mr. Johnson, but Mr. Riggs had not mentioned the conflict

at that time, despite testifying under oath that he was satisfied with Mr. Threatt's representation.

(Cr. Doc. 114 at 6–8). And the court asked Mr. Riggs about his testimony that he had not been

threatened into entering the plea agreement. (*Id.* at 11). Mr. Riggs stated that he had lied to

protect his family. (*Id.*).

The Government called Mr. Threatt to testify at the hearing on Mr. Riggs' motion to

withdraw. (Cr. Doc. 114 at 37). Mr. Threatt testified that, at Mr. Riggs' meeting with the United

States deputy marshal on September 5, he had told Mr. Riggs that the interview should take place

"outside [his] presence because [he] believed that [Mr. Riggs] was going to give information

about a client of [his] at the time." (*Id.* at 39–40). He testified that Mr. Riggs never told him he

was entering the plea agreement because of fear for himself and his family. (*Id.* at 43). And he

testified that he and Mr. Riggs had, on at least three occasions, watched a videotaped confession

in which Mr. Riggs admitted to sending the emails and text messages, including the obscene

photographs. (*Id.* at 45). Mr. Threatt testified that Mr. Riggs had never refuted that confession.

(*Id.*).

After the Government and defense counsel questioned Mr. Threatt, the court permitted Mr. Riggs to question Mr. Threatt directly. (Cr. Doc. 114 at 55–84). In response to Mr. Riggs' questions, Mr. Threatt testified that he "spoke to at least eight of [ten people who Mr. Riggs wanted to subpoena] on the phone about the matters that [Mr. Riggs] had asked [him] about." (*Id.* at 55). He also testified that he and Mr. Riggs had several conversations about an alibi defense, and Mr. Riggs had filed a *pro se* notice of alibi defense. (*Id.* at 74). Mr. Threatt testified that he told Mr. Riggs he would not file the notice because "alibi means that an individual is asserting that they were at a place other than the place that a crime was committed. When an individual—when the criminal allegation is that you were sending text messages from a phone, it does not matter whether you were doing that in this building or across the street. That's the conversation we had." (*Id.* at 74–75). In addition, Mr. Threatt testified that he felt an alibi defense would be inconsistent with Mr. Riggs' confession. (*Id.* at 75).

The court found that Mr. Riggs' plea was knowing and voluntary, and that sufficient evidence existed to justify a finding of guilt. (Cr. Doc. 114 at 88). The court also found that Mr. Threatt and his predecessor attorneys had provided Mr. Riggs with effective assistance. (*Id.* at 88–90). As a result, the court denied the motion to withdraw the guilty plea. (*Id.* at 90).

The court sentenced Riggs to two concurrent 120-month sentences. (Cr. Doc. 89). Mr. Riggs appealed. On appeal, Mr. Bloomston filed a brief under *Anders v. California*, 386 U.S. 738 (1967), stating that he believed no issues of arguable merit existed. (Doc. 13-2 at 55–72). In response, Mr. Riggs filed a *pro se* brief, contending, among other things, that all of his attorneys had provided ineffective assistance, that his guilty plea was invalid because Mr. Threatt and other federal public defenders coerced him to enter that plea, and that he was actually innocent. (Doc. 13-2 at 75–93). Specifically, Mr. Riggs argued that Mr. Threatt "knowingly and willingly hamper[ed] the prosecution of the murder of one DeAndre Washington . . . reported by the accused." (*Id.* at 85). He also argued that the plea agreement was void because he entered it based on Mr. Johnson's threats against his family and his erroneous impression that it was the only way to protect them. (*Id.* at 89–91).

After an independent review of the record, the Eleventh Circuit affirmed Mr. Riggs' convictions and sentences. *United States v. Riggs*, 589 F. App'x 523 (11th Cir. 2015).

II.   DISCUSSION

Mr. Riggs primarily raises three issues in his § 2255 motion: (1) Mr. Riggs' guilty plea was not knowing and voluntary; (2) trial counsel was ineffective because of his conflict of interest; and (3) he is actually innocent.[2] (Doc. 63).

1. Invalid Guilty Plea

Mr. Riggs' first claim is that his guilty plea was involuntary. He asserts that after he gave a statement against Mr. Johnson and before he entered the plea agreement, he told Mr. Threatt that Mr. Johnson had threatened Mr. Riggs' wife and children. (Doc. 63 at 4). According to Mr. Riggs, Mr. Threatt told him that the United States Marshals Service would protect Mr. Riggs' family only if he pled guilty. (*Id.*). Mr. Threatt allegedly also told Mr. Riggs that, if

---

[2] Mr. Riggs states at various points throughout his § 2255 motion and in his briefs that counsel's alleged conflict of interest resulted in the *denial* of counsel at each of the conflict-of-interest hearings. (Doc. 63 at 8–9, 14, 17–19; Doc. 75 at 2–5). To the extent that Mr. Riggs attempts to raise a denial-of-counsel claim, the court denies it because the record confirms that Mr. Riggs was represented by counsel at every stage of his criminal proceedings.

Mr. Riggs also alleges that another federal public defender, Sabra Barnett, who was not representing him, shared information about him with one of her clients. (Doc. 63 at 18–19; 75 at 7). But an attorney who was not representing him cannot have provided him with ineffective assistance. To the extent that Mr. Riggs attempts to assert a claim of ineffective assistance about Ms. Barnett's actions, the court denies that claim as well.

he pled guilty, he would receive a sentence of time served for substantially assisting the Government. (*Id.* at 14–15).

Of relevance to Mr. Riggs' § 2255 motion, a movant seeking to challenge his sentence faces two procedural hurdles to raising a claim. First is the procedural bar, which provides that "once a matter has been decided adversely to a defendant on direct appeal it cannot be re-litigated in a collateral attack under section 2255." *United States v. Nyhuis*, 211 F.3d 1340, 1343 (11th Cir. 2000) (quotation marks omitted). The other is the doctrine of procedural default, which precludes any claim that the defendant could have, but did not, raise on direct appeal. *Lynn v. United States*, 365 F.3d 1225, 1234 (11th Cir. 2004).

The procedural bar and procedural default rules—the first prohibiting claims that the movant raised on direct appeal and the second prohibiting claims that the movant did *not* raise on direct appeal—may seem to place the movant in an impossible position. The movant may navigate the narrow passage between those two rules by raising in his § 2255 motion a claim that he *could not have raised* in his direct appeal—for example, a claim of ineffective assistance or a claim based on newly discovered evidence. *See, e.g., Bousley v. United States*, 523 U.S. 614, 621–22 (1998) (noting the "exception to the procedural default rule for claims that could not be presented [on direct appeal] without further factual development"); *Brown v. United States*, 688 F. App'x 644 (11th Cir. 2017) ("One example of a claim typically requiring further factual development through a § 2255 proceeding is a claim based on ineffective assistance of counsel.").

But Mr. Riggs' claim challenging the validity of his guilty plea does not rest on the ineffectiveness of his attorney or on evidence that he discovered *after* his appeal. Instead, Mr. Riggs' claim is simply that his guilty plea was invalid because (1) he entered the guilty plea based on his belief that pleading guilty was the only method to protect his family from Mr. Johnson, who had threatened them; and (2) Mr. Threatt told him that was the only way to get a lower sentence for substantially assisting the Government. (Doc. 63 at 4, 14–15).

The court finds that his claim is procedurally barred in part and procedurally defaulted in part. As to the part of his claim relating to Mr. Johnson's alleged threats against Mr. Riggs' family, the claim is procedurally barred. In his *pro se* brief on appeal to the Eleventh Circuit, Mr. Riggs argued that his guilty plea was invalid because he entered the plea agreement under the erroneous impression that it was the only way to protect his family. (Doc. 13-2 at 90–91). The Eleventh Circuit, in affirming his convictions, rejected that argument. *Riggs*, 589 F. App'x 523.

The Eleventh Circuit has held that a *pro se* brief filed in response to counsel's *Anders* brief triggers the procedural bar because "an issue presented is presented, even if raised only in the *pro se* response to an *Anders* brief." *Stoufflet v. United States*, 757 F.3d 1236, 1242 (11th Cir. 2014) (quotation marks, alteration, and citation omitted). Because Mr. Riggs challenged the validity of his guilty plea based on the alleged threats by Mr. Johnson against his family, and the Eleventh Circuit rejected that challenge, the procedural bar prevents this court from considering that claim on collateral review.

Less clear is whether the portion of Mr. Riggs' claim relying on Mr. Threatt's alleged promise of a sentence reduction is also procedurally barred. Mr. Riggs' *pro se* brief on appeal did not mention any promise of a sentence reduction, even though Mr. Riggs had already raised that alleged promise in the district court as a ground to withdraw his guilty plea. (*See* Cr. Doc. 57 at 1–2; Doc. 13-2 at 90–91). But the court need not decide whether that portion of the claim is procedurally barred because, even if it is not, Mr. Riggs procedurally defaulted it.

189

Mr. Riggs' motion to withdraw his plea alleged that Mr. Threatt had induced him to plead guilty by telling him that such a plea was the only way to get a reduction in his sentence. (Cr. Doc. 57 at 1–2). He *could have* raised that argument in his *pro se* brief on appeal—he had already raised it in the district court by that point—but his *pro se* brief on appeal challenged his guilty plea only on the basis that he entered the plea to protect his family. (*See* Doc. 13-2 at 90–91). And his § 2255 motion does not allege any newly discovered evidence supporting the claim; it does not bring to light any information that was not already in the record of the trial proceedings. As a result, he procedurally defaulted his challenge to the guilty plea based on Mr. Threatt's alleged promise of a sentence reduction.

Two exceptions to the procedural default rule exist. Under the first exception, "a defendant must show cause for not raising the claim of error on direct appeal *and* actual prejudice from the alleged error." *Lynn*, 365 F.3d at 1234. Mr. Riggs has not alleged any facts that could support a showing of cause or prejudice. Under the second exception, a court may excuse the movant's procedural default "if a constitutional violation has probably resulted in the conviction of one who is actually innocent." *Id.* (quotation marks omitted). Mr. Riggs relies on the second exception by arguing that he is innocent of his crimes of conviction. (Doc. 63 at 5).

To establish actual innocence, a § 2255 movant must demonstrate that, in light of all the evidence, "it is more likely than not that no reasonable juror would have convicted him." *Bousley v. United States*, 523 U.S. 614, 623 (1998) (quotation marks omitted). Mr. Riggs makes two arguments in support of his allegation that he is actually innocent. First, he alleges that, unbeknownst to him, his housemate at the time of the crimes was a confidential informant named Joy Brown, using the alias Laney Jones, who was working with police in exchange for a lighter sentence. (Doc. 63 at 22–23). Mr. Riggs contends that she used a SIM card from one of his broken cellphones to send the texts and explicit photographs to the other undercover agent who was posing as a young girl, all in a scheme to frame him and stop his work as an informant exposing the involvement of public officials in the drug trade. (*Id.* at 4–5, 22). He states that, while he was in jail, Ms. Brown admitted to him that she sent the nude pictures of him from her cellphone. (*Id.* at 22). Second, he alleges that ten alibi witnesses would have proved that he was not "even present when the alleged conduct occurred." (*Id.* at 12, 23).

Mr. Riggs has not established that, "more likely than not . . . , no reasonable juror would have convicted him." *Bousley*, 523 U.S. at 623. Law enforcement officers arrested Mr. Riggs on the date and at the time and place that he had arranged to meet with someone he believed was 14 years old, after he had sent numerous explicit text messages and emails, including nude photographs of himself, to that person. (*See* Doc. 55 at 4–5). Furthermore, at the hearing on Mr. Riggs' motion to withdraw his guilty plea, Mr. Threatt testified that Mr. Riggs had made a videotaped confession to the police in which he admitted to sending the emails, text messages, and nude photographs.[3] (Cr. Doc. 114 at 45). Although the Government did not submit that confession during Mr. Riggs' criminal proceedings, it would be entitled to do so now. *See Bousley*, 523 U.S. at 624 ("[T]he Government is not limited to the existing record to rebut any showing [of actual innocence] that petitioner might make. Rather, on remand, the Government should be permitted to present any admissible evidence of petitioner's guilt even if that evidence was not presented during petitioner's plea colloquy . . . .").

In contrast to that evidence, Mr. Riggs presents his own allegation that Ms. Brown was an informant who framed him. Because he does not include any affidavit from Ms. Brown or any

---

[3] In his reply brief, Mr. Riggs mentions in passing that Mr. Threatt "presented an edited version of the videotaped interview," but he does not explain that statement any further. (*See* Doc. 75 at 7).

other witness, the court can only assume that he is proffering his own testimony in support of that allegation. Even if Mr. Riggs had taken the stand at trial and testified about the alleged conspiracy to frame him, the court cannot find it more like than not that his testimony would have overcome the strong evidence against him such that "no reasonable juror would have convicted him." *Bousley*, 523 U.S. at 623.

As for Mr. Riggs' assertion of an alibi defense, the court notes that an alibi is "[a] defense based on the physical impossibility of a defendant's guilt by placing the defendant in a location other than the scene of the crime at the relevant time." *Alibi*, Black's Law Dictionary (10th ed. 2014). Mr. Riggs does not set out how his ten alibi witnesses would have proved the "physical impossibility" of him using his phone to send text messages, emails, and photographs to the undercover agent. (*See generally* Doc. 63; Doc. 75 at 6). The court notes that, at the hearing on Mr. Riggs' motion to withdraw his plea, Mr. Threatt testified that he spoke to "at least" eight of the witnesses Mr. Riggs said would provide him with an alibi, but he had declined to file an alibi because "when the criminal allegation is that you were sending text messages from a phone, it does not matter whether you were doing that in this building or across the street." (Cr. Doc. 114 at 55, 74–75). And, as discussed above, police arrested Mr. Riggs at the appointed time of an arranged encounter with a girl he believed to be underage, after exchanging multiple text messages and emails from his phone. Again, the court cannot find that, more likely than not, "no reasonable juror would have convicted" Mr. Riggs if he had presented his alibi defense. *See Bousley*, 523 U.S. at 623.

Mr. Riggs' claim that his guilty plea is invalid because he entered it under duress is procedurally barred in part and procedurally defaulted in part. And Mr. Riggs cannot excuse the procedural default because he cannot establish his actual innocence. As a result, the court WILL DENY this claim.

2. Ineffective Assistance Based on Conflict of Interest

Mr. Riggs' second claim is that Mr. Threatt provided ineffective assistance because he was operating under a conflict of interest by representing both Mr. Johnson—who allegedly confessed to Mr. Riggs that he had committed an unsolved murder—and Mr. Riggs. (Doc. 63 at 7, 12). Mr. Riggs contends that, to protect Mr. Johnson, Mr. Threatt had to "silence" Mr. Riggs. (*Id.*). This claim fails because, even if Mr. Threatt had a conflict of interest, Mr. Riggs waived the conflict on the record.

In a typical claim of ineffective assistance of counsel, the movant must demonstrate that (1) his counsel's performance fell below an objective standard of reasonableness; *and* (2) he suffered prejudice because of that deficient performance. *Strickland v. Washington*, 466 U.S. 668, 684–91 (1984). But the standard is different when a movant alleges ineffective assistance based on a conflict of interest. A movant who can "show[ ] that a conflict of interest actually affected the adequacy of his representation need not demonstrate prejudice in order to obtain relief." *Cuyler v. Sullivan*, 446 U.S. 335, 349–50 (1980). To obtain the presumption of prejudice in this type of case, the movant must "demonstrate[ ] that counsel actively represented conflicting interests and that an actual conflict of interest adversely affected his lawyer's performance." *Strickland*, 466 U.S. at 692. But a defendant can waive the right to conflict-free counsel. *United States v. Garcia*, 517 F.2d 272, 276–78 (5th Cir. 1975),[4] *abrogated on other grounds by Flanagan v. United States*, 465 U.S. 259 (1984).

---

[4] In *Bonner v. City of Prichard*, 661 F.2d 1206, 1207 (11th Cir. 1981) (en banc), the Eleventh Circuit adopted as binding precedent all decisions of the former Fifth Circuit handed down before October 1, 1981.

During Mr. Riggs' criminal proceedings, a magistrate judge found that Mr. Threatt did

not have a conflict based on his concurrent representation of Mr. Riggs and Mr. Johnson, and the

court found that Mr. Threatt had provided effective assistance despite Mr. Riggs' charge of a

conflict. (Cr. Doc. Minute Entry, Sept. 5, 2013; Cr. Doc. 114 at 88–90). Mr. Riggs did not

challenge those findings in his direct appeal. (*See* Doc. 13-2 at 55–72).

Nevertheless, because Mr. Riggs' current claim is one of ineffective assistance based on

the alleged conflict, the court will not deny the claim as procedurally defaulted. *See Massaro v.*

United States, 538 U.S. 500, 509 (2003) ("We . . . hold that failure to raise an ineffective-

assistance-of-counsel claim on direct appeal does not bar the claim from being brought in a later,

appropriate proceeding under § 2255."). But the court also will not reevaluate the underlying

finding that Mr. Threatt had no conflict, because Mr. Riggs had the opportunity to challenge that

finding and failed to do so.

In light of the magistrate judge's and the court's earlier findings that Mr. Threatt had no

conflict, Mr. Riggs cannot now establish ineffective assistance based on a conflict of interest.

See Cuyler, 446 U.S. at 349–50 (requiring the movant to show *both* an *actual* conflict of interest

and that the conflict affected the adequacy of his representation).

And even if the magistrate judge had not made a finding that Mr. Threatt had no conflict,

or if that finding were somehow wrong, Mr. Riggs would not be able to demonstrate that

Mr. Threatt's representation of him violated the Sixth Amendment, because Mr. Riggs waived

the right to conflict-free counsel. To establish waiver, the record must demonstrate "that the

defendant was aware of the conflict of interest; realized the conflict could affect the defense; and

knew of the right to obtain other counsel." *United States v. Rodriguez*, 982 F.2d 474 (11th Cir.

1993).

194

The record demonstrates each of those requirements. Mr. Riggs was clearly aware of the alleged conflict of interest, aware that a conflict could affect his defense, and aware of the right to obtain other counsel, because he filed not one, but two *pro se* motions based on the alleged conflict, expressly seeking a new attorney in one of those motions. (*See* Cr. Doc. 51; Cr. Doc. 57 at6). Yet at the hearing on his first motion about the conflict, he told the magistrate judge that, after he had placed his motion in the mail, he had discussed the alleged conflict with Mr. Threatt and they had "determined this was not going to be an issue." (Cr. Doc. 109 at 7). Finally, the court notes that, at his change of plea hearing, which took place *after* the conflict hearing, Mr. Riggs responded "yes" when the court asked if he was satisfied with Mr. Threatt's representation of him. (Cr. Doc. 62 at 24).

The court finds that, even *assuming* that Mr. Threatt had an actual conflict of interest—an assumption that the court doubts—Mr. Riggs validly waived that conflict. And to the extent that Mr. Riggs asserts that his other attorneys had conflicts of interest, he has not explained what the conflict of interest was or how it adversely affected their representation of him. *See Cuyler*, 446 U.S. 335, 349–50 (requiring both an actual conflict of interest and that the conflict affected the adequacy of counsel's representation). As a result, he cannot establish that he received ineffective assistance of counsel. *See McCorkle v. United States*, 325 F. App'x 804, 807–08 (11th Cir. 2009) (concluding that the movant did not receive ineffective assistance of counsel because he waived his trial attorney's conflict of interest). As a result, the court WILL DENY this claim.

3. Actual Innocence

Mr. Riggs contends that a confidential informant, Joy Brown, sent the explicit text and email messages that formed the basis for his convictions. (Doc. 63 at 5). As the court discussed

195

above, Mr. Riggs cannot establish that he is actually innocent. But even if he could, a freestanding claim of actual innocence is not cognizable in a § 2255 motion. *Jordan v. Sec'y Dep't of Corr.*, 485 F.3d 1351, 1356 (11th Cir. 2007) ("[O]ur precedent forbids granting habeas relief based upon a claim of actual innocence, anyway, at least in non-capital cases."); *see also Herrera v. Collins*, 506 U.S. 390, 400 (1993) ("Claims of actual innocence based on newly discovered evidence have never been held to state a ground for federal habeas relief absent an independent constitutional violation . . . ."). As a result, the court WILL DENY this claim.

4. Certificate of Appealability

Rule 11 of the Rules Governing § 2255 Cases requires the court to "issue or deny a certificate of appealability when it enters a final order adverse to the applicant." Rule 11(a), Rules Governing § 2255 Cases. The court may issue a certificate of appealability "only if the applicant has a made a substantial showing of the denial of a constitutional right." 28 U.S.C. § 2253(c)(2). To make such a showing, a "petitioner must demonstrate that reasonable jurists would find the district court's assessment of the constitutional claims debatable or wrong," or that "the issues presented were adequate to deserve encouragement to proceed further." *Miller-El v. Cockrell*, 537 U.S. 322, 336, 338 (2003) (quotation marks omitted). This court finds that Mr. Riggs' claims do not satisfy either standard. The court WILL DENY a certificate of appealability.

III.   CONCLUSION

The court WILL DENY Mr. Riggs' § 2255 motion. The court WILL DENY AS MOOT Mr. Riggs' motion for appointment of counsel. The court WILL DENY Mr. Riggs a certificate of appealability.

The court will enter a separate order consistent with this opinion.

DONE and **ORDERED** this 2nd day of May, 2018.

Karon O. Bowdre

KARON OWEN BOWDRE
CHIEF UNITED STATES DISTRICT JUDGE

IN THE UNITED STATES DISTRICT COURT
FOR THE NORTHERN DISTRICT OF ALABAMA
SOUTHERN DIVISION

KELLY PATRICK RIGGS,   ]

       Plaintiff,   ]

v.   ]   **2:15-cv-08043-KOB**

UNITED STATES OF AMERICA   ]

       Defendant.   ]

FINAL ORDER

This matter comes before the court on Kelly Patrick Riggs' amended 28 U.S.C. § 2255

motion to vacate sentence (doc. 63) and his motion for appointment of counsel (doc. 67). For the

reasons set out in the accompanying memorandum opinion, the court DENIES Mr. Riggs'

§ 2255 motion; DENIES AS MOOT Mr. Riggs' motion for appointment of counsel; and

DENIES Mr. Riggs a certificate of appealability.

DONE and **ORDERED** this 2nd day of May, 2018.

Karon O. Bowdre

KARON OWEN BOWDRE
CHIEF UNITED STATES DISTRICT JUDGE

**UNITED STATES DISTRICT COURT
NORTHERN DISTRICT OF ALABAMA
SOUTHERN DIVISION**

KELLY PATRICK RIGGS   :

             :

V.   :   CASE NO. : 2:15-CV-8043-KOB

             :

UNITED STATES OF AMERICA   :

             :

NOTICE OF APPEAL

Mr. Riggs gives notice of appeal from this Courts final judgment to deny him a certificate of appealability and/or denial of evidentiary hearing to settle contested factual issues.

Mr. Riggs shows that the district judges' ruling is in direct contradiction with *Clisby v. Jones*, 960 F.2d. 925(11th Cir. 1992) (en banc). The order handed down by the Court addresses only three of Mr. Riggs' four claims and the three it did address are incomplete. In Mr. Riggs' petition, to request a certificate of appeal- ability will particularize that the district court left unanswered the following:

1. his claim of Conflict of Interest with the Federal Public Defenders office as a whole.

2. his claim of outright denial of counsel at a critical stage of the criminal proceeding. (Ground Three)

3. his claim that Glennon F. Threatt and Sabra Barnett conspired to murder Mr. Riggs in a jail cell by discussing his case with cartel associate Lois Rodriguez.

4. his claim that Brett Bloomston provided ineffective assistance of trial counsel by failing to refine and/or clarify Mr. Riggs' claims in his motion to withdraw his plea agreement.

5. his claim that Glennon Threatt failed to provide effective assistance of counsel by presenting a version of a police video, edited to appear to be a confession, rather than challenging the governments evidence.

6. that Glennon Threatts representation was in fact a constructive denial of counsel where he "testified that he felt an alibi defense would be inconsistent with Mr. Riggs confession." Thus, failing to provide adversarial testing of governments evidence.

7. Mr. Riggs expressly moved for the appointment of conflict free counsel, yet the Court dispatched Glennon Threatt to counsel Mr. Riggs concerning the conflict of interest. Thus, Mr. Riggs did not know, "of the right to obtain other counsel" where the Court failed to advise him and failed to appoint unconflicted counsel. Moreover, Mr. Threatt counseled, likely at the behest of the Court, that Mr. Riggs wouldn't get new counsel because he was getting time served for his assistance anyway.

8. The claim that Brett Bloomston abandoned Mr. Riggs at appeal, making it highly unlikely that Mr. Riggs could articulate meaningful appeal claims on his own. An inability the Court now relies on to deny Mr. Riggs his right to an evidentiary hearing. §2255(b).

9. In this action it is the Court itself that obstructs justice by concealing the contested video confession, the alibi witnesses, and the presiding judges personal and church relationship with Brad Taylor and the Hazelrig family. Researching the murder of Samfco Hazelrig and the attempted murder of Mr. Riggs in 2011.

10. The district court commits fraud on the American people of the Northern District of Alabama by falsifying established Court record in her memorandum. The record reflects that on December 20, 2013 Id at 74, states "we actually filed a Notice of Alibi" and "we subpoenaed at least ten people in the case." Id at 55 That Mr. Riggs claims that the ineffectiveness of counsel has facilitated the conviction of someone who is actually innocent.

11. The facts of the criminal case show that Mr. Riggs was in a pool with his wife and children at the time the Court has testified that Mr. Riggs answered agents' messages.

12. Mr. Riggs will show that neither the government nor the Court has provided a single affidavit from anyone on anything the Court currently is testifying to.

13. Mr. Riggs' claim that he was not appointed unconflicted counsel at a conflict of interest hearing. The Court tries to dismiss the claim by not addressing Mr. Riggs' Ground Three and addressing the claim, in part, in a foot note on page eight of the Courts memorandum. The facts are:

    a. Mr. Riggs has filed no briefs and set his claim out clearly in Ground Three of his amended § 2255 Motion.

    b. The Court refuses to "re-evaluate the underlying finding that Mr. Threatt had no conflict, because Mr. Riggs had the opportunity to challenge that finding and failed to do so." But, the Court fails to state that Mr. Riggs' only opportunity to challenge the finding was while he was deprived of counsel.

    c. Mr. Riggs challenged Mr. Threatts loyalties in a *pro se* motion.

    d. The Court dispatched Mr. Threatt, to address Mr. Riggs' motion with Mr. Riggs, rather than unconflicted counsel.

    e. The Court failed to advise Mr. Riggs of his right to unconflicted counsel at the conflict hearing and failed to appoint unconflicted counsel to advise Mr. Rig$$.concerning his right to conflict free counsel at the conflict hearing.

    f. At the hearing Mr. Riggs interest was to prove that counsel was conflicted, Glennon Threatts interest was to prove there was no conflict. This represents a second independent conflict of interest where Mr. Riggs was without counsel.

    g. The Court did not advise Mr. Riggs of his right to unconflicted counsel to assist him in deciding to waive the conflict of counsel. Nor, did the Court conduct a Ferretta hearing to decide if Mr. Riggs could represent his own interests or understand the impact of his decision; to represent himself in waiving his right to conflict, free counsel.

14. Finally, the Court has rushed Mr. Riggs to judgment where the Court issued an "order regarding summary disposition," in which it "gives Mr. Riggs until May 15, 2018... to supply any additional evidentiary materials or legal arguments...," but yet issued a "Final Order" to deny Mr. Riggs § 2255 on May 2, 2018. Mr. Riggs moves this Court to designate the record for appeal.

Submitted on May 14, 2018, By:

Kelly Patrick Riggs

KELLY PATRICK RIGGS

CERTIFICATE OF SERVICE

I have served a copy of this notice on the clerk of this Court, the United States of America, the 11th Circuit Court Clerk, and the Release of Innocent Prisoners Effort, Inc. All in the interest of justice and publication on social media. "What we do in the dark will come to the light."

Submitted on May 14, 2018, By:

Kelly P. Riggs

Kelly Patrick Riggs

**IN THE UNITED STATES DISTRICT COURT
FOR THE NORTHERN DISTRICT OF ALABAMA
SOUTHERN DIVISION**

KELLY PATRICK RIGGS,　　　　　　}

　　　　Plaintiff,　　　　　　　　}

v.　　　　　　　　　　　　　　　}　　　　2:15-cv-08043-KOB

UNITED STATES OF AMERICA　　　}

　　　　Defendant.　　　　　　　}

ORDER

This matter comes before the court on Kelly Patrick Riggs' "Objection and Opposition to the Court's Order Regarding Summary Disposition" (doc. 78) and "Request for Judicial Notice" (doc. 79). In his "Objection and Opposition to the Court's Order Regarding Summary Disposition," Mr. Riggs seeks an evidentiary hearing on his 28 U.S.C. § 2255 motion to vacate sentence. (Doc. 78). In his "Request for Judicial Notice," Mr. Riggs requests that the court take judicial notice of various parts of the record in Mr. Riggs' underlying criminal record and in this § 2255 proceeding. (Doc. 79).

This court denied Mr. Riggs' § 2255 motion on May 2, 2018. (Doc. 77). As a result, the court DENIES AS MOOT Mr. Riggs' motions.

DONE and **ORDERED** this 17th day of May, 2018.

KARON OWEN BOWDRE
CHIEF UNITED STATES DISTRICT JUDGE

UNITED STATES COURT OF APPEALS
FOR THE ELEVENTH CIRCUIT

ELBERT PARR TUTTLE COURT OF APPEALS BUILDING
56 Forsyth Street, N.W.
Atlanta, Georgia 30303

David J. Smith
Clerk of Court

For rules and forms visit
www.ca11.uscourts.gov

May 21, 2018

Appeal Number: 18-12111-F
Case Style: Kelly Riggs v. USA
District Court Docket No: 2:15-cv-08043-KOB
Secondary Case Number: 2:12-cr-00297-KOB-JEO-1

This Court requires all counsel to file documents electronically using the Electronic Case Files ("ECF") system, unless exempted for good cause.

The referenced case has been docketed in this court. Please use the appellate docket number noted above when making inquiries.

Upon notification from the district court concerning whether the filing fee is paid or a motion to proceed in forma pauperis is filed, we will advise you regarding further requirements.

Every motion, petition, brief, answer, response and reply filed must contain a Certificate of Interested Persons and Corporate Disclosure Statement (CIP). Appellants/Petitioners must file a CIP within 14 days after the date the case or appeal is docketed in this court; Appellees/Respondents/Intervenors/Other Parties must file a CIP within 28 days after the case or appeal is docketed in this court, regardless of whether appellants/petitioners have filed a CIP. See Fed.R.App.P. 26.1 and 11th Cir. R. 26.1-1.

On the same day a party or amicus curiae first files its paper or e-filed CIP, that filer must also complete the court's web-based CIP at the Web-Based CIP link on the court's website. Pro se filers (except attorneys appearing in particular cases as pro se parties) are **not required or authorized** to complete the web-based CIP.

Attorneys who wish to participate in this appeal must be properly admitted either to the bar of this court or for this particular proceeding pursuant to 11th Cir. R. 46-1. In addition, all attorneys (except court-appointed counsel) who wish to participate in this appeal must complete and return an appearance form within fourteen (14) days. Application for Admission to the Bar and Appearance of Counsel Form are available on the Internet at www.ca11.uscourts.gov. The clerk

POST-CONVICTION RELIEF: ADVANCING YOUR CLAIM

may not process filings from an attorney until that attorney files an appearance form. See 11th Cir. R. 46-6.

Pursuant to Eleventh Circuit Rule 42-1(b) appellant is hereby notified that upon expiration of fourteen (14) days from this date, this appeal will be dismissed without further notice by the clerk unless the docketing and filing fees are paid to the **DISTRICT COURT** clerk, with notice to this office, or appellant requests leave to proceed in forma pauperis on appeal in the district court. See Fed.R.App.P. 24(a). A form which may be filed in the district court to accomplish this is enclosed.

Sincerely,

DAVID J. SMITH, Clerk of Court

Reply to: Dionne S. Young, F
Phone #: (404) 335-6224

Enclosure(s)

HAB-1 Ntc of dktg COA IFP pndg DC

ABOUT THE AUTHOR

Kelly P. Riggs led a relatively unremarkable life for most of his years. He was quite content and very pleased with his role as a loving father and guide to his children. His life, however, was ultimately redirected by a rogue court, operating under the guise of dispensing justice, in Birmingham, Alabama.

Riggs always recognized the products of his choices, both good and bad. He applied his choices over the years to achieve the best possible outcomes available. One of those choices included providing information to the F.B.I.

In 2011, Mr. Riggs was forced to report the activities of a D.E.A. agent to the F.B.I. The rogue agent was trafficking large quantities of drugs into the Birmingham, Alabama area. This one choice started an investigation into Mr. Riggs's life. Once arrested, he was held for a crime that the Chief district judge freely admits he did not commit. After Mr. Riggs's refusal to change his testimony, the district judge, at sentencing, stated that it was about time he learned to tell the truth, as she said it would be.

His growing up in the home of an abusive alcoholic father, who consequently died in a car accident in 1981, gave way to extreme culture shock for the remaining family members as they moved from Hinkley, California to Blountsville, Alabama in 1983. In 1985 Mr. Riggs dropped out of high school and signed to join the United States Army. In the Army, he finished his studies at Aberdeen Proving Grounds, Maryland, which were subsequently accepted by J.B. Pennington high school in Blountsville Alabama.

With high school behind him, Mr. Riggs began his study of military law with aspirations of becoming a J.A.G. lawyer. After over two years of intense correspondence study and hours under the scrutiny of various proctors, Mr. Riggs discovered that the prospective oath required to become a J.A.G. lawyer was in conflict with his military oath, "… to defend the constitution …" and his own personal strict moral code. His choice to forego a career as a J.A.G. lawyer lead to an unprecedented career change. Mr. Riggs used the skills he learned in the Army to become a valuable asset in the electrical trade as a leader, problem solver, and teacher.

Over the next two decades, Mr. Riggs quietly continued his studies to satisfy his own desire to possess an intimate knowledge of the law and provided only limited assistance to those in the practice thereof.

In the course of his assistance, Mr. Riggs found himself ethically bound to report the corruption of public officials and federal agents, some of which are now under indictment. By May of 2012, he was charged with a crime he did not commit by the same Federal district he made his report in.

Mr. Riggs entered a guilty plea as a vehicle to gain protection from a death threat against his family, that was later discovered to have been propagated by the Federal public defender's office in the Northern District of Alabama (see case no's: 2:12-cr-297-KOB-JEO, and 2:15-CV-8043-KOB). Mr. Riggs thereafter dedicated his every waking moment to his study of advanced criminal procedure. Over the last five years, he has become a skilled and treasured legal writer who assists underprivileged victims of the judicial machinery. He is one of the founding members of Release of Innocent Prisoners Effort: RIPE Inc. and has assisted over 750 federal prisoners, directly or indirectly, acquire their desired relief.

In the beginning of Mr. Riggs' service to his country he vowed to fight for those who couldn't fight for themselves. In this capacity, he, here now, vows to dedicate the remainder of his life to the fight for justice, by bringing awareness to the American people through his fiction and non-fiction writing concerning the law, government, and injustice.

In 2011, he donated a kidney to a fellow soldier. The man was on dialysis and quickly losing his battle. He had a young child who needed his father. With that in mind, he was inspired to donate one of his kidneys to a stranger.

FREEBIRD PUBLISHERS

Thanks for your interest in Freebird Publishers!

We value our customers and would love to hear from you! Reviews are an important part in bringing you quality publications. We love hearing from our readers-rather it's good or bad (though we strive for the best)!

If you could take the time to review/rate any publication you've purchased with Freebird Publishers we would appreciate it!

If your loved one uses Amazon, have them post your review on the books you've read. This will help us tremendously, in providing future publications that are even more useful to our readers and growing our business.

Amazon works off of a 5 star rating system. When having your loved one rate us be sure to give them your chosen star number as well as a written review. Though written reviews aren't required, we truly appreciate hearing from you.

Sample Review Received on Inmate Shopper

 poeticsunshine

⭐⭐⭐⭐⭐ **Truly a guide**
Reviewed in the United States on June 29, 2023
Verified Purchase

This book is a powerhouse of information. My son had to calm/ground himself to prioritize where to start.

CURRENT FULL COLOR CATALOG

92-Pages filled with books, gifts and services for prisoners

We have created four different versions of our new catalog A: Complete B:No Pen Pal Content C:No Sexy Photo Content D:No Pen Pal and Sexy Content. Available in full Color or B&W (please specify) please make sure you order the correct catalog based on your prison mail room regulations. We are not responsible for rejected or lost in the mail catalogs. Send SASE for info on stamp options.

Freebird Publishers Book Selection Includes:

- Ask. Believe. Receive.: Our Power to Create Our Own Destiny
- Celebrity Female Star Power
- Cell Chef 1 & 2
- Cellpreneur: The Millionaire Prisoner's Guidebook
- Chapter 7 Bankruptcy: Seven Steps to Financial Freedom
- Convicted Creations Cookbook
- Cooking With Hot Water
- DIY for Prisoners
- Federal Rules of Criminal Procedures Pocket Guide
- Federal Rules of Evidence Pocket Guide
- Fine Dining Cookbook 1, 2, 3
- Freebird Publisher's Gift Look Book
- Get Money: Self Educate, Get Rich, & Enjoy Life (3 book series)
- Habeas Corpus Manual
- Hobo Pete and the Ghost Train
- Hot Girl Safari: Non-Nude Photo Book
- How to Write a Good Letter From Prison
- Ineffective Assistance of Counsel
- Inmate Shopper
- Inmate Shopper Censored
- Introduction to Financial Success
- Kitty Kat: Adult Entertainment Resource Book
- Life With a Record
- Locked Down Cookin'
- Locked Up Love Letters: Becoming the Perfect Pen Pal
- Parent to Parent: Raising Children from Prison
- Penacon Presents: The Prisoners Guide to Being a Perfect Pen Pal
- Pen Pal Success: The Ultimate Guide to Getting & Keeping Pen Pals
- Pen Pals: A Personal Guide for Prisoners
- Pillow Talk: Adult Non-Nude Photo Book
- Post-Conviction Relief Series (Books 1-7)
- Prison Health Handbook
- Prison Legal Guide
- Prison Picasso
- Prisoner's Communication Guidelines for Navigating in Prison
- Prisonyland Adult Coloring Book
- Pro Se Guide to Legal Research & Writing
- Pro Se Prisoner: How to Buy Stocks and Bitcoin
- Pro Se Section 1983 Manual
- Section 2254 Pro Se Guide to Winning Federal Relief
- Soft Shots: Adult Non-Nude Photo Book
- The Best 500 Non-Profit Organizations for Prisoners & Their Families
- Weight Loss Unlocked
- Write & Get Paid

CATALOG ONLY $5 - SHIPS BY FIRST CLASS MAIL
ADDITIONAL OPTION: add $5 for Shipping and Handling with Tracking

Made in the USA
Middletown, DE
08 July 2024

57032181R00124